Studies in Systems, Decision and Control

Volume 653

The series "Studies in Systems, Decision and Control" (SSDC) covers both new developments and advances, as well as the state of the art, in the various areas of broadly perceived systems, decision making and control–quickly, up to date and with a high quality. The intent is to cover the theory, applications, and perspectives on the state of the art and future developments relevant to systems, decision making, control, complex processes and related areas, as embedded in the fields of engineering, computer science, physics, economics, social and life sciences, as well as the paradigms and methodologies behind them. The series contains monographs, textbooks, lecture notes and edited volumes in systems, decision making and control spanning the areas of Cyber-Physical Systems, Autonomous Systems, Sensor Networks, Control Systems, Energy Systems, Automotive Systems, Biological Systems, Vehicular Networking and Connected Vehicles, Aerospace Systems, Automation, Manufacturing, Smart Grids, Nonlinear Systems, Power Systems, Robotics, Social Systems, Economic Systems and other. Of particular value to both the contributors and the readership are the short publication timeframe and the world-wide distribution and exposure which enable both a wide and rapid dissemination of research output.

Indexed by SCOPUS, DBLP, WTI Frankfurt eG, zbMATH, SCImago.

All books published in the series are submitted for consideration in Web of Science.

Suparna Biswas · Chandreyee Chowdhury ·
Sarmistha Neogy

Adhoc and Sensor Networks: Security and Applications

Springer

Suparna Biswas
Department of Computer Science
and Engineering
Maulana Abul Kalam Azad University
of Technology
Haringhata, West Bengal, India

Chandreyee Chowdhury
Department of Computer Science
and Engineering
Jadavpur University
Kolkata, West Bengal, India

Sarmistha Neogy
Department of Computer Science
and Engineering
Jadavpur University
Kolkata, West Bengal, India

ISSN 2198-4182 ISSN 2198-4190 (electronic)
Studies in Systems, Decision and Control
ISBN 978-981-95-5838-4 ISBN 978-981-95-5839-1 (eBook)
https://doi.org/10.1007/978-981-95-5839-1

This Springer imprint is published by the registered company Springer Nature Singapore Pte Ltd.
The registered company address is: 152 Beach Road, #21-01/04 Gateway East, Singapore 189721, Singapore

I am dedicating this book to my parents, husband and daughters

—Dr. Suparna Biswas

I am soulfully thankful to my grandparents who had opened the windows of knowledge and inspired me to explore it further

—Prof. Chandreyee Chowdhury

Kiaan, Roshni and Prince Bose

—Prof. Sarmistha Neogy

Preface

Computer Network has evolved through different forms from centralized-static to distributed-dynamic, with or without infrastructure support, nodes and links being homogeneous and heterogeneous, etc. With this continuous evolution, in different advanced forms of networks, along with advantages, several challenges have been inherent. While discussing such advanced networks, like Wireless Sensor Network, Mobile Adhoc Network, Internet of things, etc., it is felt that a 360° tour on architectures, protocols, security issues, applications must be included. We have put our best effort to contribute exactly in that way. What more if some recent case studies, prototype demonstration, funding data in related field of research could be added to make the journey of the reader through this book embedded with utmost interesting knowledge? Also it should not be very good if we miss mentioning the "Problem Section" that comprises Questions and sample Answers to quench the thirst of our readers of their queries that could be ignited in their mind while they read the book.

Salient Features of the Book

- **What Interesting Aspects for the Readers?** This book is a combination of fundamental concepts, Case Studies, Prototype demonstration while utilizing WSN, WBAN, MANET, etc., in different applications along with detailed addressing to the security, privacy, trust issues, and challenges taken care of.
- **Target Audience**:

  i. **Undergraduate and Postgraduate Students**: Exposure on WSN, MANET with challenges, opportunities are given to the students studying computer science and Engineering and allied fields.
  ii. **Researchers**: To be enriched with the innovative research motivations that could be addressed in different problems discussed.

iii. **Faculty Members**: This book can be used by the faculty members as a reference book on different aspects such as design, development, analysis, problem identification, solving on WSN, MANET related applications.

Case Studies

Extensive case studies have been illustrated highlighting implementation perspectives, prototype development, prototypes that are being used in practice, etc., to have an idea of the achievability of the advanced.

Structure

The book is comprised of ten chapters to provide scope to the readers to be able to venture in the world of adhoc, sensor, and advanced networks. Chapter 1 provides detailed overview of the domain of both infrastructure based and infrastructure less networks. In Chap. 2, we try to cover the varied application domains of adhoc and sensor networks and beyond. Chapter 3 details about architecture of adhoc network and working of its several components individually and together in coordination with each other. Chapter 4 describes several algorithms and protocols developed in the domain of adhoc, sensor networks and beyond. Chapter 5 enhances the proneness of advanced networks suffering from various challenges toward failures at hardware, software, node or link level. In Chap. 6, these issues are addressed both from the theoretical and real-world point of view to study their effects on performance of networks. Chapter 7 deals with all security issues and challenges and solutions. Chapter 8 presents important case study on smart and remote healthcare applications. Chapter 9 details out the implementation of a complete, secure, end-to-end smart healthcare application using sensors, smartphone, IoT and cloud. The whole write-up concludes in Chap. 10 showing a pathway to travel independently after applying acquired knowledge, in theory and practice by venturing through this book.

Haringhata, India Suparna Biswas
Kolkata, India Chandreyee Chowdhury
Kolkata, India Sarmistha Neogy

Acknowledgments

We would like to express our sincere thanks and gratitude to all those who contributed to the writing and development of this book. We would also like to thank our research scholars and research team, our Department and our University for their valuable insights and support. Also we are thankful to our family members for their unconditional support to successfully complete this endeavor. To be very specific in acknowledgment, Dr. Suparna Biswas wants to acknowledge her University, Department and her research team comprising of PG students and Ph.D. scholars. On security aspects of WSN based systems research contribution of Dr. Sohail Saif, Dr. Pratik Bhattacharjee's work on healthcare prototype development, Dr. Ramesh Saha's work on body sensor based health monitoring, etc., are to be acknowledged for enriching the book content. Professor Chandreyee Chowdhury would like to express her sincere thanks to her Masters students Mr. Kaustav Kundu and Ms. Arijita Banerjee whose works on trust management of sensor networks were crucial in shaping the chapters of the book. She extends her heartfelt thanks to the Ph.D. scholars Ms. Moumita Roy and Ms. Mohana Bakshi as their studies and findings on wireless body area networks and Internet of Things have been duly cited and discussed in the chapters of the book. Professor Neogy is grateful to her husband Mr. Prasun Neogy for encouragement and emotional support throughout this journey. He has also helped immensely by providing necessary and useful insights regarding the illustrations. She is very happy and indebted to as well, to work closely with her two former research students Dr. Chandreyee Chowdhury and Dr. Suparna Biswas as co-authors of this book. We like to express our gratitude and sincere thanks to our teachers and research students who are always imbibing us with knowledge. This book aims to be a valuable resource for anyone interested in learning about and utilizing Wireless Sensor Networks, Adhoc Networks. We hope that it will inspire readers to explore the vast possibilities of this exciting technology and contribute to its further development.

About This Book

Our book has covered evolution of computer networks from its advent to its current advanced form along with several characteristics, issues, challenges of some of the much used advanced computer networks. Advanced computer networks are well demonstrated in terms of architecture, protocols, security and modern applications. Performance related concerns such as security, trust, privacy, fault tolerance, energy efficiency, routing, etc., have been travelled through from the specific type of network and application perspective. To have a 360° view from fundamental concepts to real life applications, case studies, scenarios, prototype development have been augmented to complete the journey. Last but the not the least, the book is comprised of Problem section at the end of each chapter to illustrate related questions, problems with answer clues or probable answers for ready reference of the readers.

Contents

About the Authors

Dr. Suparna Biswas is working as an Associate Professor in the Department of Computer Science and Engineering in Maulana Abul Kalam Azad University of Technology, WB. She has received M.E. and Ph.D. from Jadavpur University, West Bengal. She has been an ERASMUS MUNDUS post doctoral research fellow in cLINK project in Northumbria University, Newcastle, UK. She has successfully completed two funded research projects in the capacity of PI and Co-PI in the area of smart healthcare using WBAN, IoT. She has successfully guided six Ph.D. research scholars in the broad domain of Wireless Body Area Network, IoT based Healthcare and Network Security, 80 UG and 40 PG final year projects. She has been the lead Editor in publishing edited book, has been lead organizing chair, session chair, session organizer in the International Conferences, etc. She is Technical Committee Member of many International conferences of repute, has served as Reviewer in reputed journals, conferences, etc. She has delivered a number of Invited lectures in seminars, Workshops, Webinars, Invited Tutorial Lectures in International Conferences. She has published more than 100 research papers published in reputed journals with good indexing and high impact factors including Q1 journals in association with national and international collaborations, in International conferences and as book chapters of repute. She has been granted with two International patents for innovation in development of a Smart Health Monitoring Assistance prototype for Parkinson's diseased people and as recognition the work has been published in leading National News Paper as well. She has 20 years of teaching experience and is teaching subjects like Computer Network, Network Security, Internet of Things, Machine Learning. Her areas of research interests are Wireless Body Area Network, Internet of Things, Smart Healthcare, Precision Agriculture, Network Security, Machine Learning, etc. She had executed administrative responsibilities as Head of the Department during 2020–2022. She has been University MOOCs coordinator, is SPOC of NPTEL-SWAYAM of MAKAUT, WB, since 2017. She has organized Seminar, Training, Workshop, AICTE funded ATAL FDPs as Coordinator, etc. She is a senior member of IEEE.

Chandreyee Chowdhury is a Professor in the department of Computer Science and Engineering at Jadavpur University, India. Her research interests include IoT in healthcare, indoor localization, and human activity recognition. She was awarded Post Doctoral Fellowship by Erusmus Mundus in 2014 to carry out research work at Northumbria University, UK. She has served as technical program committee members of many international conferences. She has published more than 140 research papers in reputed journals, book chapters and international peer reviewed conferences. Her works have been published in many Q1 journals. She has coauthored three edited volumes. She holds two international patents and two copyrights. She has successfully supervised six Ph.D. scholars. She has 18 years of teaching experience and taught courses on Wireless Networks, Web Technology to name a few. She is a member of IEEE and IEEE Computer Society.

Sarmistha Neogy is Professor in the department of Computer Science and Engineering, Jadavpur University, Kolkata. She received her Ph.D. degree in Engineering and Masters degree and Bachelor in Computer Science and Engineering degree from Jadavpur University, Kolkata, India. Dr. Neogy's research interests are in the areas of Fault Tolerance in Distributed Systems, Reliability and Security in Wireless and Mobile Systems, Wireless Sensor Networks, Security and Privacy in Healthcare and Healthcare Data Analytics. She is a Senior Member of IEEE and IEEE Computer Society. She has a number of publications in international journals and proceedings of international conferences. She has supervised Ph.D. students and currently supervising few more. Dr. Neogy is member of Government of India mirror committee for Joint Technical Committee (JTC1) and member of two international subcommittees of ISO/IEC JTC1. She has co-authored four books, including one on Wireless Sensor Networks and another on Big Data, both published from CRC Press.

List of Figures

List of Tables

Chapter 1
Introduction

Abstract This is the first chapter of the book. This chapter introduces the idea about the book in general. It tells about the different types of networks: wired and wireless. Since the focus of the book is on wireless network, this chapter explains in details the types of wireless networks, including Adhoc network and Wireless Sensor Network (WSN). The chapter ends with providing future research directions so that interested readers can pick up their area of research.

Keywords Wired network · Wireless network · Adhoc network · Wireless sensor network

The twentieth century marked its debut with airplane and went on adding an unparalleled list of remarkable scientific inventions and discoveries along with technological advances. The list kept ever growing and overflowed to the twenty-first century as well. Every aspect of human life was touched upon. Needless to say, humanity was greatly influenced by these inventions and discoveries. They changed the ways of our lives forever!

There were activities in every sphere, from invention of antibiotics to invention of radio, television and digital computers, installation of world-wide telephone networks, launching communication satellites, to name a few, to the last but not the least, the Internet. Starting last couple of decades of the twentieth century, computer industry saw an unprecedented rapid growth. Much to our delight, the technological progress is also advancing at a pace much faster than we are able to cope. Every now and then it seems to be slipping out of our hands. As we get prepared to embrace the latest, a "later than the latest" pops out.

Availability of computers and the advancement in communication technologies required to keep the computers "in touch" with each other is the focus of this book. As we build our way into this process of "keeping in touch", we are amazed to find that not only computers, but other things are also in "touch with each other". Answers to the "hows" and "whys", and such other volley of questions can be found in the convergence of different technologies that are becoming sophisticated with every passing day.

S. Biswas et al., *Adhoc and Sensor Networks: Security and Applications*, Studies in Systems, Decision and Control 653, https://doi.org/10.1007/978-981-95-5839-1_1

1.1 Computer Network: Wired and Wireless

Centralized computer systems dominated the first couple of decades after computers came into being. However, they became almost obsoletes, as small computer systems like personal computer, laptop, tablet and other similar and even smaller systems filled the market and made their way into our lives. Alongside telecommunication technologies were also making rapid progress. Thus, merger of computers and communications was imminent. So what we get is a collection and system of interconnected autonomous computers that are able to exchange information, and share resources among them. Thus Computer Networks is born. What becomes more interesting is the fact that copper wires may not be the only way of interconnection; interconnection can be via fiber optics, microwave, infrared, even via communication satellites! The network can be small with a handful number of computers or medium spread over an organization or large spread over a country or very very large spanning continents. The network may be Local Area Network (LAN) that interconnects computers within a limited area like in a laboratory, a school building, residence, or a college campus. Wide Area Network (WAN) covers larger geographical area and distance. A Metropolitan Area Network (MAN) stands in between LAN and WAN with respect to area, referring to a geographic region, generally in the range between 5 and 50 km. IEEE 802 standards family deals with LANs and MANs. A WAN may connect several LANs and MANs. Thus, the network (WAN) can also be a network of networks, Internet being the most well-known example.

1.1.1 Wired Network

Wired network comprises computers that are connected and that communicate with each other over wired connection or wire-based communication technology. Wired communication examples include telephone networks, cable television, fiber optic communication. Ethernet is mostly used as the communication technology for interconnecting personal computers. Wired LANs generally use twisted pair cables and fiber optics cables and network switches. Ethernet data transfer rate has phenomenally increased from a mere 2.94 Megabits per second (Mbps) to 400 Gigabits per second (Gbps). The roadmap of Ethernet Alliance expects speed of 800 gigabits per second, which is projected to be IEEE standard of 1.6 Terabits per second possibly during 2023–2025. Wired network technologies offer enhanced speed and nil interference. Among other advantages are provision of better security, ability to connect across long distances. However, infrastructure requirements lead to expensive installation and high replacement cost, as well.

The most common wired LAN is IEEE 802.3 standard for Ethernet technologies. Computers with Network Interface Controllers or Network Interface Cards (NIC) as they are commonly known as, join network via a switch with point-to-point link. Each port of a switch connects to an individual computer. The switch sends the packet (data or control, etc.) meant for a particular computer to that computer only by determining the destination address a packet refers to. A computer connected in a network is generally referred to as host. A WAN may look like a large wired LAN that connects, say branches of an organization in different parts of the country. Each such branch will have hosts connected via subnet. The subnet consists of transmission lines (here only wired connection is considered) that may be leased lines from telecommunication companies and routers. However, this simplified concept of WAN is now replaced with the concept where communication aspects (subnet) and application aspect (hosts) are not one and the same. They are controlled by different entities, such as, network service provider is responsible for the subnet, and hosts are controlled by organizations owning them. Routers are also expected to work with different networking technologies. The hosts themselves may not be individual hosts, but separate LANs. Thus, as the concept of WAN implementation changes, the network service provider will also enhance its service by connecting to other networks that are part of the Internet. Such network service providers are called Internet Service Providers (ISPs). As networks expand, there will be routers (say, R1 and R2) with no direct connection or communication link between them, but wishing to communicate with each other. Hence an indirect communication link has to be established via other routers. There may also be more than one path that connects R1 and R2, say one path is like this: R1–R5–R9–R7–R2, another one is: R1–R12–R3–R6–R4–R19–R2, and so on. Thus there has to be a decision as to which path to take. Routing algorithms help in taking these decisions (Fig. 1.1).

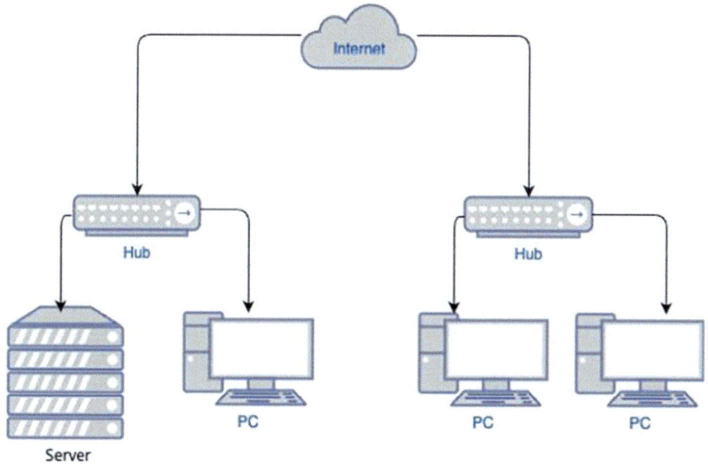

Fig. 1.1 Wired network

1.1.2 Wireless Network

Wireless networks are computer networks in which computers are not connected by cable or any wired connection. The term wireless indicates any kind of wire-free connection. Wire-free connection and communication technologies include cellular, microwave, WiFi, Bluetooth, satellite. The communication technology allows devices to be connected to the network. Devices may be roaming around too within the network coverage. Network communication can be established by compatible devices through wireless access points or access points (AP) with each other, to wired devices and the Internet, as well. However, the nodes in wireless networks are not only computers, nodes can be wireless sensor nodes, as well. This type of network is known as Wireless Sensor Network (WSN). There are a large variety of sensor nodes with which a WSN may be built of.

Cellular network, commonly known as mobile network, is a communication network whose last link is wireless. This type of network spans a geographical region which is divided into "cells", that are hexagonal in shape. A cell uses a set of frequency that is different from its neighbors' and these sets of frequencies can be reused for non-neighbor cells. Thus adjacent cells are on different frequency ranges while cells far apart use the same set of frequency. This technique of re-use increases both capacity and coverage. Base Transceiver Station (BTS) or Base Station takes the responsibility of facilitating wireless communication between the user equipment (mobile phone, any device with wireless connectivity) and the network. The network may support any of the wireless communication technologies like GSM, CDMA, WiFi, WiMAX, or any other WAN technology. Data services have now become an integral part of the mobile networks. Internet protocols are used on mobile devices to set up audio and video connection over packet data networks. Mobility of users is also seamlessly handled via handover or handoff.

Wireless LANs enable users to walk around their office premises with network connected laptops in their hands. IEEE 802.11 belonging to the IEEE 802 set of LAN protocols, is the world's most widely used wireless computer networking standards. IEEE 802.11 specifies the set of media access control (MAC) and physical layer (PHY) protocols for implementing WLAN, Wi-Fi communication in the following frequencies, including but not limited to 2.4, 5, and 60 GHz frequency bands. The IEEE 802.11 is a family of different generations starting with 802.11b in 1999, followed by 802.11a (1999), 802.11g (2003), 802.11n (2009), 802.11ac (2014), the latest being 802.11ax (2019).

IEEE 802.11 can be operated on two basic modes: infrastructure and ad hoc mode. In infrastructure mode, mobile hosts communicate via access point that acts like a bridge to connect with other networks, like Internet or LAN. An Access Point (AP) is a hardware networking device that connects directly to a wired LAN, typically, Ethernet. The AP then provides wireless connections using wireless LAN technology, typically Wi-Fi, for other (mobile) devices to use that wired connection. An AP supports the connection of multiple wireless devices through its only wired connection. In ad hoc mode, mobile units transmit directly peer-to-peer.

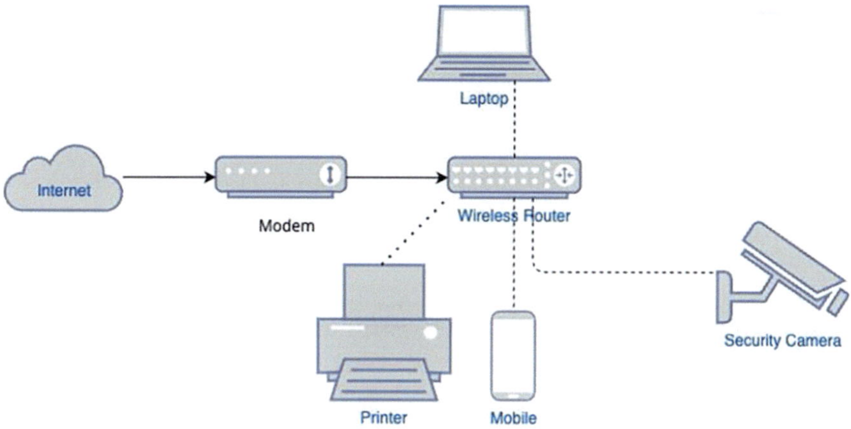

Fig. 1.2 Wireless network

As technologies were invented, market requirements became varied. Wireless technologies for connecting mobile phones to laptops and other devices were looked into. SIG (Special Interest Group: a consortium) was formed in 1998 for developing a wireless standard that will connect computing and communication devices and accessories. However, this standard was different from other existing standards of the time as it used short-range, low-power, inexpensive wireless radios. Thus Bluetooth technology made its way into the market. Bluetooth protocols enable different types of devices, such as mobile phones and laptops to headsets, printers, keyboards, watches, music players, washing machines, ovens and many others, to find and connect with each other and transfer data securely after pairing (Fig. 1.2).

1.2 Types of Wireless Networks

Wireless Networks are very different from their wired counterparts in more than one way. Wired networks are always based on infrastructures, whereas wireless networks can be both with infrastructure (referred to as "infrastructure" henceforth), and without infrastructure (infrastructure-less) as well. Cellular network may be considered to be one of the well-known examples of infrastructured wireless network.

Infrastructure-less networks are popularly known as Adhoc networks, since they can be set up and run without the need of any infrastructures, at all. It must be mentioned here that, portable devices (laptop, mobile phone, smart device, etc.), being wireless in nature, are components of wireless adhoc network. Since these devices may move, wireless adhoc network may become a Mobile adhoc network (MANET). However, a wireless adhoc network may still contain wireless stationary devices (for example, desktop computer with wireless network card) along with mobile devices. Hence adhoc networks are essentially decentralized networks with no dependence on pre-existing infrastructures, like routers (in wired networks) or access points (in wireless networks). As has already been pointed out in the earlier section Wireless Sensor Network (WSN) is one of the very important type of wireless networks with a wide range of applications.

The scope of this book is adhoc and sensor networks. We shall talk about adhoc networks and sensor networks in different subsections as each of them is a separate area for study by itself.

1.2.1 Adhoc Networks: Characteristics and Challenges

Adhoc network, as the meaning goes, can be set up whenever necessary. Since this is a type of network, so it can be set up wherever necessary, too. Thus it can be set up from the scratch without the need of any existing infrastructure, as per requirement. Essentially this means that whenever two or more wireless and/or mobile devices are within the transmission ranges of each other, they are able to communicate and voila! an adhoc network is up. However, it is not essential that all nodes in the network will be connected to each other. A node may be able to connect to another node via another node or other nodes. A message M meant for a particular node (N_d) may be sent by node (N_s) via nodes N_1, N_2. It is also important to note here that the task of N_1, and N_2 should be simply to forward the message M to the required destination node N_d. Thus all nodes in an adhoc network also take part in routing, besides their own computational tasks. Characteristics of this type of network include wireless and/or mobile node, communication over wireless media, topology change, routing activity at each node, among others.

First and foremost, the nodes in this network are not ordinary in nature, even physically. These are wireless and mobile nodes. So, they have to be portable which requires a node to be not heavy, not large in size, battery driven, and so on. Thus the network is constrained by the nodes from the very beginning. The varied requirements of the mobile node put limits to the capability of the processor, power usage, and user friendly features. Next comes the wireless medium. Types of wireless transmission media used in communications include infrared, broadcast radio, cellular radio, microwaves, and communications satellites. Main concerns with this type of media include coverage area, interference, security. The wireless communication itself is a major concern since it may not always offer the best of the data transfer rate. In addition to the above concerns, another important issue to be dealt with is that of mobility of the nodes. Hence, the task of forwarding and finding an appropriate route becomes an uphill task in the ever changing topology of a mobile adhoc network.

The challenges to design and develop a network with portable devices are many. A portable device needs to be lightweight (as it has to be carried from place to place). The main source of weight in such devices is the battery. Battery weight may be reduced to make the device lighter. However, that would lead to frequent recharging of the battery or carrying a spare battery, either of which may not be feasible. Instead, attention may be given to minimizing power consumption, thereby lengthening battery life. Power can be conserved by designing power-efficient hardware and power management software. Size constraints have forced portable devices to have small user interfaces. With smaller display size may come other ways of communication mechanisms, such as voice recognition and handwriting recognition. Limited storage capacity is another concern for portable devices.

Wireless transmission is a form of unguided media. Radio waves, one of the widely used transmission medium for wireless networks, have a wide frequency range. Although lower frequency radio wave can travel through walls, their power decreases with distance. Higher radio frequencies can travel in straight line and bounce back, but are prone to absorption by rain and other obstacles. High frequency radio waves have more power. Microwave transmission is a line of sight transmission medium. This transmission depends on the weather condition and the frequency in use. As we know, infrared propagation, also line of sight, is used for very short range communication purposes. It is unable to cross walls because of high frequency range.

Wireless communication has to deal with various environmental obstacles that interacts with the signal resulting in blocking signal paths, introducing noise, interference, echoes, etc. Thus it becomes a low bandwidth error-prone communication. Higher error rates and lower bandwidth contribute to frequent and spurious disconnection too. Communication latency may increase due to retransmissions, timeouts, protocols handling error-control or correction and disconnections. Wireless communication establishes connection with wired and infrastructured network via transceivers. A cell is known as the area that is covered by the signal of a transceiver. However, sizes of cells are not fixed. An infrared transceiver can cover the area equivalent to a small meeting room, whereas a cellular telephone transceiver can cover a few kilometers, and a satellite beam can cover an area of diameter more than 600 km.

The challenges faced while adopting wireless networking include disconnection, low bandwidth with variability of bandwidth, heterogeneous network and to top it all, risks due to security.

Disconnection can be handled in several ways, such as, asynchronous operation, prefetching and caching, delayed write-back. Instead of the synchronous remote call paradigm, an asynchronous procedure may continue without having to wait for acknowledgements or replies of each request that the client makes. An application may beforehand download and cache the data or some other file that may be required, on the mobile device. These may be utilized for computation during the time the device is disconnected from the network. Similarly, the application may temporarily save and store data on the mobile device before writing it back to server or other device in the infrastructured network.

As wireless networks inherently have low bandwidth, concerns regarding handling this bandwidth is much more. That the bandwidth is divided among the users in a cell further raises this concern. Hence deliverable bandwidth per user becomes the measure of the network capacity. However, this measure depends on the size and population density. So capacity of a wireless network was recommended to be measured by its bandwidth per cubic meter. Evidently, installation of more wireless network cells to service a user population will increase the network capacity. One way of achieving this is by overlapping cells on different wavelengths. But with scarce public electromagnetic spectrum, the scalability becomes an issue. Although this technique seems flexible as software is used to allocate bandwidth among users. The other technique is to reduce transmission ranges so that more cells can fit in a given area. Since transmission range is reduced, it also decreases power requirement and interference for signal. Also, transceivers covering less area can achieve higher bandwidth. Since bulk operations are considered to be generally more efficient than a number of short ones, so many such short ones can be buffered and made into a large request. Compression technique may be used with large buffered data.

Low bandwidth with variability in bandwidth is a cause of concern in wireless networks. This is due to the variation in the number of users that may be using the network at the same time. Hence applications have to be designed with this in mind such that they can utilize the available bandwidth at that time. Some applications may always ensure high bandwidth, some others may try to adapt to the currently available, and still some others may assume low bandwidth to work with always. The choice may depend upon the application itself.

With wired network, the devices being stationary are generally connected to the same network. But this may not be true for mobile devices as they roam and try to connect to any available network. This may affect the transmission speed, protocols, interfaces, etc., to which the devices have to adapt. Thus heterogeneity of network makes adhoc networking challenging.

The very characteristic of a wireless network that makes it easy for devices to connect, becomes the risk to the device and to the network. Appropriate methods must be in place to properly identify and permit a user to use network resources. Communication over insecure channels need to be handled using encryption.

The challenges involving node mobility arise from different perspectives. Mobility empowers a node to be in touch with network resources even while a node is on the move. The ability of changing locations may increase volatility of some information as the node which was nearer to a data server has now moved away, but still needs to be served all the same. As the address changes continuously, handling of ever changing addresses, location-dependent information, become difficult.

How does a sender know where the recipient is at present? Several ideas were floated that culminated in the proposals for "mobile IP". Among these, the concept of having a central service that will maintain the current addresses of all mobile nodes or a distributed central service termed as home base, where locations of a number of mobile nodes will be known to one single server only (without replication), or the forwarding pointer, in which the new address of a node will be kept in the old address of that node. Of course, each of these schemes had their own advantages and disadvantages, and hence the working best features from all these are seemed to be adopted in the design of mobile IP.

Users of mobile devices generally have queries regarding locations of certain services. This is because as they are moving they may not be familiar to the new environment or region and hence have these queries. The answers to the queries may be generated easily, however the answers have to travel via the network from the server to the user location, thereby revealing the user location in the process. This may adversely affect the privacy of the user.

Adhoc networking has enabled access to resources (infrastructured and without infrastructure) that eliminates the need of time and place restrictions. It can be conceived to be an interesting and challenging extension to the existing and conventional networking system. Hence the challenge of developing wireless and mobile adhoc network is quite formidable.

1.2.2 Wireless Sensor Networks (WSN): Characteristics and Challenges

Unprecedented advances and tremendous improvements in wireless technologies and electronics design technologies have made possible the design and deployment of low-cost multifunctional wireless sensor nodes. A sensor node is a tiny device which has a sensing subsystem, processing subsystem, a communication subsystem, and a power subsystem. The sensing subsystem is used to sense, that is, gather data for the purpose for which it is designed. The processing subsystem usually consists of low level computation with small storage facilities. The communication subsystem deals with maintaining contacts, that is, transmitting and receiving data and/or control information. The power subsystem is the source of energy of the sensor node unit. Typically, a WSN consists of several sensor nodes deployed over a certain region, but specifically for a particular application. WSNs have a large number of varied applications in all spheres of life. Applications span from surveillance in border areas to monitoring environmental pollution to tracking traffic flow in thoroughfares to remote patient monitoring, to name a few. Some WSNs may be deployed for mission-critical tasks too.

Why is WSN considered to be similar, and yet vastly different from traditional adhoc networks, is an often asked question put forth to researchers. The salient features of WSN are as follows:

- Number of sensor nodes in a WSN is generally very large anytime in comparison to ad adhoc network.
- Sensor nodes can be densely deployed as they are low-cost than the computing devices of other adhoc networks.
- Since deployment may be in any terrain, sensor nodes are always prone to failures while facing rough environments and their own limited power resources.
- Due to the failures of nodes (even if these are static), topology of WSN may change frequently.
- Sensor nodes have their own constraints in power, computational capability, memory and storage and transmission ability.

The challenges faced by the designer and developer of WSN and its applications are inherent in the salient features of the sensor node network themselves.

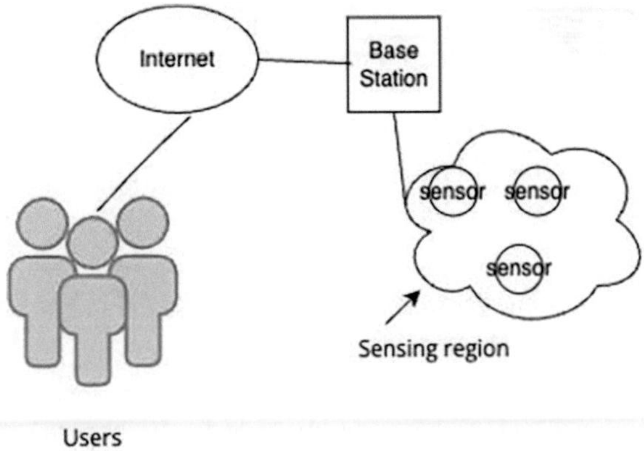

Fig. 1.3 Wireless sensor network (WSN)

As mentioned the range of WSN applications varies from civil to military, so challenges are also unique and particular to an application. Of course a large number of general challenges do exist as well.

The deployment of sensor nodes may be random in many cases. Hence location information, other than a GPS enabled node, may be rarely available. Other than the batteries with which they come, these nodes do not have any other alternative source of power. Hence energy conservation in WSN is one of the most important issues. With dynamic topology due to node death, path loss will happen. Hence routing and that too in an energy-efficient manner is highly challenging. With large number of nodes, utilization of redundancy becomes one of the interesting challenges. Many WSN applications require exchange of sensitive data. So adequate measures have to be taken so that this data don't fall into the hands of unwanted recipients. Thus security is a major challenging issue that needs to be faced.

However, even with all its limitations, it is expected that the sensor network with such resource-constrained nodes will be able to meet application requirements within its lifetime. Most of the applications are long running applications, typically one moth to one year. So, the WSN has to be working and meeting the application requirements during this entire time. Hence the pertinent and important requirement is to prolong the network lifetime, keeping all other considerations in mind (Fig. 1.3).

1.3 Research Directions

With wireless and mobile adhoc networking and computing getting popular, high demand for advanced wireless technology is in place. Researchers are also getting more and more involved as it means novel areas and issues for research are opening up. The challenges in this broad area of wireless and mobile adhoc networking are many. A variable number of subdomains in this field exist, such as, Mobile Adhoc Network (MANET), Vehicular Adhoc Network (VANET), Wireless Sensor Network

(WSN), Wireless Body Area Network (WBAN), and the network of networks Internet of Things (IoT), among others.

The common strand in all types of networks is the routing of message or data from sender to destination or multiple destinations. Depending on the type of application a network is running, some networks may require more security than others, some may require implementing privacy, yet some others may only focus on real-time execution, and so on. Hence research directions are too many to be considered only for routing.

Similarly, if one considers the amount of data generated and handled in these networks (particularly any type of sensor network, such as, WSN, WBAN), then research is open for data (often big data) management. A healthcare application may run using WBAN, MANET and/or VANET and/or IoT. This type of application particularly needs data privacy, as it is concerned with health data. This type of application also has to prioritize the freshness of data, that is, real-time data. Thus, research avenues are open on the security and privacy front for real-time as well as non-real-time applications. On the other hand, if we come to think about the huge amount of data that is generated, then one might wonder why not explore this data to obtain insights. Thus, application may also be used to gain knowledge from ever expanding limitless data and environment so that the knowledge can be used sometime to infer or predict a situation. Hence data analytics also becomes an integral part of research in adhoc networks too.

However, depending on the type of application and its environment of execution, research for suitable routing protocol is always going on. Considering different types and layers of a network, requirements are different and varied. The choice of the next hop and ultimately the entire route may be derived from other fields of science and everyday life, such as, bio-inspired network, genetic algorithms, fidelity, to name a few. There may not be any generalized protocol for all types of applications. A general guideline may help in designing and choosing a suitable protocol for the intended purpose.

Considering mobility to be an issue, different mobility models are in place. But existing models may not always be fit into the required application scenarios. Thus, mobility modeling still remains an area for exploration.

As we have seen in the earlier sections that adhoc networks are fraught with several constraints. Quality of Service (QoS) in such networks always remains one of the most important issues. Apart from this, now a days, there has been a growing focus on security. This is more so, because security lapses have already caused great misfortune. Hence design and development of secured adhoc network and applications are much sought after.

1.4 Summary

This chapter provides a detailed overview about the different types of networks. Wireless networks are also quite a handful in number. The chapter describes the characteristics of wireless networks and the challenges faced in designing such network. The chapter concluded with a direction toward probable research areas on wireless adhoc networks.

Questions (Indicative)

Q1. What are the differences between an infrastructured network and a network without infrastructure?

Q2. Do you think although it is easier to set up an adhoc network, but it is costly to maintain? Justify your answer.

Q3. How is Wireless Sensor Network (WSN) similar and dissimilar to an adhoc network consisting of laptops only?

Q4. What are the security concerns in Mobile Adhoc Network (MANET)? How can these be handled?

Q5. How does mobility of nodes affect the execution of applications in MANET? What probable solutions do you suggest?

Q6. What are the salient features of Wireless Sensor Network (WSN)? What are the challenges for executing applications in a WSN?

Bibliography

1. Tanenbaum, A.S., Wetherall, D.J.: Computer Networks 5e, 5th edn. Prentice Hall (2013)
2. Siva Ram Murthy, C., Manoj, B.S.: Adhoc Wireless Networks: Architectures and Protocols, 6th printing. Prentice Hall (2008)
3. Forman, G.H., Zahorjan, J.: The Challenges of Mobile Computing, pp. 38–47. IEEE Computer (1994, April)
4. Jain, J.K., Chauhan, D.: Recent research work on adhoc networks: a literature survey. Int. J. Mod. Comput. Sci. Appl. (IJMCSA) **4**(2), 1–6 (2016)
5. Yoneki, E., Bacon, J.: A survey of wireless sensor network technologies: research trends and middleware's role. University of Cambridge Technical report No. 646, UCAM-CL-TR-646. ISSN 1476-2986 (2005, September)
6. Mukherjee, N., Neogy, S., Roy, S.: Building Wireless Sensor Networks: Theoretical and Practical perspectives, 1st edn. CRC Press (2015)
7. Wang, Y., Attebury, G., Ramamurthy, B.: A survey of security issues in wireless sensor networks. IEEE Commun. Surv. Tutor. **8**(2), 1–23 (2006)
8. https://en.wikipedia.org/wiki/IEEE_802.11
9. https://documentation.meraki.com/MS/Layer_3_Switching/Layer_3_vs_Layer_2_Switching

Chapter 2
Applications of Wireless Networks

Abstract Wireless Networks have evolved from the advancement in wireless communication and embedded systems enabling development of tiny sensors having wireless connectivity enabled with WiFi, Bluetooth, Zigbee, etc. Sensors or Personal Digital Assistants (PDAs), Smartphones, Tablet Computers, Laptops, etc., enabled with wireless connectivity forms a network of heterogeneous devices for communication among the nodes in wireless fashion, without needing wired connectivity among the end devices. These wireless networks can be of homogeneous or heterogeneous types. Also the wireless nodes may be static or mobile once deployed in the network. Such networks have immense applications in various real life applications starting from telecom industry, healthcare, surveillance, agriculture, environmental monitoring, etc.

Keywords Wireless Network · Mobile adhoc network · Wireless body area network · Wi-Fi · Bluetooth · Smart applications

2.1 Overview of Different Types of Wireless Networks

Wireless networks are modern extension of infrastructure based computer network with heterogeneous nodes and links connected mobility support. Also establishment cost of wireless networks are much less than fully infrastructure based wired network. Wireless networks are of high demand in recent past due to mainly mobility support and low cost properties of wireless networks compared to wired network. Users prioritize uninterrupted seamless mobility while doing computing, communication or information access over the wireless network. Wireless networks are advantageous from the point of view of instant infrastructure less establishment scope based on requirement during the time of natural calamities like earthquake, flood, storm, etc., along with infrastructure based networks. Infrastructure less wireless network with mobility support is called Mobile Adhoc Network (MANET). Infrastructure less or with minimum infrastructure supported wireless network can be formed among the

S. Biswas et al., *Adhoc and Sensor Networks: Security and Applications*, Studies in Systems, Decision and Control 653, https://doi.org/10.1007/978-981-95-5839-1_2

smart vehicles on road known as Vehicular Adhoc Network (VANET) or Internet of Vehicles (IoV).

Wireless Networks based on the type of connectivity among nodes can be categorized as follows:

- wireless Cellular Network,
- wireless Sensor Network,
- mobile Adhoc Network (MANET),
- vehicular Adhoc Network (VANET), and
- internet of Vehicles (IoV).

Also, in all Wireless Networks, types of nodes and types of links are not same. In Mobile Adhoc Network, nodes and links are heterogeneous. The nodes could be any node with wireless connectivity and mobility support, like Laptop, Tablet PC, Smartphones, etc. And the wireless links could be any of WiFi, Bluetooth, Zigbee, or combination of these.

In wireless Sensor Network, nodes are homogeneous in terms of type of nodes and that is, sensor nodes connected with wireless links that can be heterogeneous like WiFi, Bluetooth, Zigbee, etc., in a single network [1].

Wireless networks work at underwater as well targeted for different applications such as environmental monitoring, oceanographic data collection, etc. Through different communication mediums such as acoustic, radio frequency (RF), and optical waves, underwater wireless communications (UWCs) can be carried out. Among these, optical wireless communications (UOWCs) perform better than the other two in terms of higher data rates at low latency levels. In UOWCs, due to severe aquatic channel conditions, e.g., scattering, absorption, turbulence, etc., the maximum communication range gets reduced.

When nodes in a wireless network are majorly and mainly sensors, then it is termed as Wireless Sensor Network (WSN). Sensor nodes deployed over a region at indoor or at outdoor, enabled with wireless communication technologies such as WiFi, Bluetooth, Zigbee, etc., form a wireless sensor network. Wireless Sensor Network has different applications specifically physical data collection and monitoring—from health monitoring and care to smart home, smart surveillance, smart traffic, smart energy, smart waste management, smart environmental monitoring, smart air pollution monitoring, smart fire monitoring, smart wild animals monitoring in the remote reserve forests, earthquake and flood monitoring, prediction Health vitals monitoring, etc. A special kind of Wireless Sensor Network that is applied for health vitals monitoring using biomedical sensors is called Wireless Body Area Network (WBAN), Wireless Body Sensor Network (WBSN), Medical Body Sensor Network (MBSN). Wireless Body Area Network spans over human body for sensing and monitoring of health vitals such as Body temperature, heart rate, pulse rate, ECG, EEG, EMG, SpO_2, and foot pressure. Wearable kinetic/motion sensors as part of WBAN can be utilized for Human Activity Recognition (HAR) toward fitness monitoring and when combined with health vital parameters during different Activities performed by the human being, disease monitoring, prediction, detection would also be possible. In WBAN, smartphone can be used as a sink or coordinator device to aggregate and

transmit sensor data to the processing unit using Machine learning or Deep learning based models at cloud server.

Wireless Sensor Networks thus can be applied and utilized in various real life applications to develop the ecosystem for smart, friendly, connected living to facilitate human being in all levels, starting from daily living of people, administration, professionals, developers, etc.

2.1.1 Sensor Network

Here we will focus and illustrate Sensor Networks from point of view of application in real world and time-critical problems. Now, first of all we need to know what is Sensor Network. It is wired or wireless? It is infrastructure supported or infrastructure less? It is static or dynamic? It supports node or link mobility or nodes and links are static? How large a Sensor Network could be? How many nodes there would be? Is there any definition or limitation of minimum or maximum or ideal number of sensor nodes to form Sensor Network? Which topology the Sensor nodes and links form mostly for improved communication or any topology is suitable for efficient communication? The nodes and links in a Sensor Network should be homogeneous or heterogeneous? Sensor Networks are deployed in mostly indoors or at outdoors or anywhere as will be required. Is there is any health hazards associated with Sensor Networks in human health monitoring, sensor nodes either attached to human body forming WBAN or human body is in near proximity when it is a smart home application for smart, connected living. Before getting answers to all these questionnaires we must be aware of formal definition of Sensor Network as follows.

Sensor Node (SN): Sensor nodes in collaboration read physical data from ambience and aggregates, transmit data through the sink node to the processing unit through short range or long range communication technology for analysis and meaningful knowledge building for necessary measures by the entrusted entities. Figure 2.1 illustrates different components of a sensor node.

2.1.2 Categories of Sensor Networks

Now the node to node connectivity could be wired or wireless depending on the region to be covered, indoor or outdoor, rural or urban area, local or remote location, etc. Also, type of application in which the Sensor Network to be deployed is important and primary factor to decide the connectivity type.

Mostly the sensor nodes deployed over a region, indoor or at outdoor are connected with wireless connectivity such as Bluetooth, WiFi, Zigbee and hence Sensor Networks are majorly or commonly termed as Wireless Sensor Network (WSN). Also in WSN there is type or category of network based on the fact that if the sensor

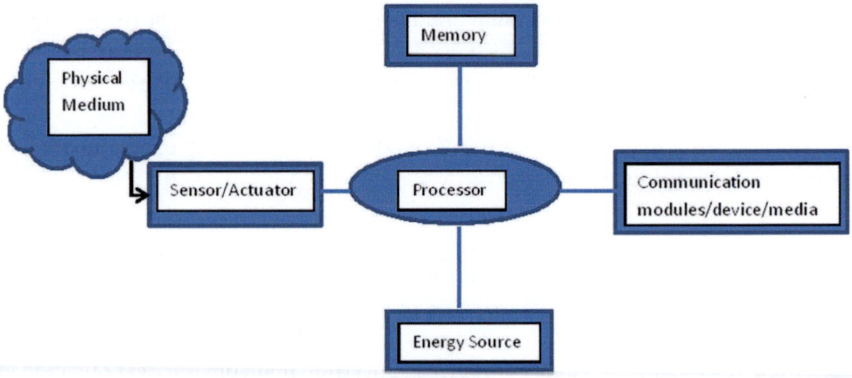

Fig. 2.1 Connected components of a sensor node

nodes are static or mobile once deployed. Another thing may differ is the sink node which may be static or mobile based on the type of the link and the application.

So, till now variations of SNs are

Static Sensor Node, Static Sink Node (S-S)
Static Sensor Node, Mobile Sink Node (S-M)
Mobile Sensor Node, Static Sink Node (M-S)
Mobile Sensor Node, Mobile Sink Node (M-M).

Another categorization or type could be of WSNs based on varying topologies that defines or describes pattern of links or connectivity among different nodes in the WSN.

If all Sensor nodes are directly connected with the Sink Node with single hop link, then this topology type is Star topology. Here the Sink node is superior than the other Sensor nodes from few perspectives like resources in terms of Memory, battery power, processing ability, size, mobility support, connectivity, etc. Also, as the Sink node is responsible for receiving, aggregating, pre-processing of data from all other sensor nodes in the network prior to transmitting the data to the local processing unit or cloud server, the Sink node must be secure and reliable enough.

Now if the infrastructure support is concerned, then Wireless Sensor Networks (WSN) can be established with or without fixed infrastructure support. WSN that needs fixed infrastructure support such as base station support or Wi-Fi access point support.

Another special type of WSN is Wireless Body Area Network (WBAN) which is deployed over a human body for collection of body vital parameters through biomedical sensors connected by wireless links such as WiFi, Bluetooth, Zigbee. So, WSN again could be broadly categorized as human body as sensing monitoring area and anything except human body as sensing and monitoring area. So, based on above discussions, Sensor Networks are of different kinds and can be summarized in Fig. 2.2.

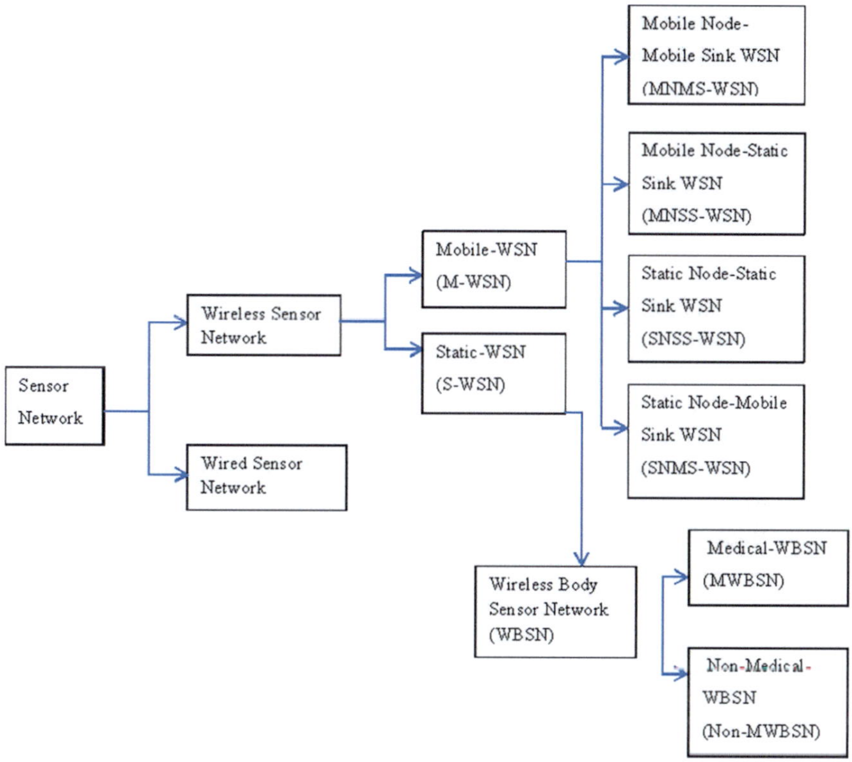

Fig. 2.2 Types of sensor networks based on connectivity, node mobility, applications, etc.

2.2 Real Life Applications of Sensor Networks

In every sphere of life, nowadays there is application of smart technologies such as Sensors, Internet of Things, Cloud, Machine Learning [2, 3] to enhance quality living enabled with automated services without or least manual interventions ranging from personal assistance to societal services to environmental monitoring, etc. Here we discuss in a nutshell several smart applications that contribute toward smart, connected, quality living.

Smart Daily Living: Human Activity Recognition, Fall Detection

Due to daily cores, all people need to move indoor or at outdoors irrespective of age, gender, diseased or fit, living in urban or rural areas. Elderly people who are mostly living alone without manual monitoring, may often face sudden illness, may fall at indoor or Types of Sensor Networks based on connectivity, node mobility, applications, etc., at outdoors and if these emergency situations get unmonitored then these may prove to be fatal, even threatening for life as well.

Another thing is that due to such unwanted events, the confidence of elderly or diseased people who are prone to fall due to suffering from prolonged diseases such as Alzheimers, Parkinsons, Diabetes, Gait issues will be lowered more and they will be scared of mobility due to daily cores at indoors or at outdoors. Thus they will be more immobile and unable to live a quality living.

Now issues need to be addressed are continuous activity monitoring and immediate measure, support in case of sudden illness or abnormal activity or posture w.r.t. location, time and duration of the day. The sensor IoT based Smart Human Activity Monitoring (HAR) to be applied for real time recognition of activity of the human being along with date, time, location and if any abnormality is found then alert message goes to the nearest caregiver, relative, hospital, health care center, ambulance, etc. Cost effective, usable, efficient, privacy aware kinematic motion sensor based, i.e., accelerometer, gyroscope based smart HAR system is a solution or friendly monitoring system of the people in need specifically elderly people. Fall Detection module also is immensely helpful for live fall detection and recovery purpose. Also, smart fall detection module harnessing the power of machine learning, deep learning, etc., is also efficiently able to predict fall event or a person is how much prone to fall. This augmented support would work to enhance confidence of the person and is helpful in rehabilitation process as well.

Smart Environment

Environment is the natural ecosystem surrounding me in smaller sense and the environment in terms if air, water, land pollutions, Weather condition, disaster outbreak, etc., in global sense. Smart environmental monitoring using sensor networks ensures efficient and intelligent monitoring of environmental pollution facts, factors, events, etc., in real time and with accurate forecast and prediction people may live a pollution aware, peaceful healthy life. Timely and accurate prediction of disasters can assure evacuation of people in safe places and also administration can arrange for appropriate measures for proactive mitigation of the disaster affected area. With air pollution forecast of a particular region could help people having breathing discomfort, Asthma, COPD, etc., may navigate themselves toward a less polluted route as frequent exposure to the polluted air may enhance the breathing discomfort related health issues. In a nutshell, Smart environment monitoring includes Air pollution monitoring, Weather forecasting, Environmental monitoring, Disaster prediction and monitoring, etc.

Health Monitoring

People suffering from prolonged age related ailments like Diabetes, Alzheimers, Parkinsons, Heart diseases, Gait issues, Arthritis, etc., need prolonged continuous monitoring of health vital parameters such as blood pressure, blood sugar, heart rate, pulse rate, SpO_2, body temperature, ECG, EEG, EMG, etc., for timely health condition analysis and proper medication for healthy living. With smart sugar level monitoring, automated dose adjustment of insulin can be done timely and with precise accuracy. Along with body vitals monitoring, Human Activity Recognition and monitoring is also very important. Why? May be heart rate, pulse rate, breathing rate or body temperature, blood pressure of a person is within normal range when the person in in sitting or standing or lying posture. But these parameters may abruptly vary when the person is performing dynamic activities such as running, jogging, stairs up or stairs down Or a person may be reluctant from performing dynamic activities and that may be related to health issues. So, combination of these to type of monitoring together may help to conclude more perfectly about health condition of a person than only considering health monitoring using body vitals monitoring.

Time-Critical Application

Time-critical applications, e.g., fire monitoring, smart surveillance, etc., enabled with sensors, WSN, Adhoc Networks have become achievable. Real time monitoring of time critical monitoring such as fire outbreak monitoring at indoors or at outdoors should be identified closest to its source of origin in real time for generating alert and taking necessary safety measure immediately. The appropriate sensors required for fire outbreak detection are deployed in strategic positions at indoors or at outdoors, even in remote areas like forests, mountains, agricultural fields or any remote areas of importance. The sensors connected through wireless links form the Wireless Sensor Network over the region of concern and through the sink node, the sensor data are being transmitted to the server for real time analysis and detection of the event closest to its source of origin for real time mitigation like to alert fire fighting services in real time, to evacuate the place, etc., could be ensured.

Nowadays the methods to identify and recognize the criminal suspects, to monitor their mobility, etc., has become more efficient, intelligent and easier with the utilization of image sensors, CCTV, motion sensors, etc., deployed in and around indoors or at outdoors across the city or regions for surveillance purposes. With analysis of captures sensory data in real time at cloud server applying intelligent models such as Machine Learning, Deep Learning, Neural Networks, Artificial Intelligence, detection of suspected people, suspected behavior combined with postures or activities of the person through HAR, real time surveillance becomes efficiently possible.

Remote Monitoring

Wild Habitat Monitoring, Underwater Marine Life Monitoring, Forest Fire Monitoring. Tiny sensor nodes in huge number are being deployed in remote areas over wide regions—that could be in forests for wild habitat monitoring, underwater for marine life monitoring, forest fire monitoring, forest ecosystem monitoring, etc. The challenge is to transmit sensor data to the server through long range connectivity, i.e., internet, Satellite links, etc.

Smart City: Smart City is comprised of different sensor enabled smart applications such as Smart Home, Smart Traffic Monitoring, Smart Energy, Smart Transportation System, Smart Pollution Monitoring, Smart Healthcare, Smart Security & Surveillance, Smart Logistics, Smart Waste Management etc to make it more livable [4]. These cities are usually very well planned and well equipped unlike the traditional big cities (which often has unplanned growth with lack of infrastructure and facilities).

However, the success of any smart city depends on several factors such as quality of good data from the smart devices, the quality of network, low-latency environment for IoT devices, Security, privacy, quality of sensors and their proper placement, proper coordination among various departments, distributed processing, etc. They may provide smart vehicle parking, smart mall, smart electricity, smart surveillance, smart park, smart hospital, and so on.

Owing to the variety of technologies that have been employed in the smart city label, it is hard to frame an exact definition of a smart city. *Deakin and Al Waer* stated the following four aspects that may lead to the classification of a smart city [4]:

- The implementation of a varied range of automated and digital machineries to societies and towns.
- The usage of Information and Communications Technologies (ICTs) to convert life and operational atmospheres in the region.
- The inclusion of ICTs in government organizations.
- The territorialization of practices which fetches people and ICTs collectively, to improve the invention and skill.

Now in all these smart real life applications, the Wireless Sensor Network primarily ensures the task of sensing data from physical environment, data aggregation, and elementary data pre-processing. Now what to do with these aggregated and pre-processed huge sensory data? Internet of Things here comes to play the pivotal role. Seamlessly these huge sensory data get transmitted to the cloud server through IoT connectivity for further analysis applying intelligent models such as Machine Learning, Deep Learning, Artificial intelligence for meaningful knowledge building. This real time knowledge development initiates communication of feedback to the entrusted authorities in concern for appropriate measure to be taken if needed.

2.2.1 Applications of Sensors in Real-Life

Sensors are eyes and ears of any system. Sensor based smart applications are spreading through almost every possible domain of human civilization [5, 6]. So much and so forth that its society implementation (Society 5.0) is being called as modern revolution toward quality living. Sensors are everywhere—Healthcare, Agriculture, Communications, Transportation, Retail, Energy, Traffic, Industry, etc., are just a few among them. The devices are becoming smart and capable of communicating with each other without human intervention. The platform is being enriched every day through newer wireless networks, ad-hoc networks, advanced level sensors and higher level of computation powers, processing ability.

We may have a look on the major sensor enabled application areas, first Consider Fig. 2.3.

Few of these applications related to smart, quality living are discussed in detail below (Fig. 2.4).

Fig. 2.3 Smart city with smart services

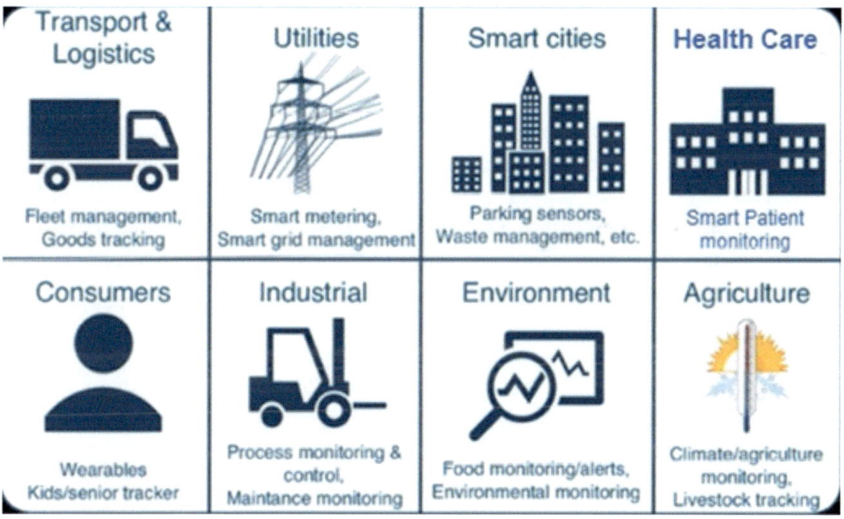

Fig. 2.4 Major smart applications where data sensing and aggregation done by wireless sensors forming wireless sensor network

Smart Cities

The IoT based digital transformation has brought a considerable change in urban life. The rapid urbanization has given rise to the concept of multiple modern, state of the art, small but smart cities [7]. These cities are usually very well planned and well equipped unlike the traditional big cities (which often has unplanned growth with lack of infrastructure and facilities).

However, the success of any smart city depends on several factors such as quality of good data from the smart devices, the quality of network, low-latency environment for IoT devices, Security, privacy, quality of sensors and their proper placement, proper coordination among various departments, distributed processing, etc. They may provide smart vehicle parking, smart mall, smart electricity, smart surveillance, smart park, smart hospital, and so on.

Healthcare

The cost of healthcare services are rapidly increasing with time. The global population is aging and there is a sharp rise in the chronical diseases. The recent pandemic due to COVID-19 shows the gap between the need and the actual manual support that is available.

Medical diagnostic is responsible for a large part of clinical expenses. Technology may help to shift the clinical assessments from a hospital-centric approach to a home-centric approach. Sensor based healthcare services enabled with Internet of things can cut down the bill by offering the following benefits:

1. monitoring and reporting,
2. end to end connectivity in affordable price,
3. data collection and analysis,
4. remote medical support.

However, there are several challenges [7] in providing the above services in unattended manner to a large group of people. Some prevailing challenges in Sensor based smart healthcare services are security and privacy of medical records, multiple devices and protocols integration, Data overload and accuracy, cost, connectivity, etc. Researchers are constantly working toward innovative and cost effective solutions to cope up with the above challenges (Fig. 2.5).

Smart Environmental Monitoring

The functions of sensors in environmental monitoring are extensive—extreme weather monitoring, environmental protection, water safety, commercial farming, endangered species monitoring in reserve forests, etc., and many more. Sensors detect and assess every kind of environmental change in such applications and accordingly the necessary action gets taken by the entrusted authority. The solutions must be 'Green' from the perspective of consumed energy as explained below.

Smart Water Management ensures there remains plenty of fresh drinking water in the planet.

Smart Energy management reduces the energy loss and lowers the carbon footprint. It encourages and implements various green energy sources (air, water, solar, etc.) for energy production and minimizes the use of fossil fuels.

Smart waste management facilitates the 3R (Reduce-Reuse-Recycle). The growing waste is a global problem. The environment protection comprises of the wireless sensors to guide the waste firms to assess fill up level in the garbage bins and boost the waste collection methods. The *Enevo* sensors can cut down the waste collection expenses by about 50%—as per the records collected from 36 countries.

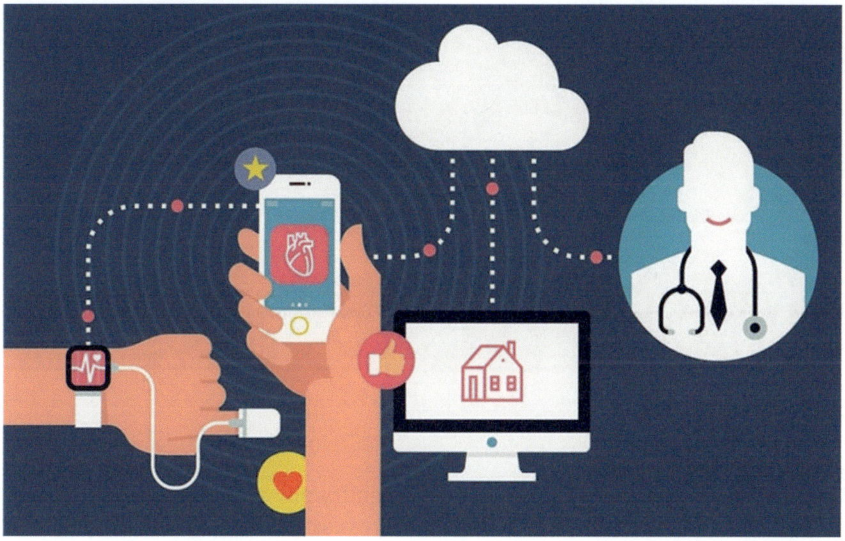

Fig. 2.5 IoT based healthcare services

The automatic wastage compression facility in smart containers can decrease waste collection rate by an average of 70–80%.

Smart Weather monitoring helps to take precautions during unprecedented weather conditions well in advance to minimize the loss of life and properties. Smart sensors along with AI based techniques can accurately predict the forthcoming weather.

Smart sensor collars can be heavily used to monitor the wildlife and save both the animals and the corps. Several non-ambulatory sensors mounted at different points in a forest may detect the forest fire and it's progress along with the movement monitoring of the wildlife (Fig. 2.6).

2.2.1.1 Smart or Precision Agriculture Enabled with WSN, IoT

The concept of smart farming is now reality with the availability of advanced technologies [8]. The capability of remote supervision of the farm environments and infrastructure can save time, labor and capital, letting the farmers to concentrate on other issues. This is also known as digital farming. The farmer can now monitor the corps and can utilize the real time weather information for good yield at minimum cost. The harvesting cost can also be minimized, and the pest control can be done with minimum pesticides. The agricultural drones are heavily used in smart farming. They can not only monitor the corps in a large agricultural area, but also can be used to spray fertilizers. The automated image processing from the drone camera can identify any exception even at a small part of a field. The sensors placed at

Fig. 2.6 Smart environment

different points in an agricultural field can identify any type of herbivorous attack (such as a herd of Deers/parade of elephants/drove of cattle, etc.) in odd hours. This can save the corps before it is too late and can provide 24 h surveillance without manual interventions. Some more benefits of smart farming are

- remote supervision of farm situations and infrastructure, reducing time and amount of labor on everyday farm assessments,
- enhancing producers' decision making via data analytics,
- faster perceptions from real-time information through the value-chain, that helps the cultivators to act toward market demand, and
- proficiency in food production with minimum wastage, convenience to market, and improved traceability to establish secure and sustainable food for consumers.

Establishing the skills for modern tools and participating in research and development for contribution toward constant innovation with enhanced productivity is demonstratated with the example of smart drone based precision agriculture and smart agriculture (Fig. 2.7).

2.2.2 Discussion on Simulation or Implementation Scope of Some of the Pioneering Works

Now, it is time to look at some real-life case studies implemented by various academic and industrial bodies. These case studies will give a brief idea about the problem and the solutions on the various fields of IoT discussed earlier.

Fig. 2.7 **Smart** agriculture scenario

2.2.2.1 Case Studies on IoT in Transportation

One of the most important examples of IoT in transport and logistics is vehicle fleet administration. It is possible to gather knowledge about the situation of the vehicle via sensors and devices implanted in the vehicles. The situation of fuel or driving behavior can also be observed remotely.

Examining the situation of the vital parts in the vehicles such as air pressure in tires, level of the coolant can decrease the amount of unpredicted failures. Maintenance becomes easier and more effective with the real time data access.

UPS Logistic

This system is one of the companies that uses the smart fleet management. The company implemented a supervising system that uses the information from the IoT sensors and GPS to minimise the amount of failures.

Sensor enabled smart solutions in transportation can also predict the behavior of the driver and their driving styles. The vehicle speed stoppage times and the driving habits such as use outbreak accelerator can be obtained in real time. These data can be used to train the drivers to drive more efficiently using less fuels.

It is possible to install sensors and devices in order to maintain the proper temperature and moisture within the transport vehicle using IoT. This is particularly important while transporting delicate foods and medicines. The system may automatically correct and control the situations when something goes out of hand.

Smart fleet management optimizes the vehicle running cost, fuel usage and finds the optimum route from source to destination.

Inventory and Warehouse Management

Modern warehouse or inventory management also implements the power of sensor, IoT, Cloud, etc., for overall increase in their performance.

Space management is an important aspect for any warehouse for efficiently managing the order and delivery. Additionally, the smart systems can help us to optimize the storage space and locate the packages in minimum time.

Smart sensors in a warehouse can automatically create orders when the supply falls below a threshold value. This may be a great method to manage constrained spaces in the warehouse.

RFID tags are frequently utilized by enterprises to handle their goods and stores. As soon as the product enters or leaves a warehouse the database is automatically updated.

A portion of **Amazon, USA** warehouse follows the above mentioned method.

Supply Chain Management

The products go through a cycle of shipments before reaching the final destination [9]. When a large number of different products are rapidly changing their locations simultaneously, it is very difficult to manage them effectively and efficiently. The IoT enabled sensors can automate the entire process in a much more effective and error proof way.

IoT logistic data can provide various information, such as real time location of the goods, theft identification and also the delay in any shipment, etc.

It is important from the sales point of view to have access to the products which are high in demand so that they can be sold quickly. Application of IoT in supply chain management may provide a great help to manage demand and also project the amount of goods being manufactured, ordered, and transported effectively. IoT can optimize the entire process that in effect can minimize the cost and maximize the profit.

The public vehicle company **Volvo** is applying the IoT technologies for acquiring auto parts from separate part of the globe and also shipping their vehicles to different suppliers.

Track and Trace

It is a tedious job to ensure that the goods are loaded in the right truck and are delivered toward right warehouses for any kind of logistics and transportation. The manual procedure not only takes a lot of time and resources but also is prone to error. RFID (radio-frequency identification) and AIDC (automatic identification and data capture) are excellent ways to track the supplies and handle them appropriately. Radio waves in RFID are used to assess the position of supplies depending on applied microchips. Such tags can provide the real time information about the product and its location as well as where the shipment is supposed to go. In contrast to the traditional scanning methods, the RFID is scanned wirelessly and automatically. Such real time data is automatically stored in a database. As a result, these information can be accessed from anywhere. **Decathlon** is applying RFID method to supply their manufactured goods to their retailers over 20 nations.

2.2.3 *Case Studies on Smart Healthcare*

There are many healthcare applications related to hygiene, and this became more imperative than ever as the COVID-19 pandemic took center stage around the world. The Internet of Things provides the right capabilities at the right time for no-contact applications and remote connectivity, all of which support more hygienic health management.

FloorBotics, a robotic software and hardware development firm, builds pioneering solutions as per the market demand for economic substitutes to labor-intensive and non-sterile clean-up systems [10]. The hospital acquired infection are managed by a series of set and forget robotic cleaners specifically designed for this purpose. Post COVID-19 pandemic, this is particularly useful to automatically handle the contaminated areas of the hospital without risking the human health (Fig. 2.8).

The FloorBotics "Sanibot™" robot provides a floor sanitation solution constantly by throwing a controlled beam of ultraviolet light for the surface disinfection. The robot design comprises of the Digi XBee® Cellular LTE CAT 1 modem, that unites 4G connectivity, built-in security, and a bundled cellular data plan in every development set. This allows the machines to communicate over the cellular network straight out of the box.

Clean Hands Safe Hands seek out to support healthcare and medical establishments to boost health and safety, employing wireless technology.

The Clean Hands Safe Hands product design uses Bluetooth based wireless communication in sterilizing stations. These stations are sensor-activated and prompt for hand sanitation. Each individual employee can be uniquely identified by the sensor and they are hand hygiene events are recorded via the health system. As the staffs

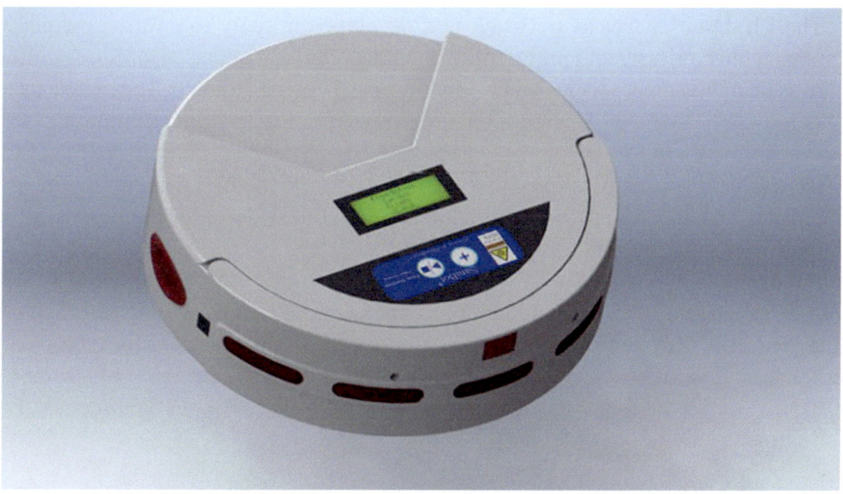

Fig. 2.8 The FloorBotics "Sanibot™"

enter or exit rooms, they must sanitize within a specified amount of time before the event is recorded by the sensor. This hand hygiene is one of the prime requirements to restrict the spread of the COVID-19 pandemic.

The sensors are associated using Digi XBee® Gateways that include Zigbee mesh topology. The collective data maintenance is possible due to the fact that the sanitizing stations are connected in a mesh network. This avoids unnecessary reminders for the person who has just sanitized hand in another nearby location.

BOS Technology not only provides monitoring solutions for critical and dangerous environments like clinics and hospitals but also extends the solution to the individual gathering places like school/college, tourist spot and other similar areas [11]. Service administrators can examine data from BOS Technology sensors in key areas, including differential pressure, temperature, tVOC (volatile organic compounds), humidity, ACPH (air changes per hour), etc.

For example, the overall building environment can be monitored for good health by analyzing the air exchanges and air supplies through HVAC systems and can deliver a range of data points which may act as a health metrics for a building's natural environment.

The **Kinetic company** has built a workplace wearable called REFLEX™ that increases worker safety via biofeedback. The workers who's task involved twisting, lifting and bending type of jobs, REFLEX is an ideal compact warning system for dangerous posture. The system provides a haptic vibration to the employee if it can identify that the posture may lead to an improper lifting or twisting which may result an injury. The supervisor and the employee can assess the progress on a dashboard at the end of the shift, based on the collected data all over the day (Fig. 2.9).

First responders play a critical role in the care cycle—responding to injury incidents and routing ambulances through city streets to get patients to hospital services—which require fast, reliable communications and GPS navigation.

The **FirstNet® wireless network** was developed initially to ensure emergency personnel have priority and pre-emptive mobile communications capabilities during large scale public emergencies when networks can become jammed. Today, IoT solutions providers like Digi International are integrating FirstNet into cellular devices and certifying them for use on these networks. These devices are then deployed for mission critical communications not only in emergency vehicles like police, fire and ambulance, but also for priority communications in transit systems, intelligent traffic management systems, and more.

For example, the New York City Department of Transportation deployed 14,000 Digi FirstNet Ready™ cellular routers to intersections across all five boroughs to improve traffic flow and support rapid response and communications for emergency responders.

Fig. 2.9 REFLEX™ by Kinetic company

2.2.4 *Case Studies on Sensor, IoT, Cloud Based Applications for Environment*

Inter vehicle communication can pave a way of allowing the smart cars to move to a new era of green driving by providing a total connectivity and communication environment with the other vehicles to convey about their decisions [12].

The system may reduce the additional fuel consumption during the speed and gear changes in a human operated vehicle by allowing the traffic to move at a constant speed keeping only a small gap between them, in an automated manner.

A driverless car called **Olli** is implemented using **IBM's Watson IoT Platform**. The large amount of data coming from various sensors in the vehicle are [13] analyzed by the Watson IoT platform and instruction is provided to speed up/down and change lanes without manual intervention.

IoT has been successful to save the extinct species with great care. The **Iberian Lynx** could be re-established in **Spain** by applying IoT tools to trace and supervise the last remaining wild lynxes. Wildlife experts and scientists were able to re-establish the species by using the smart collars equipped with the Geo mapping capability on their habits and locations and integrating them with the connector drones without disturbing the natural habitats of the animals.

Smart homes [14] can stop the unnecessary energy usage by switching off idle lights, preventing empty heating that no one will be using soon. This may help reducing the carbon footprint on the earth.

Like **the Loxone Smart Home**, programs are now available to turn on/off lights and manage the warmth and boiler parameters remotely. Smart cars may be connected to smart homes creating more sophisticated services and savings opportunity in conjugation.

Modern sensors have very small form factors and high sensitivity, so they can now be easily carried around by the people. The weather sensors can measure the air quality and can generate warnings for the users by apps on their smartphone if the atmosphere is found dangerous for the people with asthma problem. In a highly populated area, this can raise awareness of pollution and can be extremely helpful for the user. Similar type of devices are helping the people who are working in a radiation prone area or inside a mine. Such systems provide the opportunity to the government and the communities to control the rising pollution levels.

Smart sensors can also help the farmers to reduce the amount of their production waste and also can monitor the agricultural process based on sunlight, humidity, weather and other factors. People can also prevent the unnecessary watering of the soils when the sensor detect that the soil moisture levels are just perfect. So, it can save a huge amount of sweet waters which is one of the growing concern of modern world. An IoT based methodology can help to decrease the waste and enhance the energy efficiency in the agricultural domain.

2.2.5 Case Studies on Precision Agriculture

IoT solutions has revolutionized the modern agriculture and farming and the demand is constantly in rise. COVID-19 made a positive impact on IoT in the agricultural market segment. Interruptions in the supply chain, along with the scarcity of qualified agricultural workers, has propelled its Compound Annual Growth Rate (CAGR) to 9.9% [8, 14]. In fact, as per the latest reports, the smart framing market segment is set to make a mammoth $6.2 billion by 2022.

Monitoring of Climate Conditions

Weather stations are the most popular smart agricultural devices that combines various types of smart farming sensors. Installed across the farming field, they gather several environmental data and send it to the cloud. The concept of **precision farming** may be implemented by fine measurements to map the climate conditions and choose the appropriate corps and acquired methodologies to increase their capacity.

Some examples of such agriculture IoT devices are **allMETEO**, **AGRISEN** (IIT, KGP), **Pycno, and Smart Elements**.

Greenhouse Automation

In addition to tracking environmental data, weather stations has the capability to automatically adjust the conditions based on the given parameters. For example, a similar principle is used for greenhouse automation system.

Other examples include **Farmapp and Growlink** that are also IoT agriculture goods extending such abilities among others.

GreenIQ is a commercial product that operates on smart agriculture sensors. It is a smart sprinklers controller that supports the remote management of lighting and irrigation systems.

Crop Management

Crop management device is an IoT enabled sensor device that is an integral part of precision firming and crop management services. They are assigned in the field for crop specific data collection. To improve the farming procedure, the temperature and aqua-potential of the leaves as well as crop health data can be used for analysis.

Therefore, it is possible to monitor the growth of the corps and detect any inconsistencies early to avoid diseases or pest invasions which may damage the produce. **Arable and Semios** can deliver a great interpretations on how such systems may be employed in real life.

Summary

This chapter illustrates on different applications of Wireless Networks in various applications. The applications are being developed maintaining the efficiency, Quality of Service, quality, usability, etc., for convenience of the users. Wireless Networks assures ubiquitous computing enabling users to avail services with anytime, anywhere, and anything computing.

2.2.6 Problems

In this section, few basic conceptual and fundamental problems on WSN, IoT will be discussed with probable answers.

Question Q.1 What is Wireless Sensor Network?

Ans: Wireless Sensor Network is a connected network of Sensors through wireless links spread over a region indoor as well as outdoor.

Question Q.2 Nodes and links in WSN are homogeneous or heterogeneous?

Ans: Nodes and links in WSN could be homogeneous or heterogeneous depending on type of nodes or links required for a particular real life application. Nodes can be heterogeneous in terms of size, weight, resources such as battery power, memory, processor, connectivity type, mobility support Links also can be heterogeneous in terms of coverage range, bandwidth, data rate, etc.

Question Q.3 Is WSN static or Mobile?

WSN is static or mobile gets decided by the mobility of sensor nodes or sink node. Majorly sensor nodes in a WSN is static once deployed but sink node may be mobile. If WSN is a WBAN attached to a human body, then the whole WBAN or the sensor nodes at different body parts may move as per temporal mobility.

Question Q.4 Is WBAN a WSN?

Yes, WBAN is special type of WSN applied for body vitals monitoring, sensor nodes are the biomedical sensors to sense body vitals such as body temperature, blood pressure, heart rate, pulse rate, glucose level, ECG, EEG, EMG, SpO_2. Sensor node can either be attached to body or implanted.

Question Q.5 How Sensors and IoT help in Environment monitoring?

Sensors and IoT help is Environment monitoring by ensuring followings in energy efficient manner:

Smart Water Management
Smart Energy Management
Smart Waste Management
Smart Weather Monitoring
Smart Sensor Collars for wild habitat monitoring.

Question Q.6 What is Green IoT?

Green IoT is a sustainable framework aiming to reduce energy consumption and environmental impact by utilizing energy aware hardware and software.

Question 7 What are the benefits of IIoT?

Some benefits of IIoT may be listed as follows

- Better energy efficiency.
- Lower costs.
- Superior quality products.
- Enhanced decision-making capability.
- Fewer equipment downtime.

Question Q.8 What are the different types of Sensor Network based on node mobility and link type?

Ans: Based on node mobility and types of links, variations of Sensor Networks are

Static Sensor Node, Static Sink Node (S-S)
Static Sensor Node, Mobile Sink Node (S-M)
Mobile Sensor Node, Static Sink Node (M-S)
Mobile Sensor Node, Mobile Sink Node (M-M).

References

1. Khalifeh, A., Darabkh, K.A., Khasawneh, A.M., Alqaisieh, I., Salameh, M., AlAbdala, A., et al.: Wireless sensor networks for smart cities: network design, implementation and performance evaluation. Electronics **10**(2), 218 (2021)
2. Gautam, A., Mahajan, R., Zafar, S.: Big data analytics for MANET based sustainable smart healthcare solution. Recent Adv. Comput. Sci. Commun. (Formerly: Recent Patents on Computer Science) **15**(4), 601–610 (2022)
3. Tripathy, B.K., Jena, S.K., Reddy, V., Das, S., Panda, S.K.: A novel communication framework between MANET and WSN in IoT based smart environment. Int. J. Inf. Technol. **13**(3), 921–931 (2021)
4. Yustiari, S.H.: Smart governance and smart cities: a review of the literature. Jurnal Ilmiah Administrasi Publik **6**(1), 166–169 (2020)
5. Rey, A., Panetti, E., Maglio, R., Ferretti, M.: Determinants in adopting the internet of things in the transport and logistics industry. J. Bus. Res. **131**, 584–590 (2021)
6. Renugadevi, N., Saravanan, S., Sudha, C.N.: IoT based smart energy grid for sustainable cites. Mater. Today: Proc. (2021)
7. Selvaraj, S., Sundaravaradhan, S.: Challenges and opportunities in IoT healthcare systems: a systematic review. SN Appl. Sci. **2**(1), 1–8 (2020)
8. Farooq, M.S., Riaz, S., Abid, A., Umer, T., Zikria, Y.B.: Role of IoT technology in agriculture: a systematic literature review. Electronics **9**(2), 319 (2020)
9. Kaur, J., Santhoshkumar, N., Nomani, M.Z.M., Sharma, D.K., Maroor, J.P., Dhiman, V.: Impact of internets of things (IoT) in retail sector. Mater. Today: Proc. (2021)
10. https://www.prweb.com/releases/floorbotics_announces_the_successful_design_and_prototyping_of_a_revolutionary_floor_sanitizing_robot/prweb13473991.htm
11. https://healthcare.bos.com/
12. Khan, S., Nazir, S., Khan, H.U.: Smart object detection and home appliances control system in smart cities. Comput., Mater. Contin. **67**, 895–915 (2021)
13. Shahzad, Y., Javed, H., Farman, H., Ahmad, J., Jan, B., Zubair, M.: Internet of energy: opportunities, applications, architectures and challenges in smart industries. Comput. Electr. Eng. **86**, 106739 (2020)
14. Tuysuz, M.F., Trestian, R.: From serendipity to sustainable green IoT: technical, industrial and political perspective. Comput. Netw. **182**, 107469 (2020)

Chapter 3
Architectures

Abstract This chapter tells all about the architectures and network models. The chapter starts with descriptions on different types of networks. The chapter also deals in details about Mobile Adhoc Network (MANET).

Keywords Wired network · Topology · MANET · 7 layer model · TCP/IP model

3.1 Introduction

Generally, the term architecture means the art and technique of designing and building. When this is extended to "network architecture", it naturally includes at first the design of how the devices will be connected to form the network, and then, the building itself which represents the structure of the networked devices along with their services. Network devices typically include switches and routers. These will act as the connection points for different types of computing and general facilities, like, server, desktop, laptop, printer/scanner, as well as a variety of available smart devices. The inclusion of the service is due to the fact that otherwise, the structure may not serve the purpose for which it is built. The connected devices will act as both service providers, and service receivers or clients depending on the requirement of the system. By virtue of connectivity, the connected or networked devices will be able to communicate among themselves. This communication may be for resource sharing, collaborative computation requirements, among others. In a nutshell, network architecture is viewed as the physical and logical design of software, hardware, protocols and media of transmission. This implies that the connection among the network devices and the information and/or data flow depending upon the tasks assigned to them, comprise the network architecture. However, the categorization of networks may depend upon a couple of factors, like, the nature of working (assignment and execution of tasks) of the devices, the size of the network, nature of interconnection among the network devices thereby assigning a structure to the network, and number of layers.

S. Biswas et al., *Adhoc and Sensor Networks: Security and Applications*, Studies in Systems, Decision and Control 653, https://doi.org/10.1007/978-981-95-5839-1_3

It is important that before we delve deep into the architecture of networks, it is necessary to establish the connection type present in the network. The network that uses physical cables for connecting devices to other networks or the internet belongs to the category of *wired* network. Most wired networks are Ethernet networks. The category of network that uses wireless communication links, like radio waves, is known as *wireless* network. Although there are varieties of wireless technologies, the most common among them are WiFi and Bluetooth. Wireless connectivity has expanded in such a way that it has majorly impacted our daily lives. Nowadays every other thing that a house generally has can be connected with each other. This includes not only personal computers, or laptops, or smartphones, printers, scanners, but also smart TVs, speakers, house lighting, thermostats, door locks, security cameras, and if anybody wants, it includes coffee makers and refrigerators too.

Again, it can be said that as the wired networks enjoy the support of physical connectivity, they have the infrastructure support. Hence this category of network is usually the *infrastructured* network. This network may have single or multiple servers, and different computing and other devices, like printer, scanner, storage. Needless to say, that all devices including the server must have a network interface card (NIC) to stay connected to the network. A Network Interface Card (NIC) is an essential component of any computer that connects it to the network. It enables data to be sent and received between the computer and other network-connected devices, such as routers or switches. The server/s are supposed to be the controlling device in such networks. Any connected device can access the service/s offered by the server.

Wireless networks are able to operate in two modes: *infrastructured*, and *adhoc*.

Infrastructure mode is used to connect computers with wireless network adapters, to an existing wired network via wireless router or access point. The access point is basically a transceiver that actually connects to a wired network using Ethernet cables. Generally, the access points or routers are used by wireless devices to connect to some existing network server. Thus routing decisions are made using routing tables maintained in servers and the wireless devices use the infrastructure via the access points.

Ad hoc mode is used to connect wireless devices within their transmission ranges, and without the need for a wireless router or access point. An ad hoc network thus, does not need any infrastructure and hence is also known as an *infrastructureless* network. In the absence of any infrastructure, the devices themselves have the responsibility of sending and forwarding messages. Thus, the devices in an adhoc network also have to work as routers, since there are access points or routers. Routing decisions are usually made based on local information and collected information from neighbors. The neighbors in turn collect information from their neighbors, and so on.

Now let us try to understand these categories of a computer network. These categories are all applicable to wired networks. Since the transmission medium in wireless networks is not physical cable, unlike wired networks, the topology in wireless networks may be considered to be logical. The next section talks not only about the different types of networks, particularly wired networks, but also includes wireless networks, wherever applicable.

3.2 Types of Networks and Topologies

The factors mentioned in the earlier section are considered one by one and this gives rise to the following types of networks.

- Nature of working of devices
  - Peer to peer network
  - Client-server network
- Size
  - Local Area Network (LAN)
  - Personal Area Network (PAN)
  - Metropolitan Area Network (PAN)
  - Wide Area Network (WAN)
- Interconnection among Devices
  - Bus Topology
  - Ring Topology
  - Star Topology
  - Tree Topology
  - Mcsh Topology
- Number of Layers
  - ISO/OSI model (7 layers)
  - 5-layered model
  - TCP/IP model (4 layers).

  In the next section we discuss different types of wired networks.

3.2.1 *Peer to Peer Network (P2P Network)*

Even before P2P Network came into existence, there came USENET in 1979 that enabled users to read and post messages. There was no concept of a central servicing node or server. The P2P network began in the 1980s with the advent of personal computers. The first P2P network was built to share text and chat, known as the internet relay chat, in 1988. As is well known, the file-sharing P2P software (including audio) Napster was developed in June 1999. It became hugely popular. But, Napster was shut down in 2001 following a court injunction granted to Recording Industry Association of America (RIAA) as it sued Napster for copyright infringement. However the very idea that songs could be stored and/or downloaded and also shared through a network caught like wildfire. Gnutella, the first decentralized P2P file sharing network, allowed accessing files on other devices via a designated folder.

The computers in the P2P network connect with each other to share files, access the internet and any other common network resource. Each of them can share its own file with the other, and receive file from others, as well. The network is generally a small one, consisting of 10–12 devices, or nodes, as commonly called. The peer is the network device (like, computer) that can both provide and consume resources. This network is thus a distributed application architecture.

Applications of P2P Network include file sharing, block chain, Direct Messaging, content distribution, collaboration.

P2P networks are easy to maintain as nodes manage themselves and adding or deleting nodes do not involve any other node. It is comparatively less costly than other types of networks as there is no central server. However, there being no data backup becomes a reliability issue as data loss may happen if a node goes down. As nodes are independent, it becomes difficult to secure the entire network. Another issue is to properly locate the file that a node wants to access from other nodes.

For wired networks, P2P connection involves any direct physical cable connection. Hence the number of physical links associated with one wired device decides the number of fixed connections that device maintains, and thereby the number of peers. With wireless networks, since the transmission is through radio waves, any fixed number of connections cannot be foretold. Whichever device is within the transmission range of another device is actually connected wirelessly, and termed as a neighbor of that device. Thus the number of neighbors, or peers, is not known. So a P2P wireless network may not be a feasible network to work with, unless the devices are known to have a fixed location and fixed transmission range (Fig. 3.1).

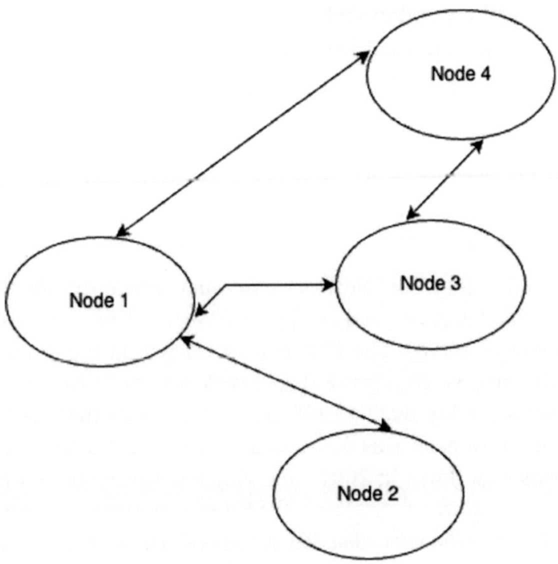

Fig. 3.1 Peer to peer network

3.2.2 Client–Server Network

A client–server network is a distributed communications architecture. The purpose of the network is to efficiently share resources. There is one centralized server and multiple clients are connected to the server. As the name suggests, the server is responsible for providing resource or service to all clients with whom it is attached. The client initiates a request for some service to a server, which will respond to the request by sending the response. A server receives and responds to requests for services from multiple clients. Similarly, on the server end, the server on receiving the client request provides the requested resource or service to the client. For example, a browser is the client program that requests data from any web server. The server may be involved in multiple tasks. It may be database server handling data storage and retrieval. This requires providing data integrity, consistency and overall security. Some other type of servers may be involved in performing computationally intensive tasks for clients. However, it is desirable that a server validates a client before proceeding to provide the client necessary service. A server also has to ensure its performance by providing timely service to the clients. This model of network architecture is suitable for any size of the clientele, ranging from small businesses to large enterprises.

The request-response pattern of exchanging messages between client and server is the example of inter-process communication. Hence both sides must agree on a common language and format and rules. These are defined in communication protocols, which are described in Chap. 4.

Since dedicated servers are used for specific task or activity, they have enhanced reliability, speed and performance. However, being dedicated also implies that these are expensive. This type of network is scalable in nature and easy to be secured due to the presence of a centralized server. And the presence of a centralized server also serves as a bottleneck in a network, as all traffic is toward it. A server also takes down the network with it when it itself fails.

Client–Server network may work both as wired and wireless network. The difference between the two being, in the type of the transmission medium only. A server may connect with its wired clients via routers, whereas a server may connect with its wireless clients via access points (Fig. 3.2).

3.2.3 Local Area Network (LAN)

A Local Area Network (LAN) is a collection of devices connected over a single, limited area, that is, a building or home or office. There may be large number of users or devices, but the characteristic of LAN is the small or limited geographical region or area.

LANS were developed in 1960s primarily for educational and research purposes. They were in use in colleges, universities and research facilities. The primary goal

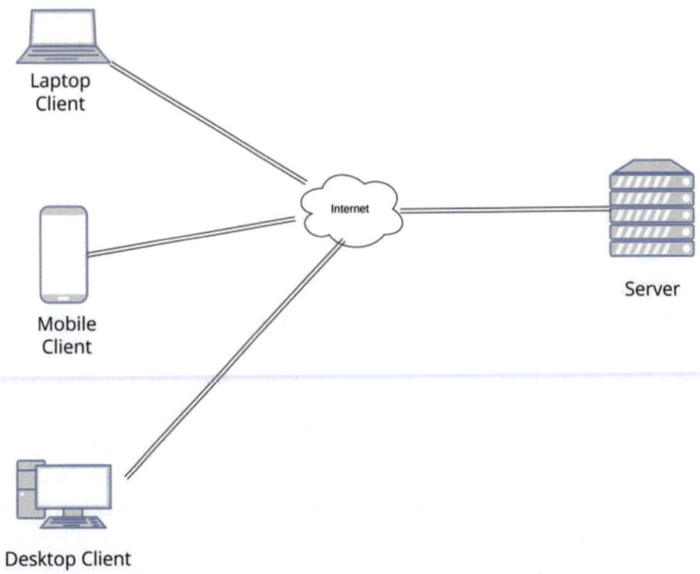

Fig. 3.2 Client–server network

was to connect computers to other computers. Development of Ethernet technology (1973), its commercialization (1980), and its standardization (1983) led to its popular choice as network and eventually wide use.

Setting up a LAN requires cables, switches, access points, routers, apart from computers that may be servers and/or desktops, laptops, workstations, smart devices, etc. The advantages of LAN are the same that any networked device would enjoy. Devices can use the same and single Internet connection, access resources shared by all them over this network.

LANS may work either in the Client/Server mode or Peer to peer mode.

The devices share resources to a switch or router in P2P LAN, which does not have any central server. In Client/Server mode, there will be a central server that manages access to resources, storage, and network traffic. The clients can connect with the server to access the service they are looking for. It is typical for a LAN server to have suites of applications that are generally required by clients.

Apart from physical LAN which may span a room, a floor, a building, several nearby buildings in an institution or a small geographical area, Wireless LANs are nowadays most popular due to their ease of setting up and usage.

In a typical WLAN configuration, the access point connects to the wired network from a fixed location using standard Ethernet cable. Besides acting as transceiver, the access point also buffers data between the WLAN and the wired network infrastructure. A single Access Point can support users and can function within a range of less than one hundred to several hundred feet. Wireless Fidelity or Wi-Fi, as it is commonly called, is a family of wireless protocols based on IEEE 802.11 standards,

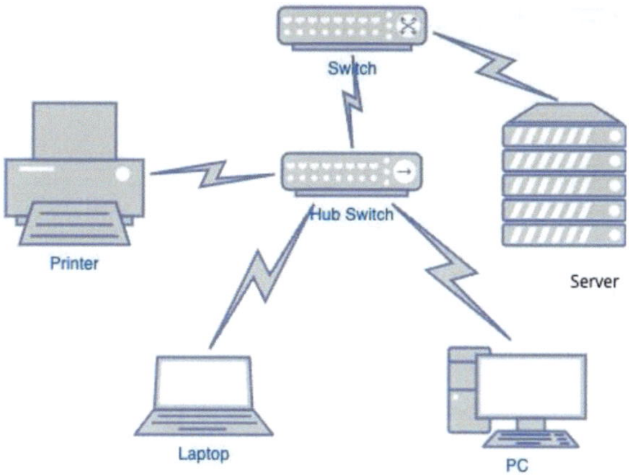

Fig. 3.3 Local area network (LAN)

are most commonly used for setting up wireless LANs. These are used globally in homes, offices, etc., that provide wireless connectivity of devices to access the internet with the help of wireless routers and wireless access points (Fig. 3.3).

3.2.4 Personal Area Network (PAN)

A Personal Area Network (PAN) is a network that generally connects several different types of devices, including desktops, laptops and other smart devices like mobile phone, tablet, Personal Digital Assistance (PDA), entertainment devices, etc., within a user's immediate area. The size of PAN may range from few centimeters to few meters. The connection between Bluetooth earpiece and the mobile phone of a user can be considered as the most popular example of PAN.

Wireless Personal Area Network can be set up by using wireless technologies such as WiFi, Bluetooth. It is a low range network (Fig. 3.4).

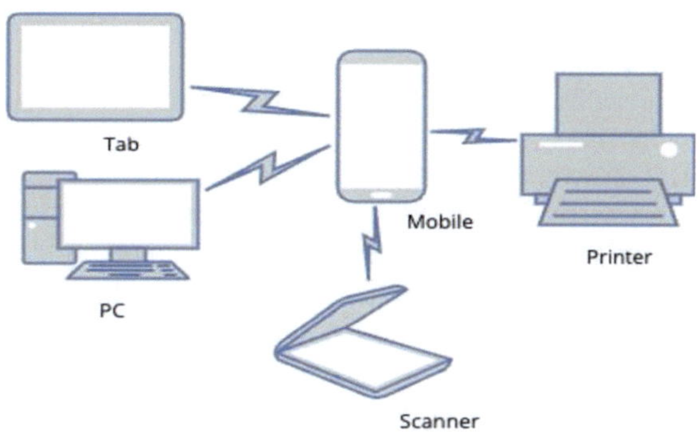

Fig. 3.4 Personal area network (PAN)

3.2.5 Metropolitan Area Network (MAN)

A computer network that connects multiple computers in a metropolitan area like city, multiple cities, or a large area with many buildings is called Metropolitan Area Network (MAN). MAN is larger in area than LAN. The range of MAN may be 5–50 km. The local cable TV company is one of the examples of MAN. Mostly, MANs are implemented using fiber optic cables. These help in maintaining speed and data capacity.

3.2.6 Wide Area Network (WAN)

As the name suggests, Wide Area Network or WAN connects multiple smaller networks, such as LANs across a large geographical area. WAN is thus a network of networks. It is aptly called wide area network because it is not limited in a single building or large campus. But it tends to include multiple locations spread across a specific geographic area, or countries, or even the world. WAN allows devices from anywhere in the world to communicate and share information, as it connects offices, data centers, cloud storage, etc. Businesses that have multiple offices in various countries use WAN to connect to their office network.

WANs generally use leased lines. Since these are expensive, WANs can also be built using circuit switching or packet switching methods, and Ethernet as well.

However, WAN may face more security challenges than LAN or any other small networks due to the use of various technologies. It is also more costly to be set up as multiple routers, switches of different capabilities have to be procured.

Apart from wired WAN, wireless WAN (WWAN) also is very popular. The technology of WWAN differs from WLAN, as the geographic area of WAN is far greater than in LAN. In WWAN, mobile telecommunication cellular technologies, like 2G, 3G, 4G LTE, 5G, 6G are in use. A wireless service provider provides these technologies, also referred to as mobile broadband.

3.2.7 Bus Topology

This structure of the network is the configuration in which all devices are connected to a single cable called the backbone or bus. This is the shared communication line among the devices. The Bus topology supports bi-directional communication in the form of half-duplex. Hence the devices can both transmit and receive information, albeit in a single direction at a time. The Bus topology is mainly used in the IEEE 802.3 and IEEE 802.4 standard network. Coaxial cable or twisted pair cable (RJ-45 network cable) is usually used as the backbone cable. The most common access method is Carrier Sense Multiple Access (CSMA). However, as two nodes may try

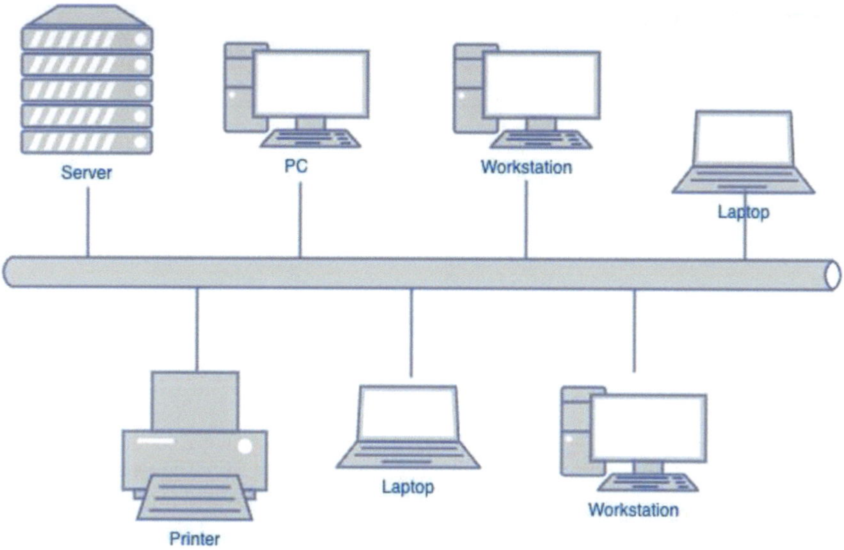

Fig. 3.5 Bus topology

to access the bus simultaneously, two methods are in place to control the data flow in the bus so that data packets are not lost. These are:

- Carrier Sense Multiple Access Collision Detection (CSMA CD)—This is used for detecting collisions. Whenever a station (device attached to the bus) detects a collision, it refrains from transmitting.
- Carrier Sense Multiple Access Collision Avoidance (CSMA CA)—This is used for avoiding collisions. So, a station tries to find out if some transmission is going on, that is, whether the bus is busy. If so, the station waits for sometime till the medium is idle, before beginning transmission. This technique helps in reducing collisions, but a station may have to wait for long or multiple times to gain access to the medium.

Advantages of this topology include low installation cost due to the common cable, support of moderate data speed up to 10 Mbps, no effect of failure of individual node in the network.

However, even with CSMA CD and/or CSMA CA, collisions could still happen, and any fault in the cable itself affects the entire network (Fig. 3.5).

3.2.8 *Ring Topology*

In this network configuration, the devices are connected in a circular pattern, creating a closed loop. So, every device is connected to two other devices, thus forming a ring.

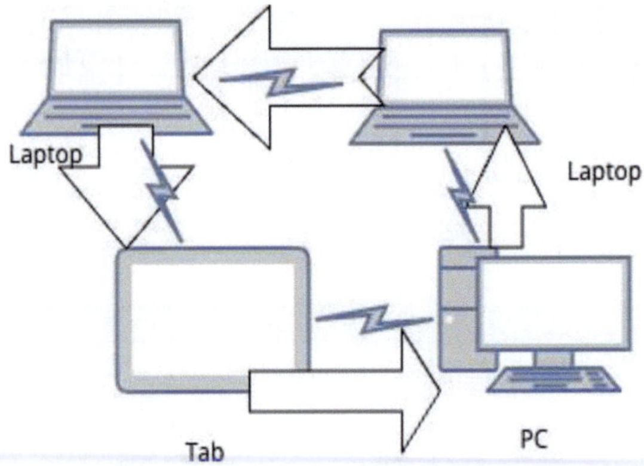

Fig. 3.6 Ring topology

Thus, a device is able to send and receive information only from the two devices it is connected to. These devices may be termed as 'neighbors'. Data in this network flows in a single loop continuously, usually in the clockwise or anticlockwise direction. An RJ-45 network cable or a coaxial cable is used to connect the devices.

The most common access method in ring topology is through token passing. Empty tokens with a place for holding data are distributed in the ring. If a node wants to send data, it captures a token, fills it with data, its own MAC address, and the MAC address of the destination. Then it passes the token to the next node and if that neighbor is not the destination, it passes that filled token to the next node and this goes on till the filled token with data reaches the destination mentioned in the token. Generally this form of data transmission is helpful for avoiding collisions. However, this topology may not be in use at present (Fig. 3.6).

3.2.9 Star Topology

Star topology is a network configuration that has a central network processor to which all network devices are connected. Hence the layout looks like a star, and thus the name of the topology. The star may be a LAN too. The central node manages the network as each device has to send the data and the destination it wants to send the data, to the central node at first. The central node checks the destination first. If valid, then data is delivered to the destination, by the central node, otherwise data is rejected. Probability of data collisions is nil. Detecting fault is easy as each connection is separate and only between the central node and the respective device. However, if the central node goes down, the network also goes down (Fig. 3.7).

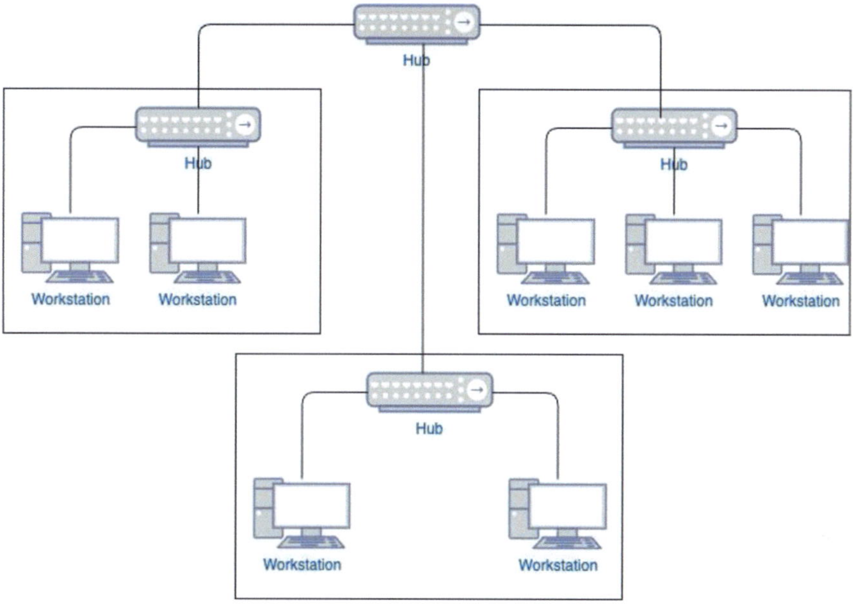

Fig. 3.7 Star topology

3.2.10 Tree Topology

The network topology resembling a "tree" with a root node (central hub) and other nodes hanging out like branches and connected to the central node through a single path is the tree topology. Tree topology is also defined to be star-bus topology. This is so called because every branch forms a star network and the main structure is designed as a bus backbone. Devices are connected hierarchically. The topology supports broadband transmission, and may provide better performance than bus topology as intelligent hubs or switches can be used. Although the topology is scalable, security issues remain as the devices can see the data going through the network (Fig. 3.8).

3.2.11 Mesh Topology

A mesh topology is the network structure in which each network device is connected to the other. Thus with redundant links, the network provides fault tolerance too. If each device is connected to every other device, the network is a full mesh network, otherwise it is a partial mesh network. Services, particularly emergency services, that require reliable communication use mesh topology. Main advantages of mesh networks are fault tolerance, redundant links, continuous connectivity, among others. However, the cost to set up a mesh network and manage it may be quite difficult.

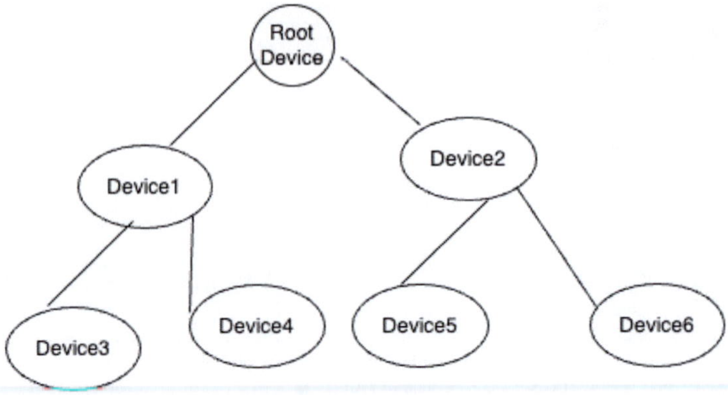

Fig. 3.8 Tree topology

Mesh WiFi, however, can be used in scenarios where a single router is unable to provide adequate coverage. It can be thought of as a LAN of multiple nodes that are able to broadcast a WiFi signal over a large area. In a Mesh WiFi system, connected devices are seamlessly handed off to the router or satellite with the strongest WiFi signal in a given area. A mesh network, in such a scenario, is a group of connectivity devices, such as Wi-Fi routers that act as a single network, so there are multiple sources of connectivity around an area (like a house or a building), instead of just a single router. Google calls the first mesh device that is set up a router, and each additional mesh device a point (Fig. 3.9).

Fig. 3.9 Mesh topology

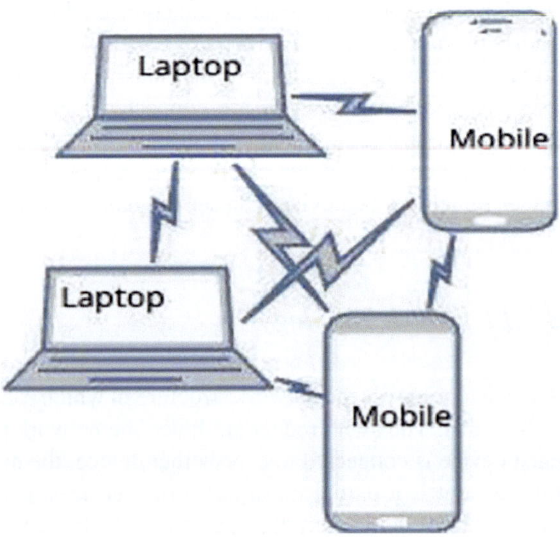

3.2.12 ISO/OSI Model (7 Layers)

The Open Systems Interconnection (OSI) model was developed by the International Organization for Standardization (ISO) in 1984, and since then it is considered to be the basic architectural model for inter-computer communications over the network. With its seven layers the model clearly demonstrates the steps of the flow of information from one software application in the sender computer to the software application in the receiver machine. The layers and their functionalities are briefly mentioned as follows:

- Physical Layer—This is the lowest layer responsible for the establishment and maintenance of actual physical connection for transmitting data/information bits. It also specifies the topology of the network, as well as all types of interfaces, like mechanical, electrical and procedural network.
- Data Link Layer—The responsibility of this layer is to deliver error-free data frames from one network computer to another over the Physical Layer. Switches and bridges are common Data Link layer devices. Overall functioning of the Data Link Layer includes framing (size of frame depends on the Network Interface Card) of the raw bits from the physical layer and putting sender address and destination MAC address. The MAC address is known through the Address Resolution Protocol (ARP). MAC address of the network computer is used for delivery of the data packet. This layer is also responsible for the error control and flow control. This layer is divided into two layers. Point-to-Point Protocol (PPP) and Ethernet IEEE 802.2 are the examples of the Data Link Layer protocols.
  - Logical Link Control (LLC)—This sublayer is responsible for dealing with the Network Layer regarding receiving packets from it at the sender end, delivering packets to it at the receiver end, and identifying the Network Layer protocol including providing flow control.
  - Medium Access Control (MAC)—Access control of the media is the main function of this sublayer.
- Network Layer—This is the Layer 3 protocol responsible for transmission of data from one computer to the other in different networks. IP addresses of both the sender and the receiver are placed in the packet header. Routers and switches work in this layer. The main functions of this layer are to find the best route between the communicating partners or routing, and internetworking which provides the logical connection between different devices. Logical addressing scheme using IP addresses uniquely and universally identifies a device in a network. The protocols used by this layer are IPv4, IPv6, etc.
- Transport Layer—The main responsibility of this layer is the end to end delivery of the message. This layer as a sender receives formatted data from upper layers of the sender device, performs Segmentation, adds both source and destination port numbers in the header and pushes the segment to the Network Layer. Flow control and error control are also implemented to ensure flawless data transmission. At the receiver end, different segments of the same message bearing

sequence numbers are reassembled to form the entire message. The port number is identified and the message is delivered to the appropriate service process. The Transport Layer provides both connection-oriented and connectionless service. Acknowledgment handling is also a functionality of this layer. The protocols used include Transmission Control Protocol (TCP), User Datagram Protocol (UDP), among others.

- Session Layer—As a network is all about connections between devices, a layer in the OSI model is dedicated to perform the functionalities with respect to connections. Session Layer is responsible for establishing, managing and terminating sessions between two devices. It also provides authentication and security. Maintaining synchronization is also one of its functionalities. Protocols used in the Session Layer are NetBIOS, PPTP.
- Presentation Layer—As the name suggests, the function of this layer is to translate the information into proper syntax and semantics and present the information. Different encoding methods, encryption methods and compression methods are also used for the purpose. Protocols used in this layer are JPEG, MPEG, GIF, etc.
- Application Layer—The uppermost layer in the network architecture or the network protocol stack, as it is commonly referred to, is the Application Layer. The applications produce data/information to be transmitted over the network. This layer also allows application services to access the network, as well as provides necessary services for displaying the received information to the user. The protocols pertaining to this layer are SMTP, FDP, DNS, among others (Fig. 3.10).

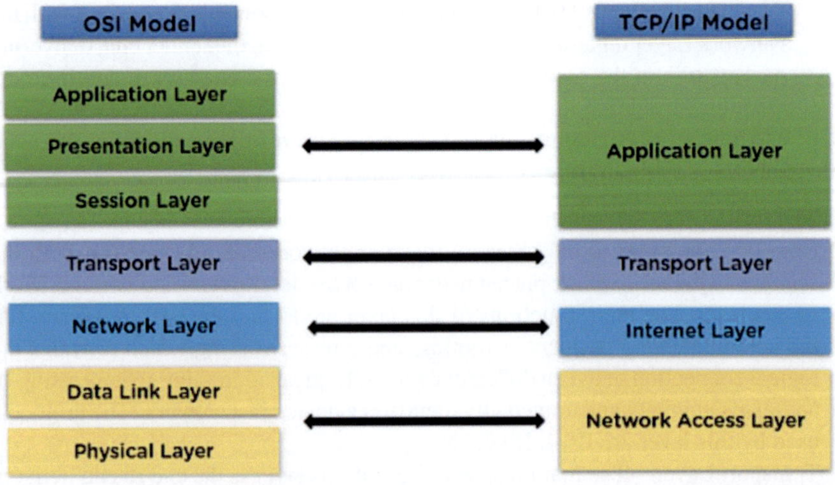

Fig. 3.10 ISO/OSI versus TCP/IP model

3.2.13 TCP/IP 5-Layer Model and 4-Layer Model

The TCP/IP model is one of the fundamental frameworks in the field of networking. The model is based on the core protocols of networking and the Internet. It stands for Transmission Control Protocol (TCP)/Internet Protocol (IP). This model also takes care of the flow of information from one computer to another ensuring data reliability, among other features.

This model is expressed in two ways:

- 5-Layer Model—The layers in this model are

  Application, Transport, Network, Data Link, and Physical.

  - Application Layer—The Application layer assumes all the tasks that the uppermost three layers of the ISO/OSI perform. Hence it can be said that those three layers (Application, Presentation and Session) are molded into one layer in this model. The functionalities and the protocols used in these three layers include proper formatting of data for making it ready for transmission, and maintaining different sessions between any two communication partners.
  - Transport Layer—The functionalities of this layer are providing reliability, flow control, and data correction.

    TCP and UDP are the protocols used in this layer. The Transmission Control Protocol (TCP) creates a virtual circuit between the sender and the destination during the entire time of communication. It is considered to be a reliable protocol, as it detects error and retransmits damaged frames. Segmentation of the information into sequenced data packets are done at the sender end and reassembly is done at the receiver end by looking into the sequence number in the packets of the same information. TCP is a connection-oriented protocol, whereas UDP is a connectionless protocol. UDP is not considered to be a reliable protocol as it does not specify errors, although it detects the error. UDP contains only the checksum, thereby identifying the error, but not the data packet segment, as it does not contain the sequence number.
  - Data Link Layer and Physical Layer—These two layers perform the same activities as that in ISO/OSI 7-Layer network architecture model.

- 4-Layer Model—The layers in this model are

  Application, Transport, Internet or Network, Network Access

  - Application Layer—The topmost layer of this model handles high level protocols and representations of data in proper formats. It also allows the user to interact with the application. The main protocols used in the Application layer are Hyper Text Transfer Protocol (HTTP), Simple Mail Transfer Protocol (SMTP), File Transfer Protocol (FTP), Simple Network Management Protocol (SNMP), Domain Name System (DNS), Terminal Network (TELNET), Network File System (NFS), Remote Procedure Call (RPC), etc.

- Transport Layer—The functionalities are same as that in the TCP/IP 5-Layer model.

  The main responsibility of this layer is to send packets to their destination by implementing IP addressing, routing through the network and also fragmentation, if the size of the IP datagram is bigger than the Maximum Transmission Unit (MTU) imposed by the lower layer. Protocols in this layer are TCP and UDP.
- Internet or Network Layer—This layer performs the functions that the Network layer in the ISO/OSI model performs. The main protocols in this layer are Internet Protocol (IP), Internet Control Message Protocol (ICMP), Address Resolution Protocol (ARP).
- Network Access Layer—This layer combines the main functionalities of the Data Link Layer and some of the Physical Layer. This layer is responsible for generating data and asking for connections. Error prevention and framing are also considered in this layer.

However, as mentioned above, we find that the TCP/IP model 4-Layer does not have the Physical Layer specifically. This is because of the fact that the Data Link Layer is considered to be the interfacing point between the TCP/IP stack and the underlying hardware. This allows the TCP/IP model to be flexible enough to adapt to various types of physical connections including Ethernet, Wi-Fi, fiber optics, etc. The Physical Layer handles the hardware components and the physical medium, like Ethernet cables or radio waves for Wi-Fi.

3.3 Adhoc Networks

In the earlier section we have introduced the idea of *adhoc networks*. A wired network generally cannot be categorized as an adhoc network as it has got its components, that is, the connected devices located in fixed locations with physical cablings. However, a wireless network can both be *infrastructured* and *adhoc*, as mentioned earlier. As we understand, devices with wireless network interface controller cards are able to connect to an existing network using radio transmission, provided the device in that network is also able to communicate in wireless mode. Apart from the wireless infrastructure mode connectivity, the other one in which the wireless devices are able to set up a network by themselves, whenever any two devices are within the transmission range of each other, is known as *adhoc* mode.

In this section we shall deal a bit with details of wireless and mobile adhoc networks. Now the question may arise: why are we saying wireless and mobile? We know that our readers are intelligent enough to understand that if your device has wireless connectivity options, then it will not require physical cabling to connect with a network. And therefore, if it does not require any physical cable or wire dangling from it for network connection, it can be taken from one to the other with much ease. Hence the term mobile also comes with wireless. So your device needs to have wireless connectivity to become mobile and here comes the added feature to the network, which was so long static, as the devices did not move from one place to the other. However, although a wireless network is essentially not mobile, a mobile network is essentially wireless!

3.3.1 Mobile Adhoc Network (MANET)

MANET can be defined as a wireless network that connects mobile devices without a centralized infrastructure. In general, it is easy to set up MANET, as it does not require any pre-existing infrastructure. It has several characteristics as mentioned below

- Wireless media—Wireless links connect the devices.
- Decentralized or No centralized infrastructure—The nodes do not depend on access points or pre-existing infrastructures to form the network.
- Dynamic topology—As the nodes are able to change locations, the topology changes every now and then.
- Path breakage—As the nodes move, the connection between them gets lost and the communication path breaks down.
- Autonomous Node—A node has to take up the responsibility of routing in the absence of any fixed infrastructure.
- Self-configuring—A node itself has to take the responsibility of aligning itself to the network in case it gets detached or any of its neighboring nodes is not available.

These characteristics throw some challenges for setting up MANET and utilizing the same for running applications.

- Error prone media—Wireless media is itself an error prone media.
- Low bandwidth—The wireless channels are relatively lower bandwidth with respect to the wired channel counterpart.
- Mobility—Mobility of the devices adds to unpredictability of the network topology and connections between the devices.
- Routing—As there is no assistance, routing is done by participating nodes with local information only.
- Security—As MANET is easy to set up, any device may join that network and pose security risk, if not properly validated.

The challenges mentioned above provide a broad view. Several more challenges show up as you try to take one broad challenge and deal with it.

There are many interesting applications of Wireless and Mobile Adhoc Network. The broad application areas of MANET are *civil* and *defense*.

As the devices or mobile nodes in a MANET have to work both as host and router, the network can be deployed very fast. Reconfiguration is also the responsibility of the node/s when communication is unavailable. Communication may be

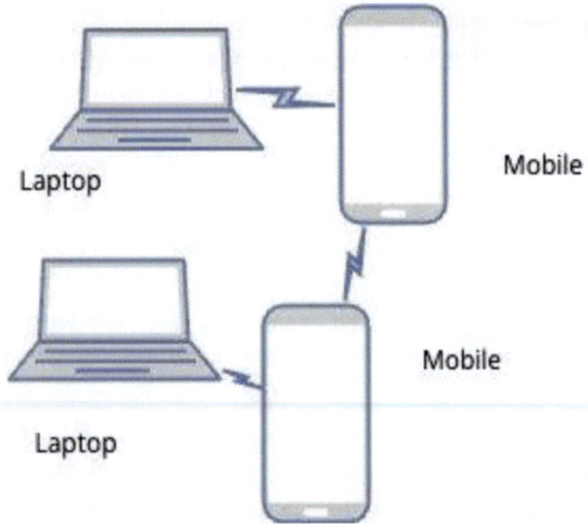

Fig. 3.11 Mobile adhoc network (MANET)

unavailable due to reasons, like, mobility, path breakage, low battery, low bandwidth. Thus topology becomes dynamic. Multi-hop transmission may be required to reach a distant node. Communication links being radio waves, we can think of having logical communication channels or links among the nodes. Hence for ease of work, the network may be considered to be divided into several groups, that are referred to as clusters (Fig. 3.11).

3.3.2 Clustering

The network can be considered to be a set of clusters. A clusterhead will coordinate the activities inside a cluster. The cluster members are supposed to be ordinary nodes and they are able to communicate only with the cluster member, as each member is directly connected with the clusterhead. The clusterheads are responsible for forwarding messages from one cluster member to another cluster member belonging to same and/or different cluster. Cluster formation may be based on different parameters, depending on application requirement or other parameters.

Clustering algorithms can be *mobility based*, *energy based*, *connectivity based*, *weighted clustering*. Cluster heads are also selected based on different parameters. Clusterhead selection algorithms may run in regular intervals or based on other suitable parameters, so that the same clusterhead does not have to continue for long. Other than clusterhead and cluster member nodes, there are *Gateway* nodes too. Ordinary nodes send their information or data packets to their cluster heads that forward these packets to other clusters or sometimes in its own cluster. The clusterheads forward the packets meant for other clusters, to the gateway nodes. Routing decisions are not the responsibility of the ordinary nodes. The clusterheads and the gateway nodes have

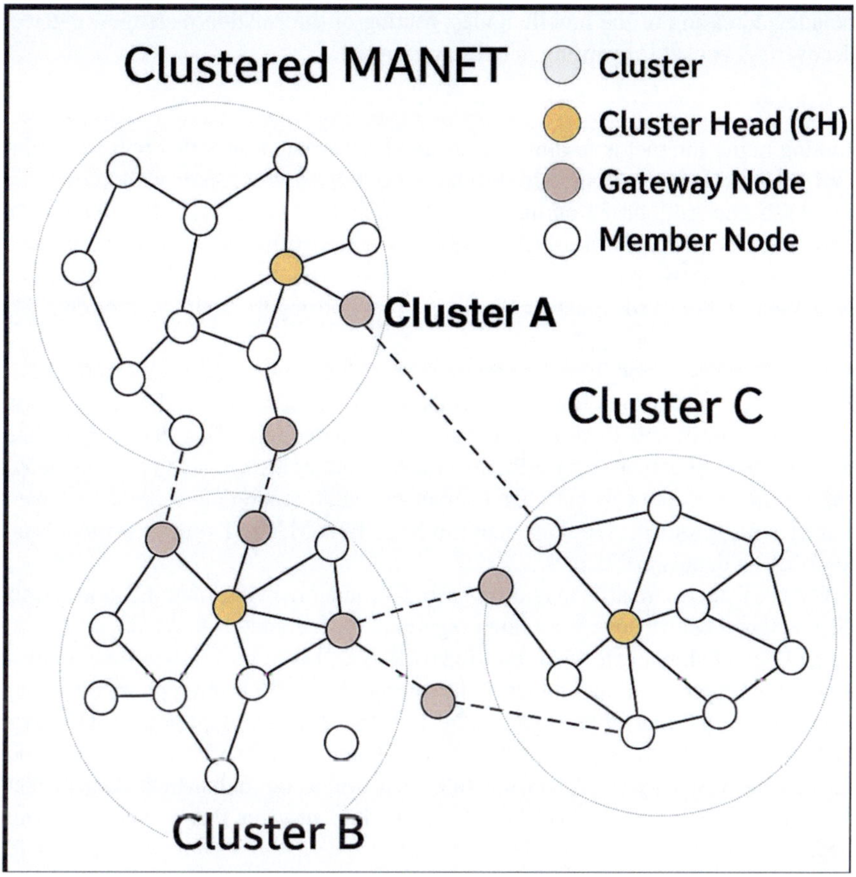

Fig. 3.12 Clustering in MANET

the responsibility for routing. They contain information regarding routing. Needless to say that a gateway node will belong to more than one cluster and hence act as the node through which messages can be routed from one cluster to another cluster (Fig. 3.12).

3.4 Integration of MANET with Internet

MANET, being adhoc in nature, does not have any central server and the network can be formed as soon as any two or more than two nodes are in the transmission range of one another. Hence, to access the Internet from any such MANET node, we face challenge and therefore need to consider a number of related issues. These include addressing of the mobile nodes, routing of information/messages, gateway discovering, packet forwarding, handover, security.

- Routing

Routing in the Internet is finding a route and/or alternate routes that will be used to send data packets from source to destination in the network. As is well known, the Internet is generally based on the TCP/IP protocol network stack, discussed in the earlier section. IP address is used in routing in the Network layer. Each IP address can be interpreted as two parts consisting of the network ID, and host ID. Routers utilize the network ID of the destination IP address for choosing the path to be followed for routing.

In MANETs, as mobile nodes can move anywhere, a node may get disconnected from another (with which it was connected till then). Hence the path between these two nodes will be lost thereby giving rise to a change in routing decision. Consequently, routing becomes very difficult as several issues are needed to be considered. There is no concept of a centralized server or router, among other issues. Conventional routing protocols are thus, misfit in MANETs. MANET routing protocols are described in details in Chap. 4.

MANET nodes are able to choose or find a route involving MANET nodes only. They will not receive any information regarding the parameters to choose a route for the nodes not belonging to MANET. Since MANET nodes generally follow wireless adhoc routing protocols and nodes in the Internet follow IP routing protocols, hence compatibility is what is needed for these different types of protocols. However, packets still need to be sent to its destination IP address in the Internet. Here comes the Internet Gateway (IGW) in the role of a bridge through which data packets enter and exit a network. The IGW is a network component that contains and runs the TCP/IP protocol suite for the Internet and the MANET routing protocols for the MANET. Packet transmission through conversion from one protocol to another happens seamlessly ensuring compatibility among the devices in the networks.

There are two ways—proactive and reactive that mobile nodes use to discover the IGW.

- IP Mobility

Mobility of MANET nodes may be either *micro mobility* or *macro mobility* in nature. Macro mobility is attained when a node moves among two or more different subnets, sometimes in heterogeneous subnets, as well. The IP macro mobility protocols are coupled with IP packet routing mechanisms to interconnect wired and wireless network. The popular standard for IP mobility are Mobile IPv4 and Mobile IPv6. When the MANET nodes move within the same domain, it is micro mobility. The mobile node's access point may change frequently in the same network. Thus handoffs also occur. Some such protocols are HMIP, EMA, AWAII, TelMIP, cellular IP, etc.

- Discovering the Gateway and Selecting the Gateway

Conventional MANET routing protocols only provide packet routing features within the MANET. So these protocols are to be extended by adding the feature for discovering IGW. The discovery of IGW can also be *proactive*, *reactive*, *hybrid*. Mobile node trying to communicate with fixed Internet node listens to the Modified Router Advertisement (MRA) of the IGW. Route entry is updated accordingly in the routing table for IGW in the MANET node. A MANET node can also send Modified Router Solicitation (MRS) message when the discovery is reactive or on-demand in nature. Once this MRS reaches the IGW via intermediate hops, the IGW sends a unicast route reply message to the MANET node that has sent the MRS message. The MANET node can now configure the route to IGW.

The hybrid approach considers the nodes to be either in the advertisement (proactive) zone or not. Mobile nodes within the advertisement zone (meaning nearby the IGW) uses the proactive method to discover IGW, whereas those not within this zone, uses the reactive method to find the IGW. A mobile node may sometimes receive more than one MRA messages from nearby IGWs. Needless to say that the mobile node will choose the IGW with better quality of service. Parameters like hop count, traffic load at the IGW may be considered when a mobile node has to select from multiple IGWs.

- Handover Decision

  Handover is required by a mobile node if it is moving and has crossed the gateway it was attached to, while communicating with some other node over the Internet. Handover decision is taken by detecting the movement of the mobile node while it is still communicating with the other node. There are two types of handovers that can happen to a mobile node.

  - Forced handover: As there may be multiple paths to a gateway from a mobile node, secondary route may be chosen if a single communication link in a multihop gateway path is lost due to various reasons.
  - Optimization based handover: If a node (while mobile) gets a better Internet Gateway with respect to service parameters than the one it is currently registered to, the mobile node may start the handover process to get registered to the new IGW.

- Forwarding

Message forwarding by IGW is based on tunneling based integrated routing or non-tunneling based integrated routing.

In tunneling approach packets are put into an envelope and thus wrapped using an external IP header and sent to the Internet Gateway. The IGW firstly unwraps the packet. Then it finds the inner IP header from the packet and uses the standard IP forwarding technique. Thus, packets are sent to their destination node IP addresses. The outer IP header in the envelope is the drawback of tunneling approach.

One of the Non-tunneling based routing approaches uses *forwarding by host route*. A host route generally means a route within the MANET. The destination node may be within the MANET, that is, a MANET node itself. If the destination node is not a MANET node, but the Internet, then IGW has to get involved. The IGW will act like another intermediary node toward the destination node.

The other approach is *forwarding by default route*. Default route is an entry in routing table. This entry refers to an Internet Gateway integrated with the Internet.

3.5 Conclusion

This chapter discusses the architecture of the wired network and wireless network. Study of wired network is well established and the problems have been identified and dealt with successfully. However, with wireless networks we may not be able to say the same in one breath. This is because there are a bunch of differences between the two types of networks. And with wireless/mobile adhoc network, the challenges are many fold. Several issues that are needed to be considered while coming up with an architecture of a wireless network are dealt with here in details.

Questions (Indicative)

Q1. Differentiate between infrastructure network and adhoc network.

Q2. What are the various topologies? Can you think of real-life example networking system for each such topology?

Q3. What are the functionalities of the ISO/OSI model layers?

Q4. What are the tasks of a node in MANET?

Q5. What are the difficulties of designing a wireless adhoc network that would consist of a number of wireless nodes doing collaborative work?

Q6. How can you integrate MANET with Internet?

References

1. Forouzan, B.A.: Data Communications and Networking (SIE), 4th edn. (2017)
2. Stallings, W.: Data and Computer Communications, 9th edn. (2013)
3. Kurose, J., Ross, K.: Computer Networking: A Top Down Approach, 9th edn. Pearson (2020)
4. Tanenbaum, A.S., Witherall, D.J.: Computer Networks, 5th edn. Prentice Hall (2011)
5. https://www.javatpoint.com/computer-network-architecture
6. https://www.cisco.com/c/en/us/products/switches/what-is-a-lan-local-area-network.html
7. https://javatpoint.com/computer-network-tcp-ip-model
8. https://ecomputernotes.com/computernetworkingnotes/communication-networks/hub
9. https://ecomputernotes.com/computernetworkingnotes/network-technologies/unguided-transmission-media
10. Prakash, J., Kumar, R., Saini, J.P.: MANET-internet integration architecture. J. Appl. Sci. **17**, 264–281 (2017)

Chapter 4
Protocols

Abstract Routing protocols have been thoroughly investigated in MANET and sensor networks as it forms the basis of packet transfer and thus is a deciding factor for application performance. This chapter describes several algorithms and protocols developed in the domain of adhoc and sensor networks and beyond such as wireless body area network and Internet of Things. Moreover, simulation scenarios, performance evaluation with realistic examples are framed to highlight implementation methods and techniques of the existing protocols and this will work as a tool to the explorer of this book to build new, effective, and efficient applications based on such protocols.

Keywords Routing · IoT · Wireless sensor network · Wireless body area network · Mobility model · Simulation

This chapter describes several algorithms and protocols developed in the domain of adhoc and sensor networks and beyond such as WBAN and IoT. Moreover, simulation scenarios, performance evaluation with realistic examples are framed to highlight implementation methods and techniques of the existing protocols and this will work as a tool to the explorer of this book to propose new, effective and efficient protocols.

The eyes of todays' smart city applications are the sensors. They are integrated with the gadgets of our daily lives such as, smartphones, refrigerators, washing machines, and so on. These sensors often form an interconnected network among themselves to sense and monitor some parameters over a particular area. Examples could be forest fire detection, industrial ambience monitoring, agricultural crop monitoring, and so on. When such sensors are attached to a human body to sense body vitals from a patient, it forms a Wireless Body Area Network (WBAN). Such networks not necessarily remain connected to the Internet. In fact, all these networks follow the same communication architecture where the sensors communicate to a sink node installed in direct or indirect coverage of the sensor nodes. This sink node is actually responsible for connecting to the rest of the world through the Internet. Thus, the sink is the component that provides the infrastructural part to such networks. As discussed previously, in MANET there is no such component.

S. Biswas et al., *Adhoc and Sensor Networks: Security and Applications*, Studies in Systems, Decision and Control 653, https://doi.org/10.1007/978-981-95-5839-1_4

Internet of Things (IoT) could be viewed as an extension of this concept where the consumer electronic devices, the "Things" would be connected directly to the Internet. Thus, in a pure IoT paradigm, the sensors of the previously known Wireless Sensor Network (WSN) would be a pure IoT infrastructure once each node gets internet connectivity. However, directly providing internet connectivity to such nodes would result in high internet traffic. Thus, in an IoT application where WSN is involved internet connectivity to the nodes could be provided through the sinks.

So, in this chapter, we mainly cover routing protocols and their behavior w.r.t MANET and its variants of wireless networks that are widely utilized today in smart city-based applications namely, WSN, WBAN, and IoT.

4.1 Routing Protocols

This section would present the routing and clustering protocols for MANET, WSN, WBAN, and IoT. The interesting fact about routing protocol design for such networks is that the protocols are designed from the perspective of one node and how it decides to route a packet to a destination. Here, the entire connected/disconnected network scenario at that point of time cannot be visible to a node when it is taking the decision to send a packet. A network is only partially observable to a node. There is no concept of a global observer in such a system.

The concept of routing and the main challenges for routing differ from one network to the other. However, all such protocols take care of some common properties listed as follows.

- The protocol should result in less no of control messages.
- Resource efficiency is an important issue to be addressed. Resource could mean energy, lifetime of the nodes, or in some cases computational facility.
- How the nodes would react when some nodes are down or disconnected.

The representative protocols and the broad categories are presented here for clarity.

4.1.1 MANET Protocols

Deployment of MANET does not need any infrastructural support in terms of routers, switches, or base stations [1]. Thus, the network configuration in a MANET consists of the set of nodes and the links among them. Though these links are a feature of time as they depend on relative position of the nodes in the network. So, links may be formed or disrupted depending on the relative movement of the nodes. Such volatility that is, the frequency of change in a MANET configuration or topology is a result of the node mobility.

In MANET, nodes access and exchange information regardless of their geographic position (location independence) or proximity to infrastructure. This enables development of ubiquitous applications to facilitate the delivery of services that are responsive to people [2].

The most trivial but robust solution to routing is flooding the network with a packet. Since MANET is a resource constrained network, so simple flooding could consume a lot of resources. Thus, a wide literature could be found on routing protocols for MANET. Routing protocols for MANET could be divided into two broad categories as follows.

i. **Proactive Routing**: It maintains routing information irrespective of the need for communication. The protocols exhibit low latency, and hence, they are suitable for real-time traffic. However, it consumes network bandwidth even at idle times due to periodic updates.
ii. **Reactive** or **On Demand Routing**: It discovers routes only when it is required. It is good for lightly loaded traffic. Such protocols could save energy and/or bandwidth during inactivity.

Three widely utilized routing protocols from both categories have been discussed here. Destination-Sequenced Distance Vector Algorithm (DSDV) [3] is one of the earliest routing protocol that was designed by Perkins and Bhagvat. Based on Bellman Ford algorithm, this proactive protocol enables exchange of routing tables where a routing table states the way to the destination and cost. Thus, the concept is that every node knows "where" everybody else (that is, other mobile nodes) are through the routing table. Thus, routing table is of complexity *O(N)* if there are *N* nodes in the network. Each node advertises its position, sequence number to avoid loops and maintains fresh routes. Routes are broadcasted from the potential receivers.

Nodes announce their presence through advertisements. Each broadcast has a Destination address: originator, no of hops, and the sequence number of the broadcast. The route with the most recent sequence is used for sending packets as shown in Fig. 4.1. This protocol has its pros and cons. For instance, to ensure availability of routes to all destinations always, much delay would be involved in the route setup process. The updates for broken links may lead to a control message overhead when the relative mobility among the nodes is high. In order to obtain information about a particular destination, a node should wait for a table update message initiated by the same destination node. This delay could result in stale routing information, that is the recommended route may not be valid anymore.

Ad-Hoc On-demand Distance Vector Routing (AODV) protocol is widely used by MANET researchers [4]. This reactive protocol is designed by Perkins and Royer. Here, a sender tries to find a destination by broadcasting a Route Request Packet (RREQ) as shown in Fig. 4.2. Every mobile node in the network maintains a route cache and use destination sequence number for each route entry. The destination sequence no determines an up-to-date path to the destination. The state is installed at nodes per destination. It does nothing when the connection between the end points is still valid. However, a route may fail as node mobility could lead to temporary change in network topology. In such a case, local recovery is initiated by the sender

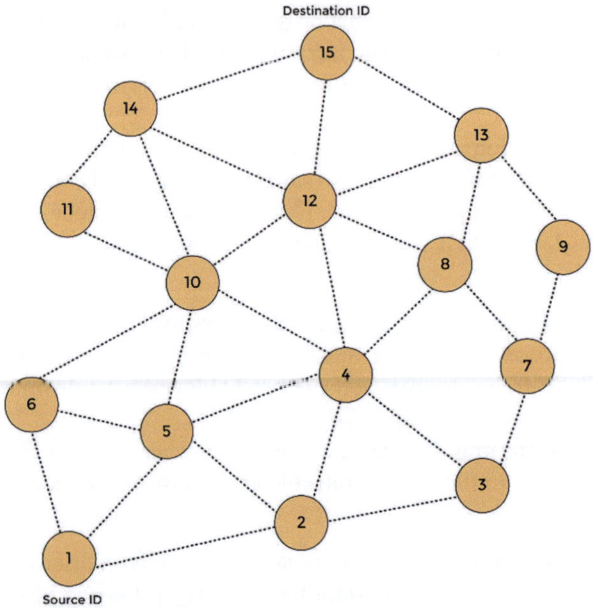

(a) Topology graph of the network

Destination ID	Next Node	Hop Count	Sequence Number
2	2	1	22
3	2	2	26
4	5	2	32
5	5	1	134
6	6	1	144
7	2	3	162
8	5	3	170
9	2	4	186
10	6	2	142
11	6	3	176
12	5	3	190
13	5	4	198
14	6	3	142
15	5	4	256

(b) Routing table for Node 1

Fig. 4.1 Working of the DSDV routing protocol

as it repeats a Route Discovery. A mobile node would monitor the link status of next hop in active routes. Route Error packets (RERR) is used to notify other nodes if a link is broken. The other nodes then remove corresponding route entry after hearing RERR.

AODV has the advantage that its connection setup delay is comparatively less. It can identify fresh routes. However, it has many disadvantages. Intermediate nodes can lead to inconsistent routes if two conditions are met- (i) the source sequence no is

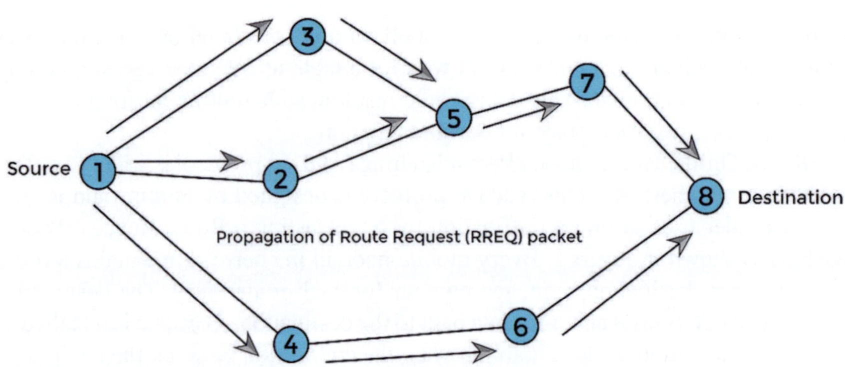

Fig. 4.2 Propagation of RREQ packets in a MANET configuration following AODV protocol

older and (ii) the intermediate nodes have higher destination sequence no but that is not the latest one signifying the destination's current position in the network. Thus, intermediate nodes may have stale entries. If multiple route replies are received in response to a single RREQ then that can lead to high control message overhead.

Dynamic Source Routing (DSR) [5] is another routing protocol that is widely adopted for several applications of MANET. The protocol defines two mechanisms as follows.

(i) Route Maintenance
(ii) Route Discovery.

Route Discovery technique is similar to that in AODV but with source routing instead. Nodes maintain route cache. A node updates its route cache entries as it learns new routes. Packets sent carry complete, ordered list of nodes signifying its path trace. Sender checks its route cache, if route exists, sender constructs a source route in the packet's header. If the route expires or does not exist, then only the sender initiates the Route Discovery Mechanism as shown in Fig. 4.3.

Two types of packets are used to indicate the status of a route in DSR namely, Route Error Packet and Acknowledgement. If transmission error is detected at data link layer, Route Error Packet is generated that is subsequently transmitted to the original sender of the packet. When a Route Error packet is received a node removes the hop entry from its route cache. ACKs are used to validate the correction of the route links.

A comparison among the three routing protocols discussed above are summarized as Table 4.1.

There are many routing protocols that are proposed based on these two categories or a hybrid of them. In [6], the concept of mobile software agent is utilized for route discovery and balancing traffic load on the route to reduce network traffic thereby improving bandwidth utilization. A mobile agent is a piece of code and data bundled together that is capable of migration among machines and performing their

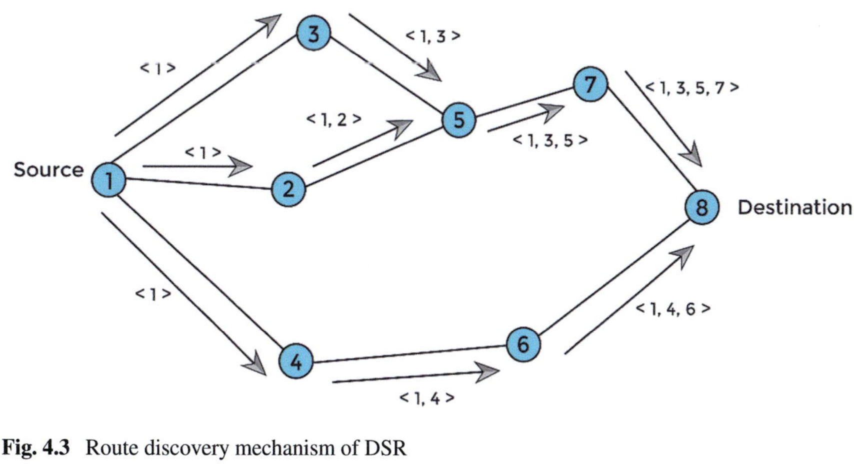

Fig. 4.3 Route discovery mechanism of DSR

Table 4.1 Comparison of MANET routing protocols

	DSDV	AODV	DSR
Source routing	No	No	Yes
Periodic message	Yes	No	No
Functioning proactively	Yes	No	No
Functioning reactively	No	Yes	Yes

task at a machine to compute the results. Drawing upon some of the computing techniques inspired by social insects such as ants [7], several mobile agent-based paradigms are designed to solve control and routing problems in telecommunication and networking. In [8], an ant-based routing algorithm for MANET is proposed that extensively uses ant like mobile agents that sample full paths between source and destination nodes. The goal of the proposed algorithm is to reduce the overhead incurred by the ants to enhance the overall performance of the system.

Mobile agents are even used for multicast routing in MANET. In [9], such a scheme is proposed that used both static and dynamic agents. The scheme first identifies the reliable nodes and then connects them through intermediate nodes. This forms a backbone for multicasting so that multicast group members can join the backbone and then manage them in case of mobility. Here, agents perform the functions of collecting and disseminating the network information. The agent system works based on the rules of blackboard architecture that is used for inter-agent communication.

Apart from routing, grouping nodes based on their geographic proximity or other criteria that is, the task of clustering them can also be performed by mobile agents. Clustering nodes actually simplify the task of routing. In [10], mobile agents have been utilized to retain routing and clustering information of each node. They also perform the task of re-clustering and cluster size adjustments. In [11], a node called master node initiates the cluster formation process. Here, the mobile agents traverse throughout the network migrating from one node to the other. The mobile agent in this process maintains a database of the nodes it visited in the format-(Node-id, Status, Visited time). A mobile agent keeps track of every node it visits through this database.

In [12], a mobile agent-based system is proposed that can process location dependent queries in a distributed fashion for MANET. Here, a mobile agent monitors the changing location trail of moving objects and efficiently refreshes answers to the queries. Here, utilization of mobile agent enhances scalability and the work ensures optimal wireless communication. Therefore, the notion of mobile agents could bring numerous advantages to the field of mobile ad hoc networks.

4.1.2 WSN Protocols

The problem of routing takes a new turn when WSNs are considered. Here, the sensors could be manually deployed in a field such as agricultural field or a factory.

So, data is routed through a predetermined path as the nodes are attached and hence, they are not expected to change their position. However, for applications such as, forest fire monitoring, nodes could be deployed from a helicopter and hence, spread across the forest in different regions. In such cases, optimal clustering is necessary to allow connectivity and energy-efficiency of the sensor nodes as it is not easy to go there and change the batteries once depleted. Multi-hop routing is also a possibility here to connect to the sink node.

There are research challenges faced by such networks. For instance, the sensor nodes could be heterogeneous with different roles and transmission capabilities. As far as routing or clustering is concerned, nodes may interact in different modalities. Some nodes could be cluster heads. All communication outside the cluster would go through such nodes. If a Cluster Head (CH) has more energy and computational capability then it can take care of transmissions to the base station (BS).

Routing protocols in WSN could be grouped into four broad categories—(i) Flat, (ii) Hierarchical, (iii) Location-based, and (iv) QoS-based.

In flat routing protocol, all nodes share equal role in establishing the routes and thus there is no distinction among the nodes based on its routing functionality. In hierarchical routing protocols, nodes are grouped into clusters with a CH responsible for data transmission and aggregation at the cluster. This data aggregation in the CH nodes reduces network traffic toward the sink. Thus, nodes could save transmission power and the aggregation of data could lead to extension of lifetime of the cluster head nodes. The overhead of cluster formation and maintenance is hence outweighed by the improvement in network lifetime for large-scale WSNs.

In location-based routing, each node's geographic position is considered in making a routing decision. The nodes also attach their position in the routing control message trails to facilitate such decision making. A packet would be routed through a node that is geographically closer to the destination.

QoS-based or QoS-aware routing protocols take any routing decision based on the QoS parameters and observable network state. Typical quality of service parameters include throughput, delay and jitter. For example, packets could be routed in such a way that congestion could be avoided thus improving overall throughput. The research in WSN routing has seen combining these different routing strategies as well. For instance, QoS parameter could be combined with geographic position in a routing decision.

Low Energy Adaptive Clustering Hierarchy (LEACH) [13] is the first hierarchical routing scheme that is also energy efficient. It works in rounds. Each node in each round chooses a random number between 0 and 1. The node becomes a cluster head for the current round if the number is less than a threshold T(n) calculated as follows [13]:

$$T(n) = \begin{cases} \frac{P}{1-P*(r \bmod \frac{1}{P})} & \text{if } n \in G \\ 0 & \text{otherwise} \end{cases}$$

where P = the desired percentage of cluster heads (e.g. P = 0.5), r = current round G = set of nodes that have not been the cluster heads in last1/P rounds, n denotes a node id.

LEACH is an extremely popular protocol in the literature that gave rise to a number of different variants of it to counter its different limitations. The limitations of LEACH are as follows:

LEACH would not perform well when WSNs are deployed over a large region. In that case, more energy would be consumed by the CHs for single hop routing to the sink.

Since spatial distribution of the nodes is not considered by T(n), good distribution of cluster heads could not be guaranteed.

To improve clustering performance for heterogeneous network, the Stable Election Protocol (SEP) [14] was proposed. It takes care of resource heterogeneity that in turn adds network stability. In this protocol, the ratio of initial energy of a node w.r.t that of a normal node is calculated. Based on this measure, each node is assigned a weight value. Thus, some nodes would get a higher weight value than the others. Hence, such advanced nodes would be more likely to be chosen as cluster heads. Thus, it overcomes the performance bottleneck of LEACH for heterogeneous networks.

Another popular multi-hop clustering protocol is the Hybrid Energy-Efficient, Distributed clustering (HEED) protocol [15]. In this protocol, relative proximity of the nodes is reflected through the cluster formation. Intra-cluster communication cost along with a node's residual energy are considered for the formation of clusters. This ensured that the elected CHs are more likely to possess better residual energy.

Advantage of HEED is that the CHs can take a single hop or multi-hop path for sending data. This approach is better than the single-hop strategy as in LEACH protocol [16] as it balances energy consumption and enhances scalability. However, HEED suffers from a few drawbacks as well. The protocol may result in more no of CHs; some of which may not even have a cluster member. Such sole clusters may consume more energy. Then, in each round, the energy overhead increases for CH selection. The CHs near the sink need to handle more traffic as compared to other CHs.

Directed diffusion is a data centric WSN routing protocol based on a flat network topology [17]. Data generated by the sensor nodes is organized as attribute-value pairs. The data items are named like that. Interest propagation and exploratory data transmission are the main functionalities of this routing protocol. At first, the sink would broadcast interests for named data as shown in Fig. 4.4. Each node then broadcasts the interest in its neighborhood and thus it diffuses through the network.

As the interest is propagated throughout the network, a gradient is set up by the nodes towards the nodes from which they received the interest. A gradient indicates a replying link pointing towards the neighboring node from which interests are received. Each node maintains an Interest cache. Upon detecting an event, a sensor node would search its interest cache for an entry matching the interest. This node acting as a source then sends data to each neighbor for whom it has a gradient. A neighbor node upon receiving the data searches its respective interest cache for an entry that matches with the data. If such an entry could not be found then the data

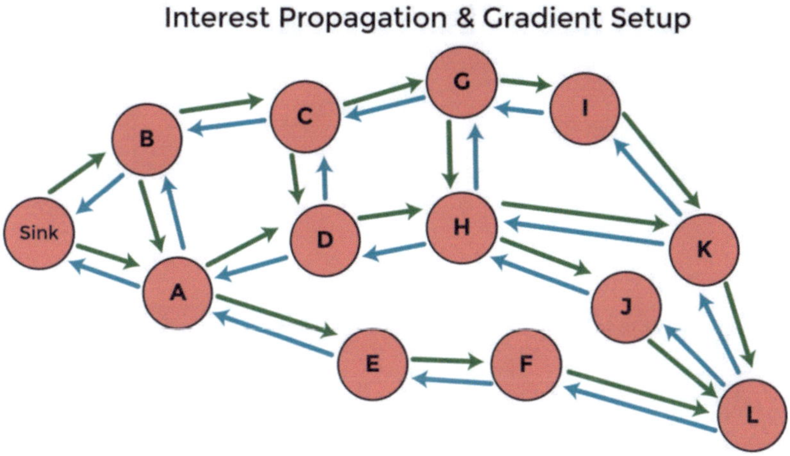

Fig. 4.4 Interest propagation in directed diffusion

message is deleted. Or else, such a message would be forwarded to the nodes having a gradient. In this way, data about an event is propagated to the sink. After receiving data, the sink reinforces a specific neighbor so that data could be pulled at higher rates. The reinforced node in a similar fashion reinforces one of its neighbors so that data could be transferred at higher rates. Such reinforcements could be positive or negative. When from a reinforced node desirable rate of data is not received, it could be negatively reinforced. The same would be positively reinforced if higher data rate could be observed from the node.

SPIN is another popular data-centric WSN routing protocol. It also follows the event-driven data delivery model. Thus, the nodes first sense data and then disseminate it across the network through negotiation as shown in Fig. 4.5. In case of SPIN, the nodes utilize three types of messages:

- ADV-This advertisement message contains metadata of the new data that the node is willing to share.
- REQ-This request message denotes the intent of the sender node to receive actual data.
- DATA-This message contains the actual sensed data.

As shown in Fig. 4.5, upon availability of data, a sensor node would broadcast an ADV message in its neighborhood. Upon receiving such a message a receiver node could respond back with a REQ message. Then the source would send the data to the REQ sender. In this way, data is propagated throughout the network. It significantly reduces energy consumption as compared to simple flooding. However, it also has some points of concern. Data advertisement here does not guarantee the delivery of data. If the interested node is far from the source, data may not be delivered. So, reliable data delivery could not be guaranteed here.

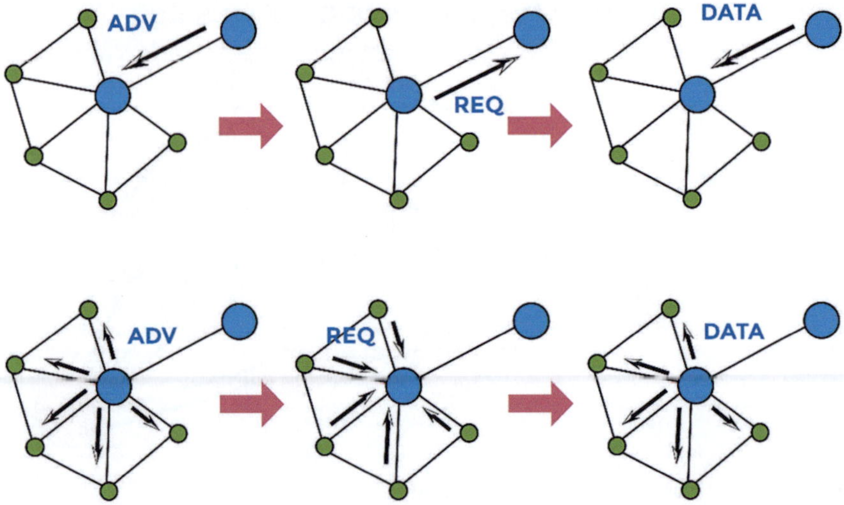

Fig. 4.5 Working of SPIN protocol

4.1.3 WBAN Protocols

WBAN can be interpreted as a network of small-size, micro, and nano-technology wearable or implantable body sensor nodes that are powered by batteries and placed in, on, or around the human body. The sole purpose of such a network is to measure and monitor physiological parameters also called body vitals. As a sensor network, it also has a WBAN coordinator that could be a smart handheld device which is responsible for connecting the network to a gateway or a sink. A coordinator is responsible for storage and local processing of the data before sending it to a remote medical server through the gateway. Thus, a WBAN enabled system follows a typical three-tier architecture as shown in Fig. 4.6. Here, tier 1 focuses on network formation. Technology like WLAN or GPRS are used by the gateway device in tier 2 to communicate to the remote server residing at tier 3 for analysis of health data by the medical personnel to provide necessary actions.

As the sensor nodes are attached to the human tissue, it is important to limit the energy dissipation rate so that resulting node heating does not damage the associated tissues. So, the sensor nodes in WBAN should maintain the prescribed Specific Absorption Rate (SAR) value from energy consumption aspect. SAR represents the rate at which energy is absorbed by the human tissue when exposed to a radio frequency (RF) electromagnetic field. It is defined as the power absorbed per mass of tissue. It is usually measured in units of watts per kilogram (W/kg). SAR is usually averaged either over the whole body, or over a small sample volume typically, 1 g or 10 g of tissue. The maximum level measured in the body part studied over the stated volume or mass is generally reported. The gross limit is 1.6 W/kg [18].

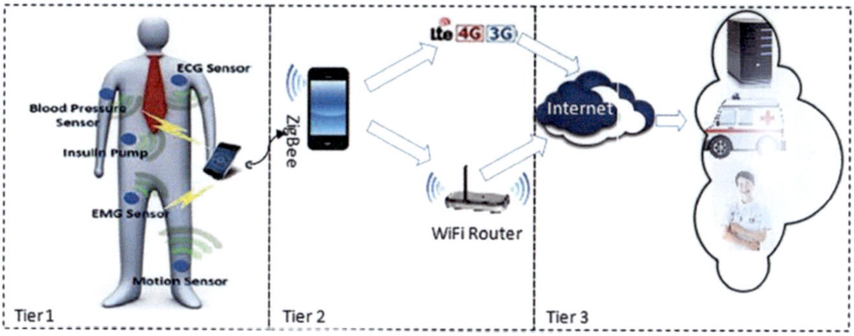

Fig. 4.6 Three tier architecture of a WBAN-based health monitoring system

Existing routing protocols are grouped into six categories focusing on their objective in solving routing problems as follows.

i. Temperature-based: Data is routed from different routes to avoid temperature rise that is to limit SAR.
ii. Cross layer: Combines the challenges in routing with medium access issues.
iii. Cluster-based: Nodes in WBAN are grouped into clusters. Each cluster is assigned a cluster head. Direct transmission from the sensor to base station is restricted.
iv. QoS-based: QoS metrics play a vital role in selecting the routes to the WBAN coordinator.
v. Interference aware: Such routing strategies are devised to oversee intra-BAN interference issue.
vi. Cost-based: Maintains a cost function that is updated periodically. The most cost-effective route is chosen always. It computes the cost based on different routing issues. It could combine aspects such as, QoS and SAR.

In early days, research works mostly aimed to address specific issues of WBAN routing such as, clustering [20], temperature control [19], and so on. However, there are limitations associated with each of the categories. For instance, temperature aware routing may not address other major issues such as, reliability and/or energy efficiency. Interestingly, cluster-based routing protocols impose hierarchy in communication through grouping the sensor nodes into clusters. Each cluster has a cluster head just like WSN and these CHs take part in data communication between sensor nodes of a cluster and the sink. Now, the cluster heads could deplete energy faster. Secondly, periodic invocation of cluster formation algorithm along with the cluster head selection process result in more overhead than benefit for a small WBAN network as the average network consists of only 15–20 nodes [21].

Consequently, WBAN research in routing moves towards addressing different issues together which could be the cross layer [22] or even incorporate modules for the QoS parameters [23]. Cross layer protocols could also address the medium access issues along with routing layer challenges. Time is divided into slots following medium access strategies and nodes need to contend for reserving slots prior to data transfer [22]. Thus, such protocols could avoid collision at the time of data transfer, thereby improving the network throughput. To conserve energy, nodes could now turn off their transceiver in sleep mode if not required. However, such protocols may not perform well due to substantial body movement. In [23], a QoS-based WBAN routing protocol is presented where depending on QoS requirements the data traffic has been divided into several categories. Each such separate module is devised to specifically address the concerns of their respective QoS category. Although such protocols could improve throughput as well as reliability, the system overhead also increases.

Another pressing trend in WBAN routing research is to address the interference issue [24]. Such strategies are designed to address the intra BAN interference issue that is, when two sensor nodes come in close contact due to change in certain body posture. Moreover, WBAN supports remote medical supervision in a hospital or home under free living conditions. This leads to a possibility of interference among coexisting WBANs especially when two patients come nearby or shake hands with sensors attached in both hands. Accordingly, solutions were attempted to address inter BAN interference complications as in [24]. However, both intra BAN and inter BAN interference comprise important concerns to be addressed by other categoris of WBAN routing protocols.

Consequently, a trade-off of different factors could be devised in cost-based routing [25] where the major routing issues such as link interference, energy efficiency, temperature control, and QoS metric are addressed through cost-based trade-off mechanisms. The least cost route would be the best route for sensing sensor data to the sink. However, the cost calculation could be handled by the WBAN coordinator centrally or it is done in a distributed manner at each individual node. In the first approach, the coordinator obtains relevant information from other sensors such as, distance from sink and remaining energy [26]. Then the overall cost is evaluated for each node. Data forwarding decisions are based on such cost values. In case of distributed cost evaluation [27] an individual sensor node estimates the cost for its neighbor nodes based on different criteria such as link quality, temperature, and remaining energy. Based on this cost so evaluated, a suitable forwarder node is chosen. However, it is important to note here that the centralized evaluation mechanisms may result in more energy consumption due to periodical gathering of information from the nodes. The forwarder nodes can be chosen opportunistically if the network connections are intermittent [28]. In this case, data would be sent in store, carry, and forward modes. Though such routing protocols would mostly select the least cost route for forwarding data; there are a few approaches where the total cumulative path cost is also considered. Such a consideration is important to ensure overall faster routes but caching of cumulative path cost could be an overhead.

It is important to note that since in a WBAN configuration, the no of nodes would not exceed 20, it is not worth to have a multi-hop connection. Most of the nodes would be directly connected to the WBAN coordinator. However, keeping in mind the rising temperature of the nodes with more transmission power, sometimes, we need to go for 2 hop connections in order to reach the coordinator.

Herewith, a cost based routing protocol has been designed in [29] where energy consumption by the sensor nodes and their effect on human body are considered in the routing decision. The authors observed that more energy consumption by the body sensors may improve performance of a particular link but as suspected it affects both the human body and the network in many ways.

The protocol supports 2-hop communication in such cases for reducing the energy consumption. Thus, it chooses a forwarder node considering factors like link reliability and remaining energy. Increase in SAR of the forwarder should also be considered while deciding about the relay traffic. Packet delivery ratio (PDR) and packet forwarding ratio (PFR) are generally considered as performance metric for WBAN routing protocols.

An extension of this protocol could be found in [30], where a 2-Hop Interference aware Energy efficient Routing protocol, HIER is developed. It has two phases- (i) setup phase and (ii) data transfer phase. During this phase node x exchanges SETUP packets with neighbors so as to know its neighborhood and test for its direct reachability to the WBAN coordinator. In the beginning of the setup phase, a node x broadcasts a SETUP REQ packet in its neighborhood. This is shown in Fig. 4.7. Setup packets are transmitted using low transmission power. The goal is to explore the reachability to the coordinator even at this low power level. This has two advantages-

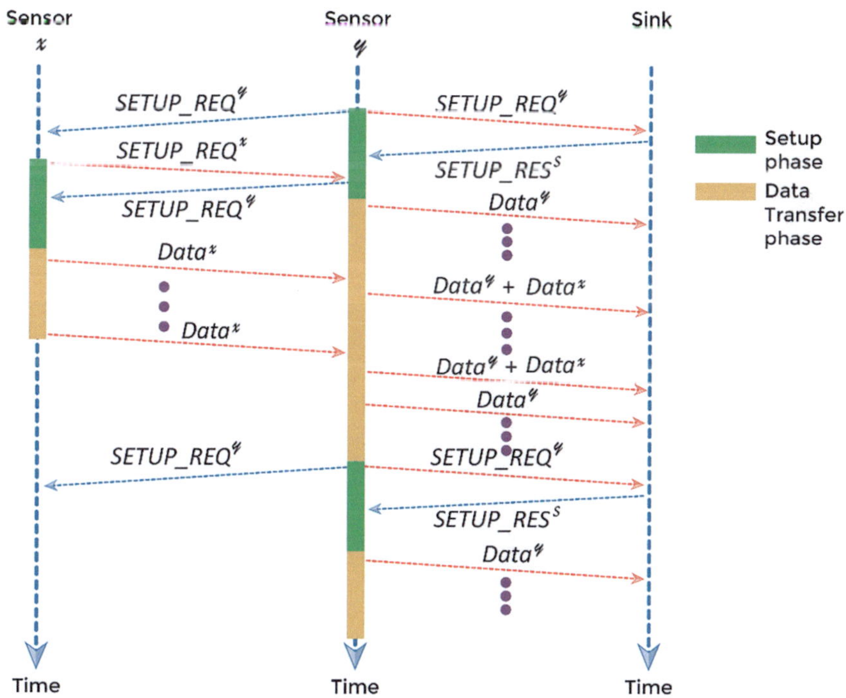

Fig. 4.7 Setup and data transfer phases of HIER protocol for WBAN routing

(i) This saves node's energy and reduces SAR as node x can further communicate with the coordinator/sink at a low transmission power.
(ii) The node x could relay data from other nodes without significant energy depletion.

Upon receiving a SETUP REQ, a node would reply with a SETUP RES packet. So, a sink would also send such a reply to its neighbors. Link reliability, energy efficiency, and specific absorption rate are then calculated for the link.

An example WBAN configuration is shown in Fig. 4.8 having 8 nodes where the SETUP RES received by the initiating nodes S5 and S8 are shown. Here, S8 has an indirect connectivity to the sink.

Node x caches the information received during the setup phase for a certain duration in its routing table so that several data packets may be sent without the setup overhead. However, node x again initiates the setup phase periodically till it has more data for the sink. Moreover, each node would discard the routes having low energy efficiency, in order to prevent buffer overflow.

Any sudden degradation of Signal to Noise Ratio (SNR) could signify a possible case of intra BAN or inter BAN interference. So, the node would wait for some time

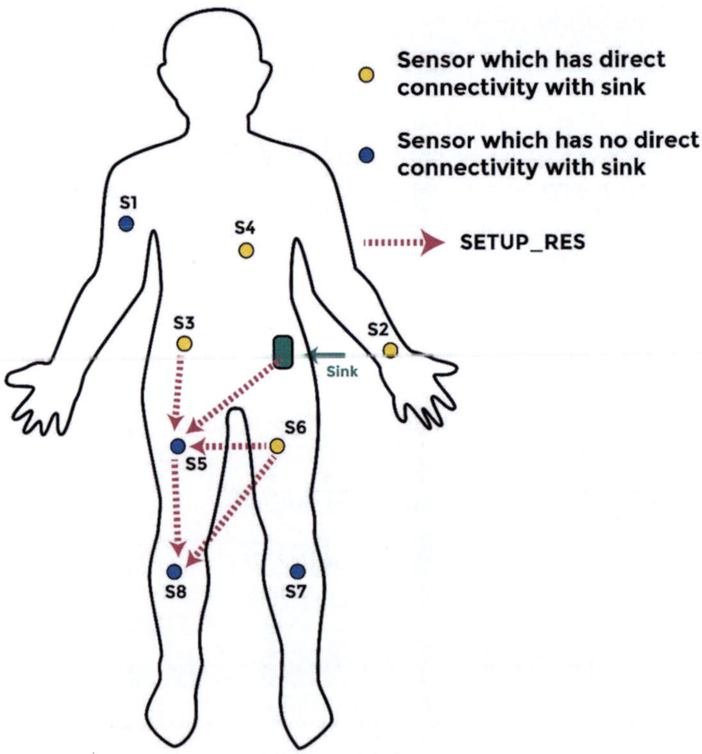

Fig. 4.8 An example WBAN topology with 1-hop (S5) and 2-hop (S8) connection to the sink

allowing the communication channels to recover from the possible interference. This waiting time would be decided by the packet urgency and upper layer timeout.

Although HIER is an on-demand protocol, it has the provision for caching the routes to reduce the setup overhead. A node would further initiate the setup phase if any of the two conditions occur.

(i) If the node suspects some problem in an ongoing data transmission process as acknowledgements for certain number of data packets have not arrived.
(ii) Certain time period has elapsed and still the node has data for the sink.

Moreover, since the broadcast of SETUP_REQ is limited to only one hop neighbors of the source node, it reduces the control message overhead even further.

4.1.4 IoT Protocols

An IoT device typically contains sensors that sense data and communicate to a remote server over the Internet. It is important to efficiently store, retrieve, and process the data sensed by the IoT devices. The conventional method involves sending the real life data gathered from multiple sensors, to cloud servers for additional processing and archiving. Sometimes, the data is locally processed, in limited manner before transferring it to a cloud server for storage and further processing. However, with wide variety of IoT applications in place, such an approach would incur huge Internet traffic and latency issues. This highlights the necessity for a different paradigm that can carry out computations nearer to the sensors or data sources. Interestingly, edge computing enables the processing of IoT data closer to the sources, in a local network such as base stations. So, the edge servers could be placed at the sink of a sensor network in order to provide local processing and sending the result to a remote cloud server over the Internet whenever required.

Having every IoT device communicating with the server via a separate connection might lead to an overbearing need for Internet connections and consumption of the network's wireless resources in an expansive IoT network. One of the key components of the IoT is clustering [31]. This is because, although the IoT appears to be an opportunistic network, not everything in the actual world is IP-enabled [32]. Because of its well-known benefits, clustering has been acknowledged by the scientific community as an effective strategy for achieving these goals of sharing IP connectivity to a cluster of sensor nodes. Clustering enhances energy-efficient routing by decreasing the number of nodes participating in the route formation process as it imposes hierarchy through the CHs. It also allows the possibility of data aggregation and better QoS [32]. Moreover, clustering is found to effectively improve a network's lifespan for large-scale deployments and enhances network scalability.

Among the current clustering strategies for WSNs, many of them assume the sensors in the networks are homogeneous. If a heterogeneous network is considered, the degree of the diversity is still rather low. For instance, some heterogeneous network simply assumes that some of the sensor nodes possess double power supplies than others. This assumption has become unrealistic recently, especially in IoT systems.

The most important issue comes from the essential feature of IoT systems—the enormous versatility. The "things" in the field are greatly dissimilar. It could be any consumer electronic device ranging from smartphones to microcontrollers. Hence, some nodes can have lower energy and computational capabilities.

The energy cost is still a crucial concern in IoT systems. Another emerging issue is to improve user convenience. Quality of Experience (QoE) has been highlighted significantly when configuring IoT networks. To cater for characterized usage, user profile should be in consideration. For a smart IoT network it needs to be made context aware, and for this, additional components in the core network have been projected to deliver additional functionalities.

In MHCM [33], a clustering algorithm has been proposed to reduce the internet connections while achieving optimal delay. This method focuses on choosing the smallest group of coordinators that can effectively cover all IoT nodes in a network. Then it further optimizes the overall number of coordinators selected. Meta-heuristic algorithms are found to influence the design of IoT clustering as reflected in the literature. Such strategies could effectively handle situations where the node heterogeneity increases while the traffic becomes more bursty in nature. A Balanced Energy-Efficient clustering algorithm, BEE, is developed by the authors in [34], which identifies cluster heads by considering energy consumption and sensor layout. This approach has been found to maintain reliable coverage and improve the network's longevity. Additionally, the algorithm utilizes a single communication interface for the sensing nodes and employs MIMO for data transmission. If a node is selected as CH, it turns on MIMO to receive data from different sources across communication channels. Then, the CHs compress the received data and transmit it back to the base station. A sensing node could select a single communication interface and hence, one cluster head for communication.

In [35], a firefly-based clustering protocol is proposed. The algorithm has a micro-clustering phase where the "things", that is, the nodes contend among themselves. Thus, they self-organize and a cluster is formed. Then, in the macro clustering phase, the small clusters are usually integrated with neighboring clusters. This approach emphasizes self-adaptation in order to optimize performance in the network.

A clustering algorithm based on particle swarm optimization (PSO) has been proposed in [36] for WSN with mobile sink. For a typical WSN configuration of M sensors, the resultant network is grouped into N clusters. First, the partition line of the network region has been determined by applying the PSO algorithm. According to the coordinates of the nodes in each region, in the cluster head selection phase, the center of gravity of the region is first calculated. A node's distance from the center of gravity is evaluated next. For each cluster, the average residual energy is then evaluated. The node having the maximum residual energy would be selected as the CH. The mobile sink broadcasts a Hello packet in two hop range from the CH. It then chooses the cluster having the highest average residual energy. The data so collected by the CH is finally sent to the mobile sink node. The sink node then moves to the next position after some time and repeats the same process.

In [37], a Glow-worm Swarm Optimization (GSO)-based clustering algorithm is proposed. In GSO, the glow-worms always move toward the worm having the highest glow. For applying GSO to obtain IoT clusters, four factors have been taken into account in the fitness function—(i) local density of each CH, (ii) the energy consumption of nodes within a cluster, (iii) intra-cluster average distance, and (iv) the dispersibility of the CH. Initially, the nodes with residual energy higher than the average residual energy are selected as CHs. The GSO algorithm is then applied to obtain optimal clusters. After clustering, the authors formed a spanning tree of the chosen CHs. If a CH is within the communication range of the base station then, the CH directly transfers the data. Otherwise, adjacent CH with the lowest cost function which is nearer to the base station is selected as the next hop.

As we have seen the IoT clustering literature is influenced by the meta-heuristic algorithms literature. As could be observed, residual energy of the nodes and hence, energy efficiency has been found to be an important factor.

4.2 Mobility Models for MANET and WSN

It is important to simulate node mobility while testing the routing protocols. To realistically represent node movements, a literature of mobility models exists. Most of the network simulators also provide implementation of one or more of such models. The commonly used ones are listed below.

4.2.1 *Random Walk Mobility Model*

This model simulates memory less movement of nodes with speed varying in the range of $[v_{min}, v_{max}]$ and direction $(0, 2\pi)$. New speed value is determined following uniform (or Gaussian) distribution. This type of motion is similar to that of the Brownian Motion. The direction as well as the speed of the nodes could be altered at each time interval. For a time duration t, a node may move with velocity vector $(v(t)cos\theta(t), v(t)sin\theta(t))$ and then it could be bounced back at an angle $\pi-\theta(t)$ or $\theta(t)$.

4.2.2 *Random Waypoint Mobility Model*

The nodes exhibiting this type of mobility choose the speed and direction randomly and so do the destination. This choice is made independent of other nodes in the network [38]. In this mobility model, the movement of a mobile node contains periods of motion with periods of pause in between. A mobile node chooses a destination randomly on the experimental region and moves toward it at a speed chosen uniformly between [0, V_{max}]. When it reaches the destination, the mobile node pauses and the process is repeated. This continues for the entire simulation duration.

4.2.3 Reference Point Group Mobility Model

This mobile model takes the spatial dependency into account. Nodes are divided into groups and each group has a leader. The members of a group follow their leader. The leader's mobility follows random way point as discussed earlier. The members of the group follow the leader's mobility closely, with some deviation [38].

4.2.4 Smooth Random Mobility Model

This type of mobility model has memory as the current values of speed and direction are correlated to previous values which makes movement of nodes smoother than random movement [38]. The probability distribution of node speed is not uniform. Those in the set of preferred speed values would have high probability, rest are uniformly distributed. Speed control is based on 'target speeds' that is changing according to Poisson process. When a new target speed $v'(t)$ is chosen, current speed $v(t)$ is not changed instantly but incrementally changed to that speed by applying a suitable uniformly distributed acceleration or deceleration $a(t)$.

The implication of mobility models vary from one network to the other. For instance, in case of WBAN, posture selection is a vital part of a network model as it influences the network topology. The chosen posture also determines the local mobility of the sensors and hence, the whole WBAN. Link connectivity among the body sensor nodes deployed on a human body varies for different postures [30]. This influences the packet delivery ratio as well. Packet delivery ratio is a well know performance metric that is calculated as the ratio of no of packets sent vs delivered. Thus, routing protocols are expected to incorporate support for such changes in topology and link quality. For the measure of stable mobility of human body four states of human posture such as Sitting, Standing, Lying, and Running could be considered along with their transition from one state to another.

Table 4.2 shows a comparison of different random walk-based mobility models with respect to their applicability to WBAN. As could be observed Smooth Random Mobility Model could be applied to WBAN effectively. However, the model does not capture the relative node movements of the network. As a WBAN configuration is setup in, on, or around the human body, group mobility model fits well and the relative mobility of different nodes could be represented effectively.

Table 4.2 Comparison among existing mobility models

Model	Pause time	Direction	Velocity	Applicability in WBAN
Line mobility	There is no pause time	Mobility direction not change	Velocity remains almost same throughout the movement	Low
Random waypoint	There is a random pause time	Direction changes frequently	Velocity is random in nature but there is pause time so sudden stop or sudden start is there	Low
Smooth random	There is no pause time	Direction changes frequently	There is no pause time; hence velocity is smooth in nature	Moderate

4.3 Simulation and Case Studies

Simulation refers to the imitation of operations of a real-world system over time. For simulation, a model is required that represents the key characteristics of the selected physical or abstract system. The model represents the system itself, whereas simulation represents its operations over time.

OMNET++ is a popular discrete event network simulation framework that is mostly used by many researchers [30]. It is freely available. Other simulators such as, MATLAB, OPNET and NS-3 are also utilized by researchers. OMNET++ has several extensions for MANET, WSN, WBAN, and IoT that could be utilized for routing experimentation as the suitable MAC layer protocol support is given in such extensions. OMNET++ provides a generic architecture, so it has been used in various problem domains:

- protocol modeling
- modeling of multiprocessors and other distributed hardware systems
- modeling of queueing networks
- validating of hardware architectures.

OMNET++ itself is not a simulator of any specific network or system, but rather provides the infrastructure and tools for *writing* simulations. One of the basic building block of this infrastructure provided by OMNET++ is a component architecture for simulation models. Models are assembled from reusable components known as *modules*.

Modules can be connected to each other via gates, and combined to form compound modules. Modules communicate through passing messages that may carry arbitrary data structures. Simple modules refer to those at the lowest level of the module hierarchy, and they encapsulate model behavior. Simple modules are programmed in C++.

OMNET++ simulations can be executed under various user interfaces including graphical, and command-line user interfaces.

The simulator as well as user interfaces and tools are highly portable across platforms. Most common operating systems including Linux, Mac OS/X, and Windows could be utilized. OMNET++ also supports parallel and distributed simulation. It can use different mechanisms for communication among partitions of a parallel and distributed simulation.

4.3.1 Installing OMNET++

We provide detailed steps of installing OMNET++ as follows.

STEP 1 Download the OMNET++ source code (OS-specific archive such as omnetpp-4.2.2-src-windows.zip for Windows) from http://omnetpp.org.

STEP 2 Copy the OMNET++ archive to the directory where it needs to be installed. It is better to choose a directory whose full path does not contain any space.

STEP 3 Extract the zip file.

STEP 4 Start mingwenv.cmd in the omnetpp-4.2.2 directory. It will bring up a console with the MSYS *bash* shell in Windows, where the path is already set to include the omnetpp-4.2.2/bin directory.

STEP 5 For configuring and building OMNET++ enter the commands

```
$ ./configure
$ make
```

STEP 6 For verifying installation, test all sample codes given and check if they run correctly

```
$ cd samples/dyna
$ ./dyna
```

STEP 7 For starting the IDE

```
$ omnetpp
```

The subsequent subsections discuss different framework under OMNET++ for simulation of MANET, WSN, WBAN, and IoT.

4.3.2 MiXiM Framework

MiXiM [39] is a network modeling framework based on OMNET++ specifically built for wireless networks like MANET and WSN. It provides model support and protocols. The channel models radio propagation effects in terms of time variant factors of the Signal-to-Noise Ratio γ of the received signal. MiXiM supports the popular channel models for shadowing, path-loss, and fading.

MiXiM's supported protocol stack is as follows.

- **MAC protocols**- Various MAC protocols [40] utilized in the WSN MAC literature have been provided by MiXiM. For WSN-specific MAC protocols, two base classes are provided-BaseMACLayer and EyesMACLayer.
- **Network layer protocols**-A wide range of traffic paradigms are supported by MiXiM including any-to-any; source-to-sink; local neighborhood; and so on.
- **Localization**- BaseLocalization - the base layer relays messages from upper and lower layers. Unknown neighbors and a list of anchors are also kept by the framework. PositifLayer—a layer that connects the MiXiM simulation framework to the Positif algorithms.
- **Mobility models**-MiXiM can support a rich library of different mobility models. Simple modules like "circle mobility" or "constant speed mobility" are supported. New mobility modules can be created by sub-classing from the BaseMobility class.

4.3.3 Castalia Framework

WBAN has been effectively simulated in Castalia 3.2 simulator [29]. It smoothly runs in Linux and provides an appropriate platform for validating new MAC or routing protocols for WBAN. It provides support to implement protocols with advanced wireless channels and radio models illustrating a realistic node behavior particularly in accessing the physical layer. The highly parametric design of Castalia-enables a researcher to study discrete platform characteristics with respect to specific applications. For instance, IEEE 802.15.4 functionality could be exploited to prototype intra-BAN communications.

A few basic simulation parameters along with their typical values are listed in Table 4.3. A WBAN comprising of 12 nodes is simulated in [30]. The nodes are deployed at different positions on the human body with the sink placed at the waist as shown in Fig. 4.9. This network size follows the typical medical network based on WBAN which consists typically of 6 to 20 nodes [41]. Simulation area of 1m × 1m has been exploited to provide support for relative node movements due to posture change. Experiments are carried out using the Line mobility model [42]. The line mobility model gives a temporal model for body movement. Here, the programmers can define the speed and the update interval. In [30], authors have implemented the Smooth random mobility model (Sect. 4.2.4) so that smooth mobility of the nodes could be simulated.

The wireless channel module is updated based on the nodes' current position. All transmissions are typically made with –15dBm transmission power so as to contain the SAR. Radio parameters in Castalia are regulated with values from CC2420 datasheet by default [29].

Table 4.3 Typical values of parameters for a realistic WBAN configuration

Parameter	Default value
No. of sink	1 (Node 0)
No. of nodes	12
Sink location	Waist
Simulation area	1 m × 1.9 m
Mobility model	Line mobility model
MAC protocol	IEEE 802.15.4

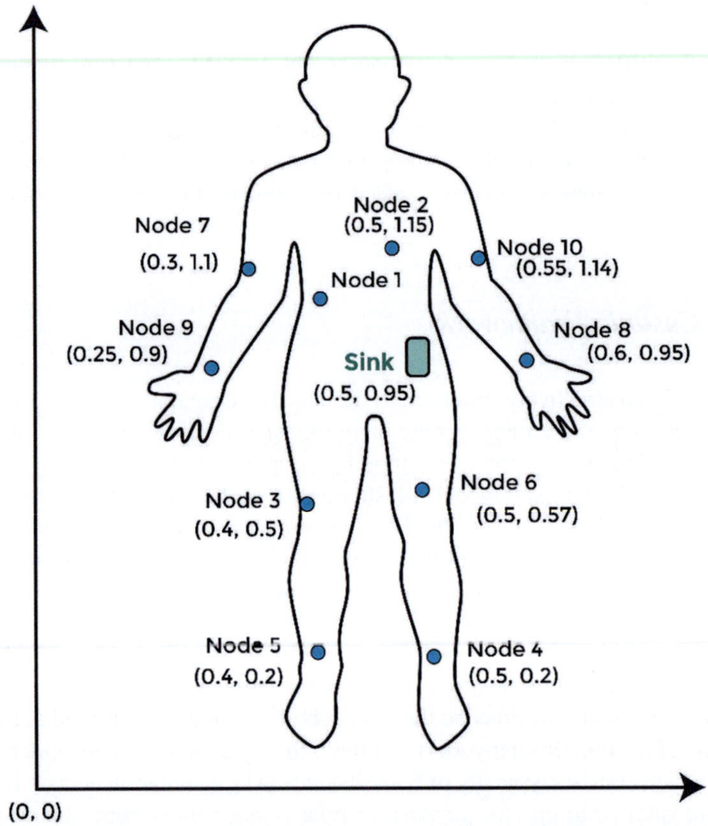

Fig. 4.9 WBAN nodes attached to a human subject representing a realistic WBAN configuration with corresponding node coordinates considering the average height and width of subjects

In Fig. 4.10, the results of HIER protocol [30] is shown with respect to the Smooth random mobility model. As shown, the sensor nodes move in a similar manner indicating overall body movement. The authors have also experimented with different transmission rate and transmission power. The results are shown in Fig. 4.11. The figure indicates that with more transmission power more packets would be delivered directly to the sink regulating the forwarding messages. However, for lesser transmission power, the more forwarding traffic could be observed as 0dBm is the highest transmission power along the rightmost x-axis. Data traffic increases with more data transmission rate and transmission power.

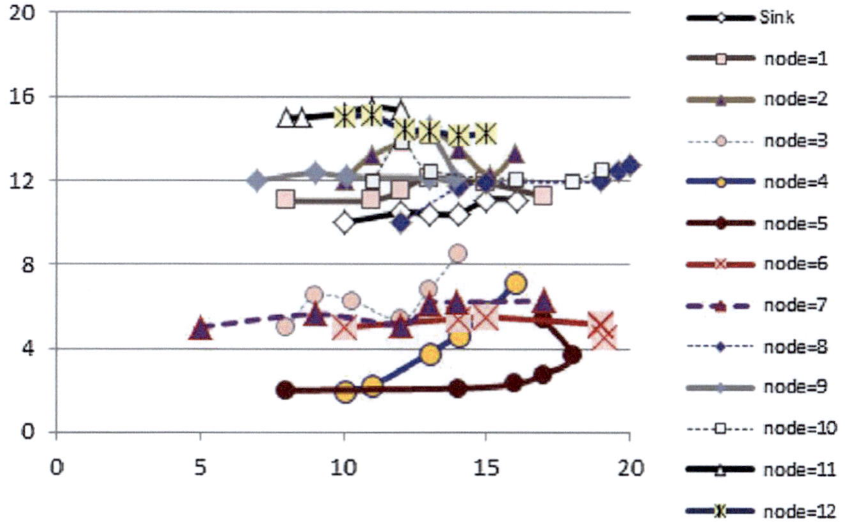

Fig. 4.10 Sensor node movements in WBAN according to smooth random mobility model

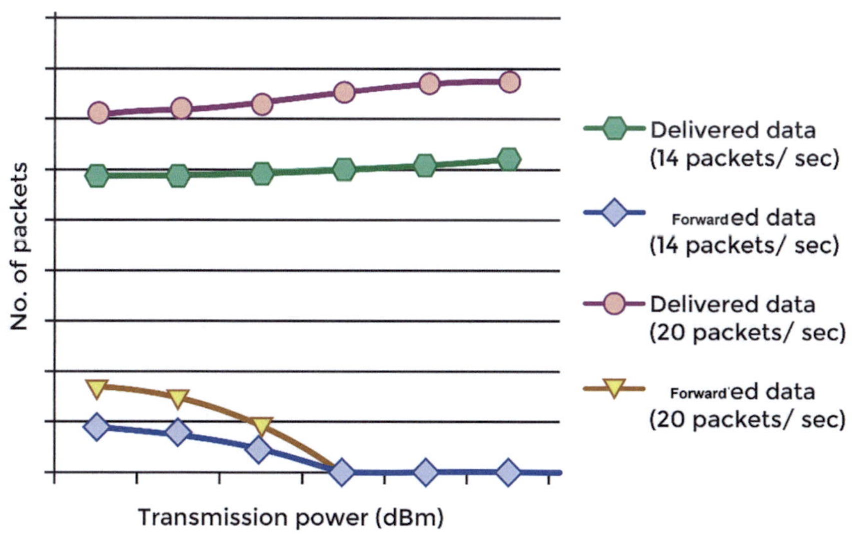

Fig. 4.11 Performance of HIER subject to different transmission power

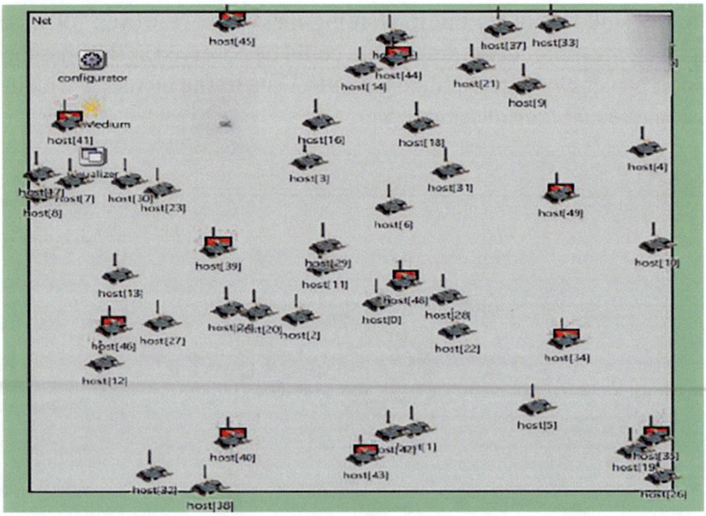

Fig. 4.12 An example IoT network configuration simulated using the INET framework

4.3.4 INET Framework

It is a framework on OMNET++ again that contains models for the Internet stack and wireless link layer protocols. This makes it suitable choice for the researchers of IoT applications. Nodes could be deployed randomly in the experimental region [43]. Figure 4.12 illustrates an example of a network deployment in the INET platform, featuring 47 nodes with the sink positioned at the center of the area. The nodes marked with rectangular boxes represent the cluster heads.

4.4 Summary

In this chapter, the routing protocols for different kinds of wireless networks are presented. We have mainly covered MANET, WSN, WBAN, and IoT protocols. These are the four wireless network variants widely used in various smart city applications. Energy efficiency and packet delivery ratio or throughput are mostly considered as important while designing such protocols by the researchers. The commonly utilized simulation platforms and the concept of mobility models applied for realistic node mobility are also discussed so that a complete view on this topic could be presented to the readers.

References

1. Pahlavan, K., Krishnamurthy, P.: Principles of wireless networks. Prentice Hall PTR (2002)
2. Muldoon, C., Hare, G.M.P.O., Bradley, J.F.: Towards reflective mobile agents for resource constrained mobile devices. The 6th International Joint Conference On Autonomous Agents And Multiagent Systems(AAMAS), pp. 927–929 (2007)
3. Nithya, S., Kumar, G.A., Adhavan, P.: Destination-sequenced distance vector routing (DSDV) using clustering approach in mobile adhoc network. In: 2012 International Conference on Radar, Communication and Computing (ICRCC), Tiruvannamalai, India, pp. 319–323 (2012). https://doi.org/10.1109/ICRCC.2012.6450604
4. Perkins, C.E., Royer, E.M.: Ad-hoc on-demand distance vector routing. In: Proceedings WMCSA'99. Second IEEE Workshop on Mobile Computing Systems and Applications, New Orleans, LA, USA, pp. 90–100 (1999). https://doi.org/10.1109/MCSA.1999.749281
5. Johnson, D.B., Maltz, D.A.: Dynamic source routing in Ad Hoc wireless networks. In: Imielinski T, Korth HF (eds) Mobile computing. In: The Kluwer International Series in Engineering and Computer Science, vol. 353. Springer, Boston, MA (1996). https://doi.org/10.1007/978-0-585-29603-6_5
6. Nehra, N., Patel, R.B., Bhat, V.K.: Routing with load balancing in ad hoc networks: a mobile agent approach. In: The 6th International Conference on Computer and Information Science, pp. 489–495 (2007)
7. Bonabeau, E., Dorigo, M., Theraulaz, G.: Inspiration for optimization from social insect behavior. Nature **406**, 39–42 (2000)
8. Ramkumar, K.R., Ravichandran, M., Hemachandar, N., Manoj Prasadh, D., Ganesh Kumar, M.: Raam: routing algorithm using ant agents for MANETs. In: The 11th International Conference on Advanced Communication Technology **2**, 1386–1391 (2009)
9. Manvi, S.S., Kakkasageri, M.S.: Multicast routing in mobile ad hoc networks by using a multiagent system. Inf. Sci. **178**, 1611–1628 (2008)
10. Denko, M.K.: The use of mobile agents for clustering in mobile ad hoc networks. In: The 2003 Annual Research Conference of the South African Institute of Computer Scientists and Information Technologists on Enablement Through Technology, pp. 241–247 (2003)
11. Anand, S., Francis, J., Rajsingh, E.B., Bhushan, S.S.: Mobile agent based AHP clustering protocol in mobile ad hoc network. Adv. Comput. Sci. Technol. **3**(1), 77–96 (2010)
12. Illarri, S., Mena, E., Illarramandi, A.: Location dependent queries in mobile contexts: distributed processing using mobile agents. IEEE Trans. Mob. Comput. **5**, 1029–1043 (2006)
13. Heinzelman, W., Chandrakasan, A., Balakrishnan, H.: An application-specific protocol architecture for wireless microsensor networks. IEEE Trans. Wirel. Commun. 660–670 (2002)
14. Aderohunmu, F.A., Deng, J.D.: An enhanced stable election protocol (SEP-E) for clustered heterogeneous WSN. Department of Information Science, University of Otago, New Zealand, p. 18 (2009)
15. Younis, O., Fahmy, S.: HEED: A hybrid, energy-efficient, distributed clustering approach for ad-hoc sensor networks. IEEE Trans. Mobile Comput. **3**, 366–379 (2004)
16. Taheri, H., Neamatollahi, P., Younis, O.M., Naghibzadeh, S., Yaghmaee, M.H.: An energy-aware distributed clustering protocol in wireless sensor networks using fuzzy logic. Ad. Hoc. Netw. **10**, 1469–1481 (2012)
17. Intanagonwiwat, C., Govindan, R., Estrin, D.: Directed diffusion: a scalable and robust communication paradigm for sensor networks. In: Proceedings ACM MobiCom 2000, Boston, MA, pp. 56–67 (2000)
18. Movassaghi, S., Abolhasan, M., Lipman, J., Smith, D., Jamalipour, A.: Wireless body area networks: a survey. IEEE Commun. Surv. Tutor. **16**(3), 1658–1686 (2014)
19. Chowdhury, C., Aslam, N., Spinsante, S., Perla, D., Del Campo, A., Gambi, E.: Energy efficient communication in ambient assisted living, In: Ambient Assisted Living And Enhanced Living Environments: Principles, Technologies and Control. Elsevier, pp. 37–59 (2016)

20. Watteyne, T., Aug´e-Blum, I., Dohler, M., Barthel, D.: Anybody: a self-organization protocol for body area networks. In: Proceedings of the ICST 2nd International Conference on Body Area Networks, pp. 1–7 (2007)
21. Cavallari, R., Martelli, F., Rosini, R., Buratti, C., Verdone, R.: A survey on wireless body area networks: technologies and design challenges. IEEE Commun. Surv. Tutorials **16**(3), 1635–1657 (2014)
22. Braem, B., Latre, B., Moerman, I., Blondia, C., Demeester, P.: The wireless autonomous spanning tree protocol for multihop wireless body area networks. In: Third Annual International Conference on Mobile and Ubiquitous Systems: Networking and Services, pp. 1–8. IEEE (2006)
23. Liang, X., Balasingham, I.: A QoS-aware routing service framework for biomedical sensor networks. In: 4th INTERNATIONAL SYMPOSIUM on Wireless Communication Systems, ISWCS 2007, pp. 342–345. IEEE (2007)
24. Sarra, E., Moungla, H., Benayoune, S., Mehaoua, A.: Coexistence improvement of wearable body area network (WBAN) in medical environment. In: IEEE International Conference on Communications (ICC), pp. 5694–5699. IEEE (2014)
25. Quwaider, M., Biswas, S.: Probabilistic routing in on-body sensor networks with postural disconnections. In: Proceedings of the 7th ACM International Symposium on Mobility Management and Wireless Access, pp. 149–158. ACM (2009)
26. Nadeem, Q., Javaid, N., Mohammad, S., Khan, M., Sarfraz, S., Gull, M.: Simple: stable increased-throughput multi-hop protocol for link efficiency in wireless body area networks. In: Eighth International Conference on Broadband and Wireless Computing, Communication and Applications (BWCCA), pp. 221–226. IEEE (2013)
27. Liang, X., Li, X., Shen, Q., Lu, R., Lin, X., Shen, X., Zhuang, W.: Exploiting prediction to enable secure and reliable routing in wireless body area networks. In: Proceedings of INFOCOM 2012, pp. 388–396. IEEE (2012)
28. Quwaider, M., Biswas, S.: DTN routing in body sensor networks with dynamic postural partitioning. Ad Hoc Netw. **8**(8), 824–841 (2010)
29. Roy, M., Chowdhury, C., Aslam, N.: Designing an energy efficient WBAN routing protocol. In: COMSNETS. IEEE (2017)
30. Roy, M., Chowdhury, C., Aslam, N.: Designing 2-Hop Interference aware Energy efficient Routing (HIER) protocols for wireless body area networks. In: Sastry, N., Chakraborty, S. (eds) Communication systems and networks, COMSNETS 2017, Lecture notes in computer science, Springer, Cham **16**(10340), 262–283 (2017). https://doi.org/10.1007/978-3-319-67235-9
31. Ansari, X.S.N.: Traffic load balancing among brokers at the IoT application layer. IEEE Trans. Netw. Serv. Manag. **15**(1), 489–502 (2017)
32. White, G., Nallur, V., Clarke, S.: Quality of service approaches in IoT: a systematic mapping. J. Syst. Softw. **132**, 186–203 (2017)
33. Sung, Y., Lee, S., Lee, M.: A multi-hop clustering mechanism for scalable IoT networks. Sensors **18**(4), 961 (2018)
34. Lina, X., O'Hare, G., Collier, R.: A smart and balanced energy-efficient multihop clustering algorithm(smart-beem) for mimo IoT systems in future networks. Sensors **17**(7), 1574 (2017)
35. Jabeur, N., Yasar, A.U.-H., Shakshuki, E., Haddad, H.: Toward a bio-inspired adaptive spatial clustering approach for IoT applications. Future Gener. Comput. Syst. **107**, 736–744 (2017). https://doi.org/10.1016/j.future.2017.05.013
36. Wang, J., Cao, Y., Li, B., Kim, H., Lee, S.: Particle swarm optimization based clustering algorithm with mobile sink for WSNs. Future Gener. Comput. Syst. **76**, 452–457 (2017)
37. Yong, L., Mufang, H., Ke, Z., Renrong, X., Xiuwu, Y., Qin, L.: Uneven clustering routing algorithm based on glowworm swarm optimization. Ad Hoc Netw. **93**, 101923 (2019)
38. Neogy, R., Chowdhury, C., Neogy, S.: Reliability of mobile agents for reliable service discovery protocol in MANET. Int. J. Wirel. Mob. Netw. (IJWMN) **3**(5), 229–243 (2011)
39. Roy, M., Chowdhury, C., Neogy, S.: Developing secured MANET using trust. In: IEEE CPS Proceedings of the International Conference on Advanced Computing and Communication (ICACC 2014), pp. 183–186 (2014)

40. Köpke, A., Swigulski, M., Wessel, K., Willkomm, D., Klein Haneveld, P.T., Parker, T.E.V., Visser, O.W., Lichte, H.S., Valentin, S.: Simulating wireless and mobile networks in OMNeT++ The MiXiM Vision
41. Fu, Y., Liu, J.: Monitoring system for sports activities using body area networks. In: Proceedings of the 8th International Conference on Body Area Networks, pp. 408–413 (2013)
42. https://github.com/boulis/Castalia/. Last accessed 10 Jul 2020
43. Bakshi, M., Chowdhury, C., Maulik, U.: Energy-efficient cluster head selection algorithm for IoT using modified glow-worm swarm optimization. J Supercomput. **77**, 6457–6475 Springer (2021). https://doi.org/10.1007/s11227-020-03536-z

Chapter 5
Fault Tolerant Network

Abstract The chapter provides the concept and idea about fault tolerance. There is an overview about the failure and recovery techniques in wireless and mobile adhoc network (MANET). The chapter then goes on to provide details about one of the frequently used techniques, namely, checkpointing and recovery in MANET. Later on, couple of checkpointing and recovery techniques used in clustered MANET are also discussed. The chapter ends with fault tolerance techniques used in Wireless Sensor Network (WSN).

Keywords Fault tolerance · MANET · WSN · Checkpointing and recovery

5.1 Introduction

In this chapter we are going to talk about fault tolerance. Before going into the details let us see what the word "fault" and "tolerance" individually mean. As we know, the word "fault" is used in many contexts, both as noun and as verb. However, the general meaning that everyone is aware of means *something wrong* or *not perfect* in the context that we are talking of. Here, we are talking about *faults* in MANET. Similarly, *tolerance* also has multiple meanings depending on the context it is used for. The general meaning, however, is *the ability to put up with something unpleasant/harmful/abnormal*. So, putting these two words together with respect to our book and the chapter, we convey the meaning that, *the MANET will be able to withstand any fault*.

Specifically put, fault tolerance in a Mobile Ad Hoc Network (MANET) is the ability of the network to continue functioning even if some component (node and/or link) does not function properly or fail partially/totally. Fault tolerance is therefore necessary for maintaining the functioning (like, connectivity among the nodes, reliable data transmission) of the network. As the network environment in which MANET works is essentially dynamic, providing fault tolerance becomes necessary even if it may incur slight overhead. But the performance gain may outweigh the loss suffered from failure.

S. Biswas et al., *Adhoc and Sensor Networks: Security and Applications*, Studies in Systems, Decision and Control 653, https://doi.org/10.1007/978-981-95-5839-1_5

The question that now springs in our mind is, why is fault tolerance relevant or important in MANET? Because if we think it is important, then we have to first identify whether there is any fault, and perhaps then depending on the fault try to take some measures so that the MANET goes on working despite that fault. As we know MANET nodes (generally denoted as Mobile Node (MN), or Mobile Host (MH)) move and hence links can break thereby leading to broken routing path/s. Since these broken links cannot be used, there will be urgent need to find other usable routes for the MANET to be working. So firstly other MANET nodes must know that a certain link is not usable any more. And this means that certain nodes are not reachable. If we want the MANET to function properly, then we have to employ means that will be able to take up the functioning of the unreachable nodes, or the network as a whole, or find an alternative path/route and continue working. Designers of routing protocols for MANET may keep this in mind and allow for multiple routes (same source–destination) to be discovered and kept, in case node/link failure happens. These measures will then ensure smooth functioning of the MANET despite faults and failure.

Here it is to be mentioned that a fault is likely to cause failure, that is, it is a potential cause for failure, while failure is the inability to function properly or in the desired manner. The users of a system or service will notice the failure and depending on the application, fault/s may be identified. It is worthwhile to mention here that if a system or service is monitored continuously, then a potential fault may be flagged and steps may be taken early on so that it does not cause failure. However, easier said than done, hence failure mitigation steps may be included while the network is being designed and developed.

Generally, we can say failure in MANET can occur when nodes move out of communication range of any other node in the said MANET, or when a node fails (due to depletion of power or any other cause), or becomes inactive (may be to conserve its energy and thus act selfishly). All of these causes can lead to link failures, which can degrade the performance of the network.

The most probable causes of failure may be listed as follows:

- Node mobility—MANET nodes, being mobile can move out of communication range of other nodes.
- Node failure—A node may fail or become inactive due to a number of reasons, including large data traffic that swamps its buffers, high energy consumption due to excessive computation/communication, or other factors, like security breach.

Whatever be the reasons, effects of the failure will be felt and the ways to deal with the failure will be crucial to maintaining the working and/or performance of the MANET. The effects of the failure will be evident in reduced network performance due to path breaks and non-functioning nodes.

Based on the characteristics of MANET and its probability of failure, *fault tolerance* comes up to be the most sought after technique in MANET.

This is where we see the role of *checkpointing and recovery* technique as one of the mostly used fault tolerant approach in MANET.

5.2 Failure and Recovery in MANET

Due to the independent nature of the MANET node, it is required to perform a lot of tasks, other than its own computing task. It is well established that MANET has limited finite resources in processing power, bandwidth, and power. In addition there is an unstable or ever changing network topology that results mainly from link failure. Change in network topology begets change in routing process and forces with the introduction of new routing paths. The routing in MANET involves not only the source–destination pair, but also the intermediate nodes or hops that only forward the data. Notable to mention here is that, these nodes have to act independently in a distributed fashion, since there is no centralized routing manager. The nodes thus have to act as computing nodes, and as routers, as well. Thus energy consumption of a node may become high. Hence a node may also die and dead nodes also cause failure in MANET as the route through it becomes unusable.

The challenges faced while deploying any measure to combat failure in MANET involve the following main factors, apart from many similar others.

- Dynamic Topology—Since it is well known, since the MHs move and links break due to the movement, topology changes frequently.
- Resource Constraint—MANET nodes have limited battery/energy, memory, processing power due to their small size and overall capacity.
- Security—It is simple and easy for a node to join a MANET, as well as leave the MANET, if the MANET in question does not have enough in-built security measures. The nature (good or suspicious or malicious) of the node being not known, poses security threat to the network.

Hence the above factors will affect the feasibility of implementing any strategy for dealing with failures and/or faults. Strategies meant for and well suited for wired networks will not work effectively in MANET.

Several techniques belonging to different categories have been proposed over the years for dealing with failures in MANET. The categories of the techniques may not be novel, but the proposed techniques are different from existing categorical techniques. The techniques can be categorized as follows:

- Redundant Routing—Multiple routes may be kept for the same source–destination pair. This will help in picking up an alternative route in case one route fails to deliver.
- Replication—There may be duplicate or triplicate nodes in the MANET, so that the replica node is able to pick up the task of the primary node, if it fails.
- Error detection and Recovery—Nodes themselves have to keep track or monitor their neighbor nodes to find whether a node has failed or not. If detected as failed, a proper mitigation plan will be taken up.
- Fault-tolerant Routing Protocols—Routing protocols may be designed in such a way that these themselves are able to detect a failure and take appropriate action, whenever necessary.

It is always easier said than done. The techniques will provide advantages as well as a couple of disadvantages.

Whenever there are multiple routes, time and space constraint come, it means that discovery of multiple routes will take more time and the requirement for buffer space for keeping the routes will also be more. Also, the limit on the number of routes poses a problem. The limit on the number of the routes to be kept will influence the searching, if one route fails. The buffer of routes also has to be updated accordingly. Whether the routes will be proactive routes or reactive routes or hybrid, may have impact on the number of routes to be kept. Likewise, if replication is used, then the MANET itself will become larger and may be difficult to manage as all nodes, irrespective of replica or primary, will be mobile. Management of the network will involve finding active modes, finding routes, updating route buffers, among other associated tasks. Thus, the MANET node MH has to be busy in these tasks apart from its regular tasks of forwarding, computation, etc. The node may employ some mechanism to keep track of whether its neighbors are alive or not. A node will worry about its neighbors only, because they are its windows to the outside world, that is, the network. The information from monitoring will be used to update route/s, whenever necessary. For reactive routing, however, this monitoring may be done only if a route is necessary. As we all know, that reactive routing has its own overheads. Even for proactive routing, the information from neighbor monitoring (which may be continuous, in this case) will be used in updating cached or saved routes. As such, routing protocols themselves are designed to deal with a failure, if it happens to encounter one such. With this special property embedded in a routing protocol, it is needless to say that the protocol will bear overhead.

However, it is not an easy task to identify dead nodes or the reasons as to why a link failure is happening. Given the limited lifetime of MANET and application requirement, it may be prudent not to specifically first try to find out the cause behind any failure. Rather it may be prudent to take action once a failure is detected. Detection of fault or failure may not be instantaneous, but it may not take much longer before it is found out. So with proper mitigation plan in place, MANET may be kept functional and the effects of a failure may be minimized. *Checkpointing and rollback recovery* is a well recommended and widely used method for fault tolerance in MANET.

5.3 Checkpointing and Rollback Recovery

The technique of checkpointing and rollback recovery has attracted many researchers. The techniques have been adopted by many researchers in their work. As is already pointed out in the earlier sections, MHs are not only prone to failures, but are also prone to security attacks [1, 2]. The security attacks may also render a MH to fail or be at fault. The technique of checkpointing allows a node to take a snapshot (known as *checkpoint*) of its process state from time to time. In a checkpoint the state of a process is saved. The state of a process saved contains process structure, register values, segments, actual data and open file information [3]. Depending on the operating system, many other related information regarding the process are also saved. Process structure of a checkpoint saved of a process running on UnixWare kernel includes process ID, group ID, parent process, process state, current directory, signal information, information of address space etc. Starting address of each segment of a process to be checkpointed, size of a segment, actual data of a segment etc. are saved in the checkpoint file. The idea is that when a process has failed due to some reasons, and wishes to resume its processing, it does not have to restart. Rather, it can resume its working from the last saved checkpoint. Since the process goes back to a previous state for resuming, the procedure is referred to as *rollback recovery*. The failed process will recover and resume execution from this state. Needless to say, that minimum information is lost in this process. The MH only has to re-execute a few of its actions (from its last saved state to the state where it failed) while it resumes.

The frequency of the checkpointing activity may depend on various factors, like, application requirement, physical state of MANET nodes, probability of security attack on that MANET, to name a few. So, checkpointing may take place at regular time intervals or irregularly, depending on the factor/s mentioned above. Whatever be the case, the old checkpoint will be erased or deleted once a new checkpoint is created.

In the next section we shall discuss a couple of *checkpointing and recovery* techniques for MANET.

5.4 Checkpointing and Recovery in MANET

MANET comprises MHs that collaborate with each other on ad hoc basis without any fixed infrastructure, stable storage and access points [4]. Nodes have transceivers so that they can perform tasks related to routing, beside normal computations. All communications are multi-hop. MANET can be modelled as: (i) Flat structure (ii) Hierarchical cluster-based structure. In flat MANET, all mobile hosts are considered to be at the same level. No supervisor node is present. Mobile hosts generally communicate with each other through broadcasting. Hence flat MANET suffers from flooding of messages. In cluster-based hierarchical network, a set of nodes are first selected as cluster heads which work as coordinators. Cluster head selection can be done based on different criteria [5, 6]. Each cluster head then finds node/s within its communication range and includes it in its cluster as cluster member. The cluster member nodes within a cluster communicate through the respective cluster heads, hence communications are 1-hop communications. However, there must be some sort of communication pathway among the cluster heads, so that message from the cluster member of a cluster reaches the cluster member of a different cluster. There are also nodes who are in the coverage area of more than one cluster heads. These nodes begin to work as gateway nodes. Inter-cluster communication takes place through cluster heads and gateway nodes. Hierarchical organization of a network is advantageous over a flat network with respect to the following performance parameters: reduced storage for communication information e.g. routing information which can be stored in cluster heads and gateway nodes, reduced overhead of information update, effective utilization of network bandwidth, optimized resource utilization etc. [4].

Checkpoint in MANET may be attributed to saving the current state of a node including its processes, and further includes routing tables, data, any other relevant information, in persistent storage. Since this saving of the state is done when there is no failure or fault detected in the network, this serves as the last known good state of the node. Hence, this state can be used successfully for restoration of the state of that node, in case, failure cripples the node.

Rollback recovery generally involves this last saved good state of the node for resumption, or restoring the node/system to a functional state. Rollback recovery therefore, requires the last saved checkpoint of the system to get the system resumed from that point. The recovery process would most likely involve restoration of the state of the node, restarting or resuming the processes that were running before the failure, and also re-establishing the communication channels in the network. But with the space constraint in MANET node, where will this checkpoint be saved so that it can be duly accessed for restoration of the node's state? And it is not the situation, that only one node will take checkpoint, all nodes will partake in the checkpointing activity. Checkpoints will be taken by each of them at some intervals (as determined by the checkpointing algorithm depending on the requirement of the process).

Checkpointing can be *Uncoordinated* checkpointing, in which nodes will take individual and independent checkpoint. Checkpointing can be *Coordinated* checkpointing. In this method all nodes/processes synchronize their checkpointing activities to coordinate their checkpoint. This eventually provides saving of a system-wide consistent state. Another type of checkpointing activity, known as *Communication-induced* checkpointing is also prevalent. This activity ensures that a process takes its checkpoint based on the information of message received from other processes in the network. As MANET is considered to be distributed in nature, Uncoordinated checkpointing may be the programmer's first choice. However, the problem in implementation of any of the above-mentioned techniques has to be considered with respect to other factors, like application requirement, network bandwidth, etc. (Figs. 5.1, 5.2 and 5.3).

At a first glance it seems that uncoordinated checkpointing may require a node/process to save multiple checkpoints in order to arrive at a system-wide consistent state. Obviously, this implies space requirement and the overhead of the checkpointing activity itself. Also, it may not be known before-hand how many checkpoints a node might store in order to fall in step with the system. In all possibility the requirement will be all checkpoints starting after the last saved consistent state till the latest saved consistent state. In case of Coordinated checkpointing in MANET, the issue is the coordination itself. This is because, nodes may move and go out of range or the battery may die down and so on. Coordination in a dynamic setup is near to impossible. Communication-induced checkpointing will increase the checkpointing activity in a node, thereby, neglecting all its other tasks which are important

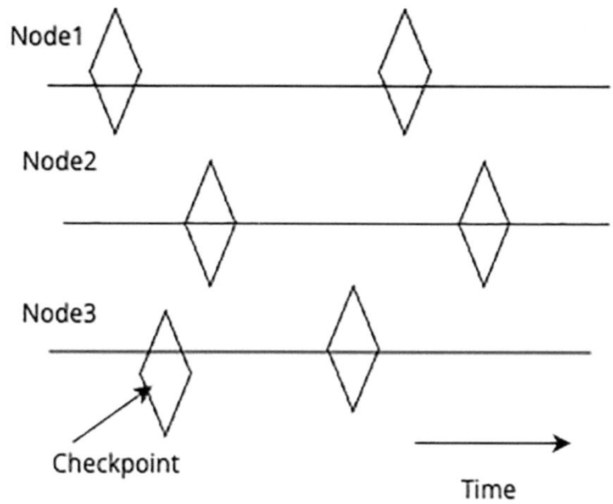

Fig. 5.1 Uncoordinated checkpointing in three nodes

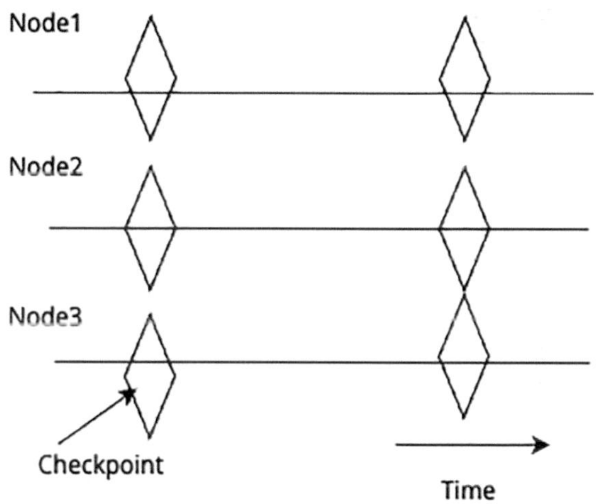

Fig. 5.2 Coordinated checkpointing in three nodes

for the MANET to execute the application without performance degradation. In this case also it cannot be known with surety the number of checkpoints to be stored for arriving at system-wide consistent state. This problem seems similar to the problem with uncoordinated checkpointing.

The challenges in implementing checkpointing and rollback recovery techniques [2, 7, 8] in MANET are many. Needless to say, these challenges have come up due to the unique nature of MANET (Fig. 5.4).

Although there is provision, that you will delete the earlier checkpoint when you take the latest one, still you need to figure out how and where to save all these checkpoints. Hence an important challenge for MANETs is to find a safe and robust storage for the checkpoint/s.

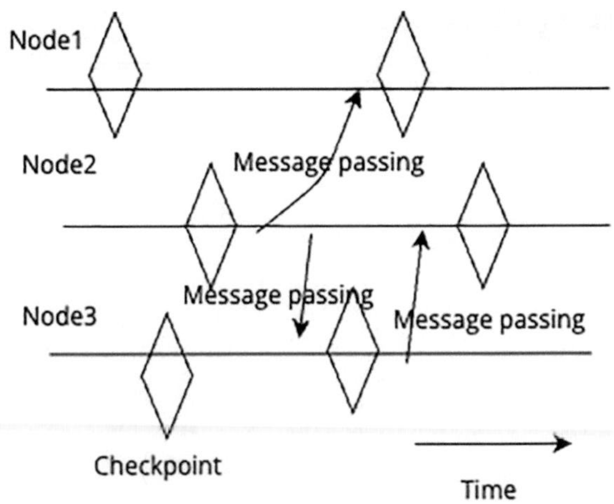

Fig. 5.3 Communication-induced checkpointing

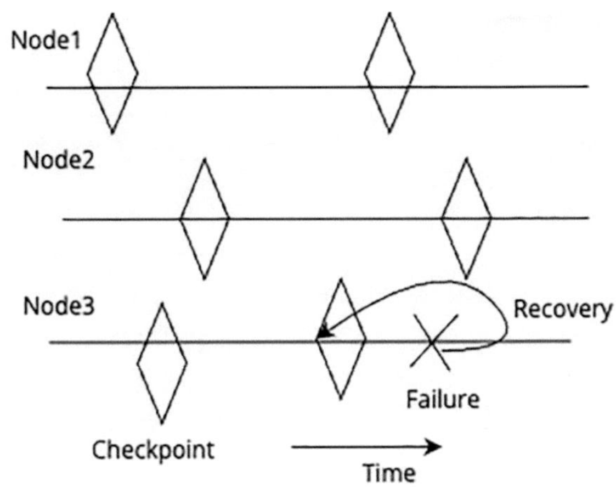

Fig. 5.4 Recovery in node 3 after failure

Firstly, as there is no fixed infrastructure support of a server, who will house the checkpoint? A mobile node is vulnerable to fail due to a variety of reasons as noted earlier, and hence may not be a good choice for storing checkpoint. This is because if the mobile host fails, how to retrieve the stored checkpoint? Even if logs of computation messages are saved, the same question still remains: where to save the lag and how to retrieve? This issue of having a storage site for the checkpoint has been addressed in [9] for Wireless Sensor Networks (WSN), which can be considered to be a specialized adhoc network. However, the WSN need not be necessarily mobile in nature. Hence the next important issue of considering node mobility has slightly less bearing in this environment. Each WSN node saves checkpoint and sends copy of its checkpoint to all its neighbor nodes because in WSNs no node has stable storage. The neighbor nodes send acknowledgement along with a probability to the sender node. This probability is inversely proportional to the number of neighbor nodes of that WSN node. As a node cannot save all checkpoints of its neighbor nodes due to limited storage space, this probability helps each node to adaptively decide on saving checkpoints of its neighbor nodes. However, in mobile cellular network, checkpoints of mobile hosts are saved in stable storage of the Mobile Service Stations, or MSSs. MSS may be assumed to be failure free. Thus, failure of a mobile host can be tolerated using last checkpoints saved in stable storage.

Secondly, since a mobile host MH is on the move, its information is likely to be scattered in several cluster heads. So, it is a gigantic task to collate all these information for suitable recovery. The task would entail both cost and time.

Thirdly, one of the important issues in any network is the behavior of the intermediate hop nodes that will be simply forwarding messages. These nodes must be trustworthy and not behave selfishly. The nodes may behave selfishly due to the fact that they may have very less battery power, or they are simply lazy and only fill up the buffers.

Last but not the least is that as both MANET nodes and links are vulnerable to security attacks or breaches, checkpoint and recovery information have to be securely retrieved, when needed.

Nevertheless, we could never ignore the issue of mobility as this is the unique characteristic of MANET. As it is well known, mobility of MHs will cause path breaks among other problems. Hence routing protocols need to be designed carefully so that reconstruction of new routes does not result in unnecessary delay. For that matter, it would be prudent to use *reliable* nodes as intermediate hops. By *reliable* nodes it is meant that nodes which may not fail all of a sudden thereby breaking the path. This also means that while setting up a route a node has to find a neighbor on which it can depend. Hence information regarding the neighbor nodes has to be made available. The information will be such that it is able to provide some sort of ranking among the neighbor nodes of a particular node. Here comes the issue of *trust*. A node will only choose one of its neighbors as its immediate next hop provided that the neighbor has fulfilled some criteria. These criteria may be several, for example, finding out whether a node will act selfishly given its power constraints, its resource constraints, activities with respect to rate of packet drop, latency regarding acknowledgement, and/or information regarding the behavior of this node from other nodes in the network. The last criteria is something like recommendation from other nodes. With such information and data, a node may be able to identify nodes which it can trust. The frequency of security attack on a mobile host can also be counted as a factor in the evaluation of its trust value.

Since we are concerned over the security of MANET, hence we consider *trusted* nodes only.

5.4.1 Trust-Based Checkpointing and Recovery in MANET

The works in [9, 10] describe trust mechanisms to enhance secure routing in MANET. As we all know different criteria can be used to effectively evaluate *trust* with respect to a MANET node.

There are trust based mechanisms [10] to implement secure routing of data through trusted nodes only.

It is observed that there are generally two types of failures in mobile system, *crash failure* and *transient failure. Transient failure* occurs for a very small time and is often too hard to detect. In the presence of some recovery mechanism, the nodes or the network undergoing *transient failure* will recover in no time and start resuming the work.

The authors in their work [7] describe a checkpointing and rollback recovery scheme for cluster based multichannel ad-hoc wireless network. This fault tolerant technique provides tolerance to transient failures. Cluster heads manage periodic checkpointing of mobile hosts. Logs of input, output, and messages are sent to gateways. This checkpointing scheme provides tolerance of computing failure of mobile hosts and gateway nodes as well.

However, *crash failures* result in lower or less permanent failures. Hence suitable *recovery* techniques are needed to be planned so that the effect on the network due to the failure is minimal. In the work in [11], the authors have studied the fundamental problem of crash recovery in mobile distributed environment. The work presented is an asynchronous recovery algorithm in MANET. The algorithm works on cluster-based network where each cluster has a cluster head which acts as the local coordinator within the cluster. As we are talking about recovery, we have to keep in mind the corresponding associated *checkpointing* technique. The accompanying *checkpointing* technique in this work is based on the concept of *event-based checkpointing.* Each MH takes checkpoint independently. So, this does not involve any synchronization and coordination overhead. Here resource limitations of mobile hosts and limited communication bandwidth have been considered.

In their work [12], the authors have designed an ant colony-based trust model to evaluate trust value of a mobile node in MANET. A trusted node is assumed to have low probability of failure and/or security attack. Hence this node may have quite high availability with positive reference from other nodes. The pheromone concept provides the network with information, such as, availability of the node, failure rate of the node, and remaining battery power of the node. Thus trust of a node is based on the above factors, unlike on single factor as proposed in [13, 14].

Another technique [15] in which checkpointing is based on mobility. Apart from mobility, that is cluster change count, remaining energy is also noted. Checkpoint is taken when either of these equals to a preset threshold either for the cluster change count or the threshold, whichever is applicable. In case of failure of the MH, its last saved checkpoint will be moved from its current storage to the current Cluster head of the MH. It is also assumed that all cluster heads and gateways in the path are trusted and thus integrity of the checkpoint is maintained. Cluster heads are selected [16] based on factors, such as, availability, failure rate, unused energy, and recommendation from other nodes.

Checkpointing and Recovery techniques are also used for detecting different attacks on MANETs.

Most of the proposed secure routing protocols in MANET work correctly only against single node attacks. They cannot provide protection against coordinated attacks from multiple malicious nodes working in collusion. Since packet transmission in MANET depends heavily on mutual trust [17–19] and cooperation among the nodes in the network, therefore determining the trust of an individual node before actually forwarding the packet to it may be considered to be an essential criteria for successful packet transmission. This trust can help in detecting malicious behavior of nodes (if present) in the network. A trusted node is one that is capable of successfully forwarding packets. In the technique proposed in [20], a node is trusted for routing if it is reliable, has sufficient resource (i.e. sufficient battery power) and has low mobility (which will reduce the chance of link breakage or topology change before forwarding the packet). Trusted MHs are selected for routing because it will ensure successful routing. Trusted MHs may also be used to save checkpoints. Hence trust calculation of a node will help in checkpointing and recovery, as well as in routing. The factors used for calculating trust in this work are also helpful for identifying blackhole node [21].

5.4.2 Checkpointing and Recovery in Clustered MANET

Clustering in MANET is one of the effective ways for performance enhancement as has already been mentioned. Consequently, researchers have proposed several checkpointing and recovery techniques for cluster-based MANETs. A selected few are described below.

In [2], Jaggi et al. presented Staggered Checkpointing and Recovery in cluster-based MANET. As concurrent checkpoint initiation can cause stable storage access contention over limited bandwidth in MANET, staggered checkpointing is proposed instead.

In their work [3], Juang and Liu presented an efficient asynchronous recovery algorithm for cluster based MANET. In this work they focused on the fundamental problem of crash recovery in mobile distributed environment.

However, not all research works addressed the mobility of the nodes in MANET.

In their work [22] the authors propose a new mobility aware checkpointing and failure recovery algorithm for cluster based MANET. In this work, a parameter ‘cluster-change-count’, maintained by each member node is used to keep count of the number of clusters a mobile node traverses through during a single checkpoint interval. A mobile node increments ‘cluster-change-count’ by 1 each time it leaves a cluster and joins another. Each mobile node saves a checkpoint independently if its ‘cluster-change-count’ exceeds a predefined threshold. Each mobile host saves checkpoint based on its movement from one cluster to another. This measure is important because each mobile node saves logs, important data required for its recovery at different cluster heads it is traversing. If the node fails, these data are to be searched and retrieved for recovery along with the last saved checkpoint. The search and retrieval costs of dispersed data of a failed node increases with increasing 'cluster-change-count' and gets added to total recovery cost for the failed mobile node. To limit this cost, a threshold for 'cluster-change-count' is set. It is assumed here that a mobile host saves back up copy of a checkpoint in one of its neighbor node that has sufficient resources as no node has stable storage. To ensure minimum cluster head change, the cluster head selection algorithm is used. Logs and other data required for recovery are saved in cluster head, log records of received computation messages are saved in gateway node, coordination at the time of recovery of a failed node is done by cluster head.

5.5 Fault Tolerance in Wireless Sensor Networks

Fault Tolerance in WSN can be described as the ability of the WSN to maintain its functionalities including data transmission and sensing, albeit failure. As already mentioned in Chap. 1 WSNs are very prone to failure due to a variety of reasons. These may range from energy or power depletion of the WSN nodes, software errors, hardware faults, environmental factors. WSNs are mainly used for data critical applications. Hence it is very much necessary for the network to be functional at all points in time. WSNs are therefore crucial due to the data they handle and the continuous nature of their sensing and transmission. Thus, introduction of fault tolerance seems to be important. The common fault tolerance techniques used for wireless networks are applicable to WSN too. However, the challenges of WSN seem to surpass the challenges of other types of wireless networks.

The research work in [23] uses two Base Stations (BS) for the entire network and two clusterheads (CH) for each cluster in the WSN: primary and backup. Using the *heartbeat* strategy faulty CH or BS are identified by other nodes. The backup CH springs into action as soon as the primary CH crashes or fails. The primary Base station saves regular updates as checkpoints and keeps the backup Base Station aware of the status of the network, so that the backup Base Station becomes alive whenever the primary one fails. The target application in this work was precision agriculture.

As we know, sensors can be body-wearable sensors and they can form Wireless Body Area Network (WBAN). In WBAN, the sensors measure different physical conditions of the person on whom the sensors are placed. The health parameters considered in the work described in [24] are heart beat rate, pulse rate, and body temperature. This work detects only node level faults. Using Artificial Neural Network (ANN) over the collected dataset faulty sensor is identified by looking into the deviations of readings from the sensors. The identification of the faulty sensor is also supported through computation of the physical parameter using the collected samples.

5.6 Conclusion

This chapter begins with the concepts of different types of failures in MANETs and the ways of handling failures. Tolerating faults that cause failure, or simply speaking, fault tolerance may be achieved with the help of the well-known technique of checkpointing and recovery. However, MANET has its unique characteristics that distinguishes it from the wired and infrastructure wireless networks. Hence checkpointing and recovery techniques or wired and infrastructure wireless networks will probably not be suitable for wireless and mobile adhoc networks. Due to the special characteristics and nature of MANETs, several new issues have to be dealt with for developing and providing suitable checkpointing and recovery techniques. Some of the main issues are mobility and security. Thus, MANET nodes must behave in a manner so that they can be trusted. Hence trust plays a major issue in MANET. This chapter briefly provides an overview of a couple of such checkpointing and recovery techniques.

Questions (Indicative)

Q1. What is fault tolerance? Why is it important in MANET?

Q2. What are the different ways of achieving fault tolerant networks?

Q3. What is a checkpoint? What is its relation with recovery?

Q4. Is security important for MANET? Justify your answer.

Q5. How can you make your MANET secure against attacks?

Q6. Give an idea of checkpointing and subsequent recovery after a blackhole attack has been identified in MANET.

Q7. What differences or similarities can you think of while designing a secure routing protocol for flat MANET and clustered MANET?

References

1. Prakash, R., Singhal, M.: Low cost checkpointing and failure recovery in mobile computing systems. IEEE Trans. Parallel Distrib. Syst. **7**, 1–38 (1996)
2. Jaggi, P.K., Singh, A.K.: Staggered checkpointing and recovery in cluster based mobile ad hoc networks. In: Nagamalai, D. (ed.) PDCTA 2011. CCIS, vol. 203, pp. 122–134. Springer, Heidelberg (2011)

3. Ying, T., Juang, T., Liu, M.C.: An efficient asynchronous recovery algorithm in wireless mobile adhoc networks. J. Internet Technol. Spec. Issue Wirel. Internet: Appl. Syst. **3**(2), 147–155 (2002)
4. Siva Ramamurthy, C., Manoj, B.S.: Ad Hoc Wireless Networks: Architectures and Protocols Pearson Education Limited. ISBN: 9788131706886
5. Gerla, M., Tsai, J.T.C.: Multicluster, mobile, multimedia network, wireless networks. J. Wirel. Netw. **1**(3), 255–265 (1995)
6. Lin, C.R., Gerla, M.: Adaptive clustering for mobile wireless networks. J. Sel. Areas Commun. **15**(7), 1265–1275 (2006)
7. Men, C., Xu, Z., Li, X.: An efficient checkpointing and rollback recovery scheme for cluster based multi channel ad-hoc wireless networks. In: International Symposium of Parallel and Distributed Processing with Applications (ISPA '08), pp. 371–378 (2008)
8. Lacharité, Y., Nguyen, D.Q., Wang, M., Lamont, L.: A trust-based security architecture for tactical MANETs. In: IEEE Military Communications Conference (MILCOM'08), pp. 1–7 (2008, November 16–19)
9. Sangho, Y., Heo, J., Cho, Y., Hong, J.: Adaptive Mobile Checkpointing: Checkpointing Facility for Wireless Sensor Networks. LNCS, vol. 3981, pp. 701–709 (2006)
10. Cho, J.H., Swami, A.: A survey on trust management for mobile ad hoc networks. IEEE Commun. Surv. Tutor. **13**, 562–583 (2011)
11. Juang, T.-Y., Liu, M.C., Yu, K.M.: An efficient asynchronous recovery algorithm in wireless mobile ad hoc networks. In: International Conference on Communications in Computing (CIC'01), pp. 25–18 (2001, June)
12. Biswas, S., Dey, P., Neogy, S.: Trusted checkpointing based on ant colony optimization in MANET. In: The Proceedings of 3rd IEEE International Conference on Emerging Applications of Information Technology (EAIT 2012), India, pp. 433–439. ISBN: 978-1-4673-1825-9
13. Fathi, A., Taheri, H.: Enhance topology control protocol (ECEC) to conserve energy based clustering in wireless ad hoc networks. In: ICCSIT, 3rd IEEE International Conference, vol. 9, pp. 356–360 (2010)
14. Li, Y., Yung, P., Jianpeng, Z.: Trust cluster head election algorithm based on ant colony systems. In: Third International Joint Conference on Computational Science and Optimization (CSO), vol. 2, pp. 419–422 (2010)
15. Biswas, S., Neogy, S., Dey, P.: Mobility based checkpointing and trust based recovery in MANET. In: Int. J. Wirel. Mob. Netw. (IJWMN) **4**(4), pp. 53-69 (2012). ISSN: 0975-3834 [Online]; 0975-4679 [Print]. https://doi.org/10.5121/ijwmn.2012.4404
16. Biswas, S., Nag, T., Neogy, S.: Trust based energy efficient detection and avoidance of black hole attack to ensure secure routing in MANET. In: IEEE Xplore International Conference on Applications and Innovations in Mobile Computing (AIMoC 2014), India, pp. 157–164
17. Cho, J-H., Swami, A., Chen, I.-R.: A survey on trust management for mobile ad hoc networks. IEEE Commun. Surv. Tutor. **13**(4) (2011)
18. Capra, L.: Toward a human trust model for mobile ad-hoc networks. In: Proceedings of the 2nd UK-UbiNet Workshop. Cambridge University, Cambridge, UK (2004, May 5–7)
19. Li, H., Singhal, M.: Trust management in distributed systems. Computers **40**(2), 45–53 (2007)
20. Biswas, S., Neogy, S.: A mobility based checkpointing protocol for mobile computing system. Int. J. Comput. Sci. Inf. Technol. (IJCSIT) **2**(1), 135–151 (2010). ISSN: 0975-3826 (online), 0975-4660 (print)
21. Tamilselvan, L., Sankaranarayanan, V.: Prevention of co-operative blackhole attack in MANET. J. Netw. **3**(5), 13–20 (2008)
22. Biswas, S., Neogy, S.: Checkpointing and recovery using node mobility among clusters in mobile ad hoc network. In: Proceedings of the Fourth International conference on Networks and Communications, NECOM, 2012, AISC 176, pp. 447–456 (2012)
23. Smara, M., Pathan, A.-S.K.: An enhanced mechanism for fault tolerance in agricultural wireless sensor networks. Network **4**(2), 150–174 (2024). https://doi.org/10.3390/network4020008

24. Karmakar, K., Saif, S., Biswas, S., Neogy, S.: A WBAN based framework for patient health condition monitoring and faulty sensor node identification applying ANN. Int. J. Biomed. Clin. Eng. (IJBCE) **10**(2), 44–65 (2021)

Chapter 6
Security Attacks, Threats, and Vulnerabilities

Abstract Wireless sensor network (WSN), Mobile ad hoc networks (MANET) and Internet of Things (IoT) are emerging and successful technologies which are being used in various application domains in real life. Implementing security solutions in such advanced networks is one of the considerable challenge due to limited resources such as energy, mobility, scalability, and computational ability among others. If any application is aware of its specific security sensitivities that means if the application is executed with sensitive information or data, for example, a smart healthcare system enabled with sensors, IoT and cloud server handles patients' health and disease-related data which is of privacy and security sensitive. In such systems the communicating nodes are geographically distributed and communicate with each other through security attack and threat prone open wireless links enabled with Wi-Fi, 3G/4G internet connection etc. In such applications security attacks, threats, vulnerabilities need to be identified properly for implanting preventive measures or providing security solutions once attacks are detected. This chapter traverses through different security attacks, threats, proposed solutions and a summary of funded research projects by different international reputed funding agencies along with budget information to reflect the importance and significance of security aware solutions in WSN, MANAET, and IoT.

6.1 Security Issues, Attacks, and Threats

Wireless Sensor Network, Mobile Adhoc Network, Internet of Things are such advanced networks that have several distinguishing features such as heterogeneous nodes, links, mobility, limited resources, constrained energy source etc. These features make them suitable for advanced applications demanding ubiquity i.e. Anywhere, Anytime, Anything computing besides making them vulnerable to security attacks and threats [1–3]. Such smart applications are widely varied and are being utilized in daily chores of our living specifically for the elderly people. Such applications are widely spread starting from sensor-based activity monitoring, health monitoring, fall monitoring and detection, disease monitoring, security and surveillance,

S. Biswas et al., *Adhoc and Sensor Networks: Security and Applications*, Studies in Systems, Decision and Control 653, https://doi.org/10.1007/978-981-95-5839-1_6

smart traffic, smart navigation, smart energy, smart city applications etc. All these applications handle with data or information that is security and privacy sensitive. Why privacy sensitive? Say in a smart healthcare application, a patient may not be willing to disclose his disease and treatment details to unauthorized entity. As we can easily understand in pandemic like scenario caused by Covid-19, information of any person having such disease should not be disclosed publicly or rather this information should be protected with utmost priority among the legitimate persons only to avoid any suffering of the person in the society, neighborhood, work place etc. Health data sensed by sensor nodes in WSN is privacy sensitive. Now how security requirements in terms of confidentiality, integrity, authentication, access control, data recentness, non-repudiation are relevant in WSN data? Sensor nodes are light weight miniaturized nodes with high portability support that can easily be under control of adversary physically, either the sensor node can be damaged giving erroneous or garbage value or may be replaced with a malicious sensor node to play with the security preventions of the network becoming the internal node. Like, if the malicious node becomes part of the routing then it easily can inject routing attacks as announcing it has the shortest path to the destination node thus inviting or tunnelling all current traffic to it. Also it can overhear neighbor nodes' communication hence information leakage will be there. The sensor node can come under the control of adversary like internal code of a sensor can deliberately be modified to hamper normal functioning, to generate erroneous data, to jeopardize routing information etc. Security attacks can be by external or internal nodes, active and passive in nature.

When WSN is connected with Internet of Things network then sensor data gets transmitted from the sensing layer to the heterogeneous communication layer comprised of several wireless and links such as Bluetooth, WiFi, Zigbee, WiMax etc., hence undergoes varying underlying security or protective measures of different communication technologies as well as different probable security attacks and threats. From communication layer the data reached to the processing layer comprised of a local server, cloud server, workstations etc. for processing and storage in the database. While getting transmitted from the communication layer to the processing layer, data passes through open, insecure internet (3G/4G wireless link) where data can be compromised in the form of information leakage, traffic analysis, content access, content modification etc. of such attacks. In the server, data saved need to be accessed by several stakeholders e.g. in smart healthcare system, patient data saved as Electronic Health Record (EHR) gets accessed by doctors, nurses, pathologists, pharmacists, medical researchers, health insurers etc. Here to ensure data access only within legitimate entities is a must to ensure data privacy of sensitive patient health information. Also, to identify any malicious traffic entering into server to be detected and blocked, might be the primary task of the Intrusion Detection System (IDS) to be designed and deployed in WSN, IoT, cloud-based smart applications. Once data is processed at the processing layer, useful information gets extracted and based on knowledge building, control layer or unit generates required feedback for proper tuning of sensing layer devices, alert or warning to the end users or stakeholders through smartphone etc. From the perspective of the healthcare system, patient vitals such as body temperature, blood pressure, pulse rate, heart rate, blood sugar level, oxygen saturation level, posture or activity or fall events monitored through smartphone sensors etc. can be sensed through. Whenever sensor data is getting transmitted over wireless links and open internet (3G/4G) connectivity, security and privacy issues must be taken into consideration and proper security measures need to be incorporated to ensure the security attributes.

Confidentiality: Data is confined within the legitimate sender and receiver only.

Integrity: Data should not be tampered while getting transmitted from sender to receiver.

Availability: Data must always be available to sender and receiver with a certain performance standard maintained.

Non-repudiation: Sender will not able to deny after sending any data to the receiver.

Authentication: Signature based authentication can be used to ensure sender and receiver both are legal entities.

Access control: Access control permissions to be set to ensure proper use of data by authorized entities.

Data recentness: Stipulated time between data origination and data analysis by intended recipient is defined by data recentness.

Off-the-shelf security techniques such as symmetric key and asymmetric key cryptography techniques can be applied to encrypt data before transmission to ensure confidentiality, hash of original message can be generated at the sender's end to ensure integrity of the received message at the receiver end, digital signature can be applied on the message to be sent to verify the authentication of the sender by the receiver before receiving message etc. But all these can be realized with additional computations which may be overhead for resource constrained WSN, MANET, and IoT applications.

Issues and Challenges that are prevalent in these types of networks are as follows.

Scalability: Huge number of sensor nodes can get added to the network based on user application requirement.

Heterogeneity: Nodes are different in terms of processing capability, available memory, battery power etc.

Pervasiveness: Anytime, anywhere, anything computing. Throughout the day and night, at indoor or outdoor, being static or mobile, with PC or away from PC, communication between human to human, machine to machine, machine to human.

Handling of huge sensory data: Sensors acquire data seamlessly from human being, ambience or environment and thus generate huge data that need to be managed/handled efficiently.

Energy efficiency: Heterogeneous nodes and links are depleted from resources, specifically sensor nodes are battery operated. Thus while designing and developing sensor based networks and applications, the energy consumption must be of utmost priority. Unnecessary energy drainage/consumption may cause the sensor node to die thus the network lifetime will be low.

Security and Privacy: Secure data transmission, processing, storage and access are of important concern in many of real life applications built up with WSN, MANET, IoT etc. due to proneness of such networks to security attacks and vulnerabilities.

6.2 Attack/Threat Model

Security attacks are of different types and nature as defined and illustrated in state-of-the-art literatures [4]. Both active and passive attacks are considered and defined in the Attack Model. When data is read or stolen by an unauthorized entity then it is passive attack. If the adversary gets access to the data, tampers or modifies it then it is active attack. In a network or an application all possible types of attacks and threats are identified and defined in an attack model.

Based on the nature of attacks, there could be following categorizations.

6.2.1 Active Attack Versus Passive Attack

Passive Attack

Man-in-the-Middle Attack

Adversary aims for passive information gathering, may claim falsely as intended recipient of data, after receiving may re-route the data causing higher end-to-end delay, authentication, and confidentiality to be violated.

Active Attack

Sinkhole Attack

Adversary falsely claims itself as intended destination, receives packets, alters and resends to the destination, wherein data integrity is lost. Denial of service attack is also considered as it is very much harmful by violating the system's availability on time.

Some MANET specific attacks/threats:

Delay Attack

The purpose of the adversary while injecting this attack is to cause delay in data transmission between the sender and receiver. This Jellyfish variants attack also exploits the RREP mechanism in AODV routing protocol used in MANET, similarly as in Sinkhole attack but with more flexibility and exploitation options as illustrated below.

Jellyfish Reorder Attack

This attack targets to jeopardize the ordering of packets sent by the sender to the receiver thus causing disruption in the functioning of the system by resulting out-of-order packet delivery, degradation in system performance, enhanced error rate etc.

Jellyfish Periodic Dropping Attack

In this variant of attack, packets are dropped periodically instead of continuously causing degradation in network performance by causing selective re-transmission of dropped packets, poor throughput etc. This strategy of periodic packet dropping makes it difficult to identify it as an attack or packet loss due to network congestion.

Delay Variance Attack

This attack is designed to introduce varying delay in selective packets being transmitted through malicious nodes. This varying delay to the packets increases the overall delay of the network thus causing successful implementation of time-sensitive applications such as healthcare.

Selfish Node

Unlike malicious nodes, selfish nodes selectively participate in routing by prioritizing their benefits on forwarding packets. If not beneficial, then selfish nodes will simply drop the packets, will not forward, and thus will save their own battery power. Thus overall network performance will be hampered and the working of the application will be disturbed.

Grey Hole Attacks

This attack is similar to black hole attack but only difference is that in this attack the adversary does not drop all the packets, instead drops packets based on some predefined criteria. Due to this nature of packet dropping, often it becomes difficult to distinguish between a legitimate node and a Grey Hole node.

Flood Attacks

The aim of this attack is to disrupt the working of the network by flooding different messages thus consuming the network bandwidth causing denial-of-service attack. There are variants of this attack:

Hello flood: Hello messages are the target of this attack to get information about neighbors and causing bandwidth consumption.

RREQ flood: Spams the network with route request messages used in reactive routing protocols, overloading nodes, and hindering legitimate route discovery.

Data flood: Floods the network with irrelevant data packets, consuming bandwidth, and hindering legitimate data transmission.

ICMP/UDP flood: Targets specific protocols like ICMP (ping) or UDP to overwhelm resources.

6.2.2 Insider Versus Outsider Attack

Insider Attack

If the attacker is injecting attacks being a part of the network, may be the adversary has stolen the ID or authentication credentials of a valid node or is able to take control over an insider node, then this category of attacks happen.

Outsider Attack

If the attacker attack injects attacks from outside of the network, not as the node of the network, then this category of attacks happen.

Attack Model in WSN

In WSN, heterogeneous sensor nodes and wireless links are prone to several types of attacks [5, 6] which are defined in this attack model as follows.

6.2.3 Some of the Security Attacks at Sensor Nodes

Node Capture Attack

This type of attack is done in the perceptual layer, where the adversary takes the control of the sensing node by replacing the node physically or tampering the hardware device of the node.

Node Replication Attack

The name of the attack reflects the fact that the legitimate nodes of a WSN may be captured by the insecure environment and may be cloned to inject attacks in the network by communicating with legal nodes with legitimate IDs and security keys. Providing secure key pairs to each node may prevent this attack.

Malicious Code Injection Attack

Here the adversary takes control of the node by injecting some malicious programs in the node, and using the malicious code the attacker can read all sensed data.

False Data Injection Attack

In this attack, the adversary can inject false data, these false data are transferred to applications, which return erroneous feedback commands or wrong services.

Replay Attack

Here the adversary uses a malicious node to communicate with destination node with legitimate data in order to gain trust.

Eavesdropping and Interference

Most of the sensing devices communicate through wireless networks, these wireless links are very much vulnerable for eavesdropping attack by non-authorized users. The adversary can also send noise or signal to interfere with the information delivered in a wireless link.

Sleep Deprivation Attacks

Nodes are made to awaken forcefully by breaking their programmed sleep routine attacks in communication links.

Node Capture Attack

This severe attack in WSN is performed by the attacker to compromise the whole network through different operations. Some of the legitimate nodes may be removed from the network by the attacker in this attack to redeploy them to inject attacks in the network.

Vampire Attack

This is a type of DoS attack in which the sensor node is completely depleted of battery power and thus the network becomes non-functional. In the paper [7] as a solution or preventive measure, an additional field, BCAST id is used in the routing field in the routing table at each node. Also used in data packets used by the AODV routing protocol, it helps to detect directional antenna attacks. A continuous check to ensure that the packets are not transmitted in infinite loops is required to prevent the network to be compromised by this attack.

Physical Attack

The sensor nodes in WSN may be deployed in remote environments such as in forests, agricultural fields etc. where they are not under closed monitoring all the time. Hence the unattended remote nodes may be destroyed in physical attack.

Tampering Attack

This attack completely damages the node taking complete control over the node. Physically the node gets damaged and the function of the network may be disrupted.

6.2.4 Communication Link Layer Attacks

Man in the Middle Attack

Here a malicious device reads all the information between two legitimate devices and keeps a copy of the data.

Routing Information Attacks

Routing information attacks focus on the routing protocols in smart applications, in which the routing information can be manipulated and resent by the adversary to create route loops in the data transmission of the network.

Sybil Attacks

A malicious device, namely a sybil device, can claim several legitimate identities and impersonate them in IoT systems. Because a sybil device has several legitimate identities, false data sent by the sybil device can be easily accepted by their benign neighboring devices.

DoS Attack

If there is denial of resources such as network bandwidth, memory etc. making the resources unavailable to the legitimate nodes, then this attack is termed as Denial of Service (DoS) attack. This attack may disrupt data transmission through the links.

Jamming Attack

This attack is deployed by utilizing a high power transmitter to interfere with legitimate wireless communication. Either the attacker may prevent the sender node from transmitting the packets or may prevent transmission of legitimate packets.

Replay Attack

The attacker replays the malicious node repeatedly for energy consumption and also the communication channels become dominated. To avoid this attack in an effective way, session tokens could be utilized and time stamp with the messages could be introduced.

Rushing Attack

The attack takes place in on-demand routings protocol. The malicious node rushes to take the data from the neighbor to the other destination node in the different tunnel. In the wormhole attack, the packets tunneled through the network can disseminate than any usual multi-hop route; if the packets are tunneled through a speedy transmission route between the wormhole attack ends, it is called a Rushing attack [7]. The countermeasure of this attack is to providing route records by embedding a node list.

Wormhole Attack

In this attack, the attacker keeps track of the packets and makes a tunnel with other nodes of different communication networks, and thus the attacker passes the packets through this tunnel; thus legitimate nodes may follow this path for faster and successful packet delivery.

Blackhole Attack

The security attacks in WSN in which the black hole attack has two distinct characteristics. The malicious node act as a black hole when the packets pass through these black holes, then the attacker can manipulate the data. First, the path is amended by announcing itself as having a route from the source to the destination node, next without forwarding the invader intercept messages for its purpose [8]. A black hole attack can be avoided by monitoring the network, changing packet routing, or using authentication mechanisms.

Traffic Analysis

Network traffic sent with or without encryption may be observed by the adversary to find the pattern, thus disclosing the gathered information to the opponent to ham and felicitate to the nodes.

Internet of things (IoT)-based smart real life applications are now everywhere in daily human life enhancing quality of living such as smart healthcare, smart traffic, smart energy etc. but due to security attack prone nodes and communication links, data/information while on rest or in movement, may not be secure always. The following scenario is an illustration of such application.

Sensor nodes are primarily sensing data from physical world and that data gets transmitted to cloud servers for processing through heterogeneous communication links. Sensor nodes and links are prone to several security attacks and threats as described above and data being sensed at nodes or being transmitted over links. Figure 6.1 illustrates over MANET and WSN having fixed infrastructure support or without support thus enabled to transmit data over limited coverage area or over wide range through 3G/4G internet connectivity. In MANET mostly sensor layer attacks are prevalent and attacks in wireless links such as WiFi, Bluetooth, Zigbee are possible. Whereas in infrastructure-based WSN, in addition. Data suffers from security attacks and threats in the open internet insecure wireless link.

6.2.5 Simulation/implementation of Secure Solutions in WSN and MANET

A rigorous knowledge on simulation or implementation of security solutions or measures in WSN and MANET based applications would enrich the interested researchers in this field. With that note, this section elaborates on a number of secure systems or implementations in practical applications using WSN and MANET.

6.2.5.1 Secure Solutions in WSN Based Applications

Wireless sensor network has already advanced significantly and is deployed to provide real life solutions successfully behind which security and privacy aware

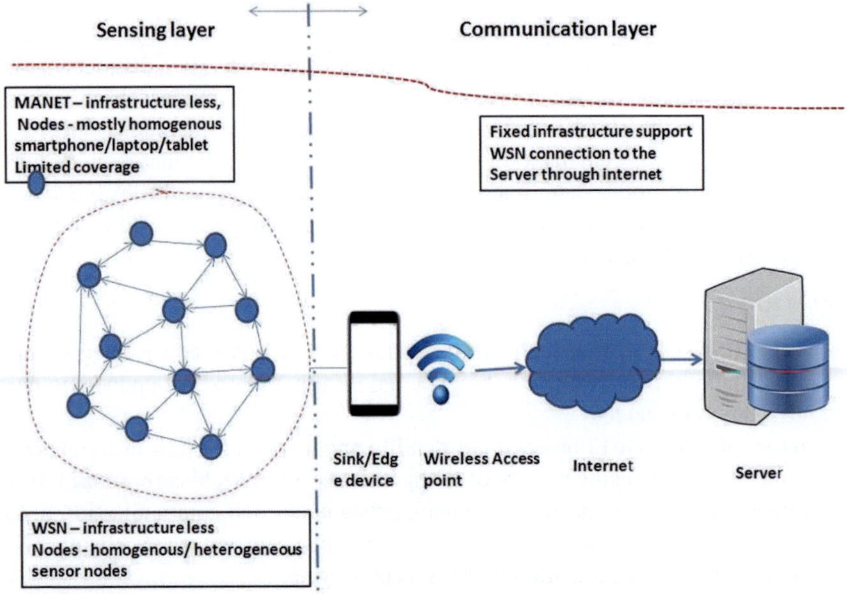

Fig. 6.1 WSN, MANET with or without infrastructure support and connection to open internet

solutions are one of the reasons of this success. Some of the recent relevant security aware solutions in WSN and MANET are being discussed here.

Elliptic Curve El Gamal (ECEG) is a very much used technique in WSNs in order to provide end-to-end privacy with better security, but the major drawback is the execution time. Efficient implementation of the mathematical functions can overcome this problem. Rafik et al. [9] has proposed a fast and secure implementation of ECEG for end-to-end secure data aggregation. This ensures data privacy between sensor nodes and sink. A fast scalar multiplication has been used in their implementation which is secure from side channel attacks. TinyECC library and MicaZ mote has been employed for the implementation and experimentation. Result shows that it takes 1.29 s to encrypt the data on MicaZ mote which is less compared to other similar techniques.

In [10], the author has presented hardware implementation of Elliptic Curve Digital Signature Algorithm (ECDSA) in IRIS node for authentication and integrity in WSN. ECDSA is a well known, efficient and secure algorithm compared to traditional cryptographic algorithms for a given key size. ECDSA uses SHA-1 for signature generation and verification. MEMSIC IRIS node has 128 KB of Memory and 8 KB of RAM and it operates on battery power. Implementation has been applied on this IRIS node with the help of TinyOS, and the experimental result shows that it takes SHA-1 to execute 39 and 941 ms for ECDSA, RAM utilization are 2.09 and 3.07 KB out of 4 KB.

One of the popular applications of WSN is the IoT based home automation system. But it suffers from various security attacks against data privacy. Pirbhulal et al. [8]

proposed a technique based on Triangle Based Security Algorithm (TBSA) which facilitates confidentiality, privacy, and integrity. This scheme uses a simple key generation procedure for encryption and decryption of the sensor data. Authors have used Temperature sensor, Intel Galileo based microcontroller and Intel Centrino Wireless N-2230 transmitter for the implementation of the proposed TBSA. Experimental result shows that the proposed method consumes 0.20 μJ of energy for Hash generation, whereas other well known hash functions such as MD4, MD5, SHA-1, HMAC consume 0.52, 0.59, 0.75, 1.1 μJ energy respectively. Experimental results also show that the proposed method consumes 0.20 μJ of energy for encryption. Experimental result shows that the proposed method consumes 0.20 μJ of energy for Hash generation, whereas other symmetric ciphering techniques such as RC4, Blowfish, AES, DES consume 0.49, 0.81, 1.20, 2.8 μJ energy respectively.

WSNs are mostly based on multi-hop communication to deliver a data packet. Data aggregation is a technique to reduce this multi-hop communication and energy consumption to enhance network lifetime. Few sensor nodes of the network can be used for this purpose, but they are not aware about the data provided by any malicious node, which can lead to large data-error. To overcome this challenge, Saravanaselvan et al. [11] proposed heavy weight security (HWS) algorithm to ensure secure data aggregation. First a random key generated using node ID and node location is assigned to each node of the network. Then the data packets are encrypted using that random key and HWS scheme. In the next step, these encrypted packets are aggregated and transmitted to the sink device, where decryption and verification is done. NS2 simulator has been used by the author with a network size of 1500×1000 and 100 nodes. AODV protocol has been used during simulation. To evaluate the scheme, various parameters of Quality of Service (QoS) such as throughput, delay, packet delivery ratio and energy have been calculated. Experimental results have been compared with an existing scheme called LOARP and it was observed that HWS out performs the other scheme. Integrating WSN with Cloud computing (WCC) is promising, since the data collected by sensors can be stored and processed by cloud service. However, cloud servers are not trusted and lacks in confidentiality, integrity, and access control. He et al. [12] proposed fine-grained and lightweight data access control scheme namely FLAC for WCC. This scheme includes ciphertext-policy attribute (CP-ABE)-based encryption algorithm which ensures the data confidentiality as well as fine-grained data access control. For integrity, attribute-based signature (ABS) algorithm has been considered. To evaluate the performance of FLAC-CP-ABE at mobile clients and sensors, experiments have been conducted on Desktop PC, Smartphone, and Intelligent sensor Imote2. Overall computation time has been reflected in the experimental results for various devices, which is relatively low and suitable for WCC. WSNs often suffer from two type attacks such as invasive and non-invasive attacks. Invasive attack affects the routing process and service availability whereas non-invasive attacks targets the power, timing of the channel, and frequency of the transmission. Denial-of-sleep attack (DOSA) is one of those attacks which exhausts the power of the nodes. In [13], the authors have proposed a technique to prevent DOSA using firefly algorithm and Hopfield neural network (HNN). This technique improves the energy efficiency and also increases the network lifetime. Firefly algorithm helps in node clustering and authentication, Hopfield neural network detects the route of the sink to send the data. This WSN-FAHN technique is assessed using NS-2 based simulation. Various QoS parameters such as throughput, network lifetime, packet delivery ratio have been calculated and compared with other similar works such as GA-DoSLD, Cross Layer, ASDA. Simulation result proved that this technique has better performance in terms of QoS.

Ullah et al. [14] proposed a scheme for health data aggregation in a secure and efficient way with the help of IoT and Fog. Peer-to-peer communications have been used between health sensors and aggregating nodes to share the sensor data to the Fog serve. In some cases the aggregating node may be not in range of the Fog server, thus unable to send the data. However, it can share the encrypted data to the Fog server with the help of a neighboring aggregator which will append with its own aggregating data. Fog server can extract meaningful information from the encrypted data and upload to the cloud database. Two algorithms have been used for data aggregation (MRA) and data extraction (MEA) at Fog server. Algorithms has been implemented and simulated using NS2 considering a network size of 1500 × 1550 m, 20–100 nodes, initial energy 1000 J, sensing radius 120 m. Experimental results have been compared with schemes such as TMT, GCEDA, and SPPDA. It is observed from the results that proposed scheme requires 40.10% less communication cost than SPPDA.

In order to overcome authentication and integrity problem in WSN, a secure authentication and integrity technique was introduced by the authors in [15]. A common key matrix is shared with both the sender and receiver and a random noise matrix is chosen by both of them. Later it is verified with the help of hamming weight. This is a basic scheme for authentication and integrity, to increase the level of security hybrid online and offline signcryption technique which serves the purpose of digital signature and encryption in a single logical step. To simulate, authors have used NS-2 simulator considering the parameters as area size of 500 × 500, 100 nodes, RSR routing protocol, packet size 1,000 bytes, transmission range 250 m, initial energy 15.1 J and simulation time of 25 s. Authors have considered evaluation matrices such as residual energy, end-to-end delay, fraction of compromised communications and average packet delivery ratio. Experimental result shows that the proposed scheme has less end-to-end delay, more packet delivery ratio, more residual energy, and less compromised communication compared to other two techniques.

To authenticate sensor nodes in WSN a digital watermark-based low overhead solution (LoWaNa) has been proposed by Sen et al. [16]. This water marking techniques includes three stages, watermark generation, embedding and detection. Authors have considered replay and masquerade attacks to design their attack model. To measure effectiveness of the proposal, cracking probability and cracking time have been calculated with a help of an illustrative example. Authors have used Cooja Simulator for simulation.

Borkar et al. [17] proposed an Intrusion Detection System (IDS) where an acknowledgement based technique has been used for malicious sensor node detection in WSN. Several security attacks such as DoS, probe, U2R and R2L has been considered in this work for IDS design. First, an efficient clustering technique called stratified sampling has been used for clustering then adaptive chicken swarm optimization algorithm has been used for cluster head selection. After this an ensemble method called Rotated Random Forest (RRF) for feature reduction from the dataset and for classification Support Vector Machine (SVM) has been employed to detect malicious and non-malicious nodes. Authors have estimated various parameters such as specificity (0.9756), sensitivity (0.22), accuracy (0.84), FPR (0.0243), FDR (0.33), Error rate (0.16), Precision (0.666), and prevalence (0.18) for the proposed system. This intrusion detection system has been simulated using python with 50 sensor nodes. Experiments have been conducted to measure QoS parameters such as throughput, delay, network life time and energy consumption before and after prevention of the attacks. For better analysis number of nodes has been varied and QoS are measured.

WSN-based healthcare applications are widely adopted in many countries but they suffer from security problem related to the privacy of the data. In [18] the privacy preservation scheme has been proposed which uses the principles of multipath routing, secret sharing, and hashing. First the health data collected using the body sensors are splitted in n components using Shamir Sharing technique and hash of each component is calculated using well known hashing algorithms. Then these n components are transmitted to the servers with the help of multipath routing and again hash is calculated. After matching the hash generated at the sensor end with the hash generated at the server, data are either accepted or rejected. Shamir sharing has been simulated using Matlab considering the secret key 1121 (role of polynomial). Original signals transmitted are plotted and the reconstructed signals are plotted where it is observed that plots are overlapping. This proves the effectiveness of the reconstruction scheme.

Bandirmali et al. [19] proposed a link layer security protocol WSNSec for Wireless Sensor Network. Scalable Encryption Algorithm (SEA) in Counter Mode (CTR) and Cipher Block Chaining-Message Authentication Code (CBC-MAC) were combined together in this protocol. This ensures confidentiality, authentication as well integrity of the data. This protocol has been simulated using OPNET modeller where it is tested with a data/block size of 192 bit and compared with the traditional TinySEC. It has been observed that this proposed protocol has a minimal increase in memory usage and energy consumption than TinySEC, but the security of this protocol is much better than TinySEC. Simulation result also shows the ratio of delay for both proposed and TinySEC where end-to-end delay converge at 13% with the increase in network load. This makes it suitable for use in highly scalable applications.

Athmani et al. [20] proposed a dynamic authentication and key management technique for heterogeneous WSN. This technique combines both authentication and key establishment in a single light weight protocol and optimizes the security standard. Key distribution algorithm includes dynamic key generation with the help of preexisting information; also sharing is not required, which improves the security standard and reduces energy and memory consumption. Behaviors of the proposed protocol have been analyzed against security attacks such as spoofing, sybil, node capturing, node injection, replay, and brute force attack. For performance evaluation this protocol has been implemented on a real testbed environment. This has been applied on two types of sensor nodes (i) LSN node consisting of a low computation CPU with 2 KB of RAM, 32 KB of RAM and 2 J of energy (ii) HSN node consisting of a high computation CPU with 96 KM RAM, 512 KM ROM, and 200 J of energy. Evaluation metrics such as memory requirement, computation complexity, and communication overhead has been considered and the result has been compared with similar state-of-the-art works.

Node capture attack is one of the common physical attack on sensor nodes where the intruder physically captures the node and removes the secret information from the node's memory. In this work [21] authors proposed the Fruit Fly Optimization Algorithm (FFOA) which is based on multiple objectives such as maximum node and key contribution and less resource expenses. Authors have presented Network model, Key predistribution model, Link model, as well as adversary model in this work. Simulation results show that FFOA achieves fraction of compromised traffic value of 1 for both single path and multi path routing. Energy consumption with respect to number of keys for both routing techniques is less than 10 μJ. Simulation result also shows that energy consumption increases if the number of nodes captures are increased. Thus FFOA achieves maximum fraction of compromised traffic and lower energy consumption compared to other similar algorithms.

Cryptographic key management is one of the bog challenge in WSN, wherein various research works have been done to deal this issue where the number of nodes are limited. Nivedetha et al. [22] proposed the Fuzzy Fingerprint Biometric based Key Security (FFBKS) scheme. Features extracted from the fingerprint are used for private key generation for users. Nodes have been clustered based on the distance between them using Adaptive Possibilistic C-means Clustering (APCMC). Fuzzy membership function has been applied on prime numbers to generate keys for the clusters. For data transmission between sensor nodes, private keys generated from fingerprint are used and for data transmission between clusters, and fuzzy membership generated key is used. This scheme has been simulated using MATLAB considering an area of 120 × 120, 100 sensor nodes, TDMA MAC protocol, and 0.5 J of energy. Experimental results show that FFBKS has better performance compared to other schemes in terms of simulation time, energy consumption, delay, and attack detection rate.

6.2.5.2 Secure Solutions in MANET-Based Applications

Mobile ad hoc network (MANET) consists of mobile nodes connected wirelessly in a self-configured network and does not require any fixed infrastructure. Due to this nature, MANET is prone to various security attacks especially DoS attack. In [23], an artificial neural network (ANN)-based intrusion detection scheme has been presented. DoS attacks refer to injecting large data packets into the network such that the network is unable to perform the regular tasks. To detect DoS attack few parameters such as packet loss (PL), packet sending (PS), packet receiving (PR) and energy consumptions (EC) can be used. In this work log files of each node have been analyzed and PL, PS, PR, EC have been extracted to train the ANN. When the values of these parameters are found high, those are marked as Attacked node and the nodes having normal values are marked as Normal. Attack simulation is done on 6 nodes for 300 s using NS-2 and 1800 log samples have been extracted. Matlab-based ANN toolbox has been used to model the ANN where 1170 samples out of 1800 have been selected for training, validation, and testing. Results show that the ANN model with TANSIG function performs better than LoGSIG in terms of Mean Squared Error and R^2 score with 12 Epoch.

Sudha et al. [24] proposed an Enhanced version of DES algorithm for MANET which consumes less energy. DES is a symmetric algorithm which provides data confidentiality by encrypting the data and traditionally uses a 64 bit secret key to encrypt a 64 bit block of plaint text where the rounds are 16. In this Enhanced version (EDES) authors have reduced the number of rounds to 8 and increased the key size to 112. EDES has been implemented using Java and tested to evaluate parameters like execution time and throughput. Experimental result show that the average execution time of EDES is less than DES and also average throughput is higher than DES. Authors claimed that this algorithm is tested with a high performance laptop but it can be applied to a resource constraint handheld device.

In [25] the authors have identified security threats on the communication layers in MANET, this includes Repudiation, data corruption, SYN flooding, Wormhole, blackhole, traffic analysis, eavesdropping, DoS etc. A light weight approach has been proposed to detect these attacks without darning out resources of the sensor nodes. System model defines a network of finite nodes spread in a geographical area and the nodes use bi-directional communication. Each node has a unique ID representing by MAC/IP address; it has been assumed that nodes contain some energy©, col© (C), power factor (PF), and reputation (R). A table containing reputation value of neighbors is present in every node. The proposed approach has methods for malicious nodes identification, In the first phase Message efficient leader election protocol (MALFA) has been used for cluster head selection. Nodes should declare their reputation value truthful in order to be selected as cluster head. In the second phase Joint Cluster heads (JCH), Co-Cluster (CCH) heads and connectors (Con) selection has been done and based on the distance nodes are marked red if they are located one hop away from CH, nodes are marked green if they are one hope away from JCH or CCH and nodes marked as gray if they are located one hope away from Con. This approach has been implemented using NS2 considering 6351×2044 m^2 area, 1.1–5.2 W energy, and reputation value 5–10. Experimental results show that the reputation value of nodes decreased with respect to time if the attack is present. Other evaluation parameters such as power consumption rate, detection rate, and false alarm rate have been shown in the results.

6.2.5.3 Research Funding

Besides enriching state-of-the-art literatures discussed above, it is also prevalent that there are various funded projects, completed or ongoing around the world in this problem domain. In a white paper published by Virginia Tech, on “Complex Networks and Security Research" (CNSR) [26], a number of funded research projects in the area of security in WSN have been detailed out.

Following are the funded research projects during 2011–2020 by different international reputed funding agencies along budget information to reflect the importance and significance of security aware solutions in WSN and IoT.

Summary

This chapter significantly illustrates various security attacks, threats, and vulnerabilities in wireless networks. Different state-of-the-art works in this domain are also highlighted for reference to the readers. Not only in terms of the research publications, the funded projects all over the world are also projected to figure out the importance of this topic in practical applications using wireless networks.

6.2.6 Problems

This section opens the pathway to explore through some brainstorming sample questions for better and clear understanding of their study.

Sample questions:

Question 1: What are passive and active attacks? Differentiate with examples. WSN, MANET are prone to which type of attacks more and why?

Answer: Passive attack—Information stolen, not modified. Active attack—Information modified.

Example: Passive attack—Login credentials overlooked by the adversary: confidentiality lost.

Active attack—Sender: "I will come tomorrow at 6 PM". Adversary—Accesses the content and modifies the content and resends. Receiver receives: "I will come tomorrow at 6 am"—Integrity lost. WSN, MANET are prone to both types of attacks but more prone to active attacks that static, infrastructure supported networks, devices being more resourceful and less mobile, more stable.

Question 2: How sleep deprivation attack can drain out energy of sensor nodes unnecessarily? What is its effect on network lifetime?

Answer: Sleep deprivation attack jeopardizes the duty cycle of the sensor node as specified by the manufacturer, thus forcibly drains out its battery power as the radio is always on by the attacker. Hence, it would cause reduction in network lifetime as sensor node may die early.

Question 3: Mobility causes frequent connection and disconnection of nodes—can this invite any specific adversary attack to happen?

Answer: Any malicious node can join the network pretending to be a legal node.

Question 4: What is eavesdropping? In which layer it occurs, node or link?

Answer: In physical layer or data link layer, any adversary can listen to the open wireless channel to overhear the communication, thus hampering the confidentiality.

Question 5: Specify security and privacy requirements in WSN, MANET, and IoT.

Answer: Based on the real-life application developed using WSN, MANET, IoT, the level of security requirements varies. In application like healthcare, health data is privacy sensitive as well as security sensitive.

1. In WSN, number of nodes is large whereas in MANET number of nodes is less in comparison. So, between symmetric key and asymmetric key algorithms, which type of security algorithm is suitable to implement in which type of above networks.
2. Why ECC is a suitable security technique to implement in resource constrained networks?

In ECC, key size is 160 bit and assures compatible security strength of RSA 102, with less overhead and computational complexity. Hence ECC is more suitable in constrained environment.

3. Specify recent security projects going on in Wireless Sensor Networks.

It is available in Table 6.1.

4. What is pervasive or ubiquitous computing and how WSN fits in to implement this?

Answer: Ubiquitous computing is 'AAA' computing, i.e. Anytime, Anywhere, Anything computing. This computing enables users to avail services or applications while on move. And the advanced WSN i.e. wireless sensor network helps to implement this because in WSN both links and nodes can be mobile enabling services to the users while they are on the move.

Table 6.1 Research projects related to WSN security

References	Project name	Funding agency	Budget	Duration
[22]	AWISSENET (ad-hoc personal area network and wireless sensor secure network)	European Union	€ 3,097,279	Jan 2008–Feb 2010
[23]	Intelligent wireless sensor networks for asset integrity monitoring	European Union	€ 71,429	May 2015–Oct 2015
[24]	Secure location-aware cooperative network-coded WSNs for better quality of life	European Union	€ 1,707,621	Dec 2011–Nov 2015
[25]	Secure connected trustable things	European Union	€ 38,792,404.47	May 2017 –June 2020
[26]	Cooperative transmission and cross-layer techniques for secure wireless sensor networks	European Union	€ 411,954	June 2008–May 2011
[27]	Tamper resistant sensor node	European Union	€ 4,323,132	Oct 2010–Dec 2013
[28]	Privacy-preserving intrusion detection and response in wireless communications	European Union	€ 165,865.20	July 2010–June 2012
[29]	SMART (secure, mobile visual sensor networks architecture)	Artemis	€ 4,460,000	Mar 2009–Mar 2012
[30]	Internet of things—interoperability framework	Croatian Science Foundation	$ 8,455,513	June 2015–May 2019
[31]	Energy-efficient protocols for sensing coverage in wireless sensor networks	IIT (BHU) Varanasi, India	INR 10 lakhs	2016–2019

References

1. Lata, S., Mehfuz, S., Urooj, S.: Secure and reliable WSN for internet of things: challenges and enabling technologies. IEEE Access **9**, 161103–161128 (2021)
2. Bharti, M., Rani, S., Singh, P.: Security attacks in MANET: a complete analysis. In: Proceedings of the 2022 6th International Conference on Devices, Circuits and Systems (ICDCS), Coimbatore, India, 21–22 April 2022, pp. 384–387. IEEE, Piscataway, NJ, USA (2022)
3. Baird, I., Wadhaj, I., Ghaleb, B., Thomson, C.: Impact analysis of security attacks on mobile ad hoc networks (MANETs). Electronics **13**(16), 3314 (2024)
4. Ávila, K., Sanmartin, P., Jabba, D., Gómez, J.: An analytical survey of attack scenario parameters on the techniques of attack mitigation in WSN. Wirel. Pers. Commun. 1–32 (2022)

5. Keerthika, M., Shanmugapriya, D.: Wireless sensor networks: active and passive attacks-vulnerabilities and countermeasures. Glob. Transit. Proc. **2**(2), 362–367 (2021)
6. Butun, Osterberg, P., Song, H.: Security of the internet of things: vulnerabilities, attacks and countermeasures. IEEE Commun. Surv. Tutor. 1–1 (2019)
7. Sharma, M.K., Joshi, B.K.: Detection and prevention of vampire attack in wireless sensor networks. In: International Conference on Information, Communication, Instrumentation and Control (ICICIC), pp. 1–5 (2017)
8. Pirbhulal, S., Zhang, H., E Alahi, M.E., Ghayvat, H., Mukhopadhyay, S.C., Zhang, Y.-T., Wu, W.: A novel secure IoT-based smart home automation system using a wireless sensor network. Sensors **17**, 69 (2017)
9. Zhan, G., Shi, W., Deng, J.: Design and implementation of TARF: a trust-aware routing framework for WSNs. IEEE Trans. Dependable Secur. Comput. **9**(2), 184–197 (2012)
10. Ahmed, M.H., Alam, S.W., Qureshi, N., Baig, I.: Security for WSN based on elliptic curve cryptography. In: International Conference on Computer Networks and Information Technology, Abbottabad, pp. 75–79 (2011)
11. Saravanaselvan, A., Paramasivan, B.: Design and implementation of an efficient attack resilient computation algorithm in WSN nodes. Cluster Comput. **22**, 3301–3311 (2019)
12. He, H., Zhang, J., Gu, J. et al.: A fine-grained and lightweight data access control scheme for WSN-integrated cloud computing. Cluster Comput. **20**, 1457–1472 (2017)
13. Fotohi, R., Firoozi Bari, S.: A novel countermeasure technique to protect WSN against denial-of-sleep attacks using firefly and Hopfield neural network (HNN) algorithms. J. Supercomput. (2020)
14. Ullah, A., Said, G., Sher, M., et al.: Fog-assisted secure healthcare data aggregation scheme in IoT-enabled WSN. Peer-to-Peer Netw. Appl. **13**, 163–174 (2020)
15. Senthilkumaran, U., Ilango, P.: Secure authentication and integrity techniques for randomized secured routing in WSN. Wirel. Netw. **21**, 443–451 (2015)
16. Sen, A., Chatterjee, T., DasBit, S.: LoWaNA: low overhead watermark based node authentication in WSN. Wirel. Netw. **22**, 2453–2467 (2016)
17. Borkar, G.M., Patil, L.H., Dalgade, D., Hutke, A.: A novel clustering approach and adaptive SVM classifier for intrusion detection in WSN: a data mining concept. Sustain. Comput.: Inform. Syst. **23** (2019)
18. Sharma, N., Bhatt, R.: Privacy preservation in WSN for healthcare application. Procedia Comput. Sci. **132**, 1243–1252 (2018)
19. NeclaBandirmali, I.E.: WSNSec: a scalable data link layer security protocol for WSNs. Ad Hoc Netw. **10**(1), 37–45 (2012)
20. Athmani, S., Bilami, A., Boubiche, D.E.: EDAK: an efficient dynamic authentication and key management mechanism for heterogeneous WSNs. Futur. Gener. Comput. Syst. **92**, 789–799 (2019)
21. Bhatt, R., Maheshwary, P., Shukla, P., Shukla, P., Shrivastava, M., Changlani, S.: Implementation of fruit fly optimization algorithm (FFOA) to escalate the attacking efficiency of node capture attack in wireless sensor networks (WSN). Comput. Commun. **149**, 134–145 (2020)
22. Nivedetha, B., Vennila, I.: FFBKS: fuzzy fingerprint biometric key based security schema for wireless sensor networks. Comput. Commun. **150**, 94–102 (2020)
23. Moradi, Z., Teshnehlab, M., Rahmani, A.M.: Implementation of neural networks for intrusion detection in MANET. In: 2011 International Conference on Emerging Trends in Electrical and Computer Technology, Nagercoil, pp. 1102–1106 (2011)
24. Senthil, S., Viswanatham, V.M., Krishnamurthy, B., Loganathan, A., Ramya, G.: Implementation of enhanced data encryption standard on MANET with less energy consumption through limited computation. Int. J. Eng. Res. Dev. **2**(4), 46–52 (2012)
25. Gaurav, A., Singh, A.K.: Light weight approach for secure backbone construction for MANETs. J. King Saud Univ. - Comput. Inf. Sci. (2018)
26. https://www.cnsr.ictas.vt.edu/projects_completed.html, 2012.
27. https://cordis.europa.eu/project/id/211998
28. https://cordis.europa.eu/project/id/671868

29. https://cordis.europa.eu/project/id/286047
30. https://cordis.europa.eu/project/id/737422
31. https://cordis.europa.eu/project/id/218163

Chapter 7
Trust and Securing Protocols

Abstract Advanced networks are resource constrained and hence any solution proposed must be aware of efficient resource utilization. On the other hand, due to the open unguided wireless medium, newer kinds of security attacks are possible in such networks that are not possible in a traditional wired network infrastructure. To prevent security attacks and threats, secure algorithms must not increase much overhead in terms of computational complexity, bandwidth, memory and energy consumption. Theory of trust and light-weight cryptography will be explored here to encourage the users to propose novel security techniques to ensure equivalent secure system by adding low overheads to the systems. This Chapter deals with all these vital concepts.

Keywords Trust · Security · Lightweight cryptography · Reputation · Directed diffusion

In MANET, WSN, and its variants the nodes may move in some fashion with or without infrastructure support. In all such networks, the nodes communicate through an open shared broadcast medium (unlicensed ISM band). These features give rise to different security threats not present in its wired counterpart. Current wireless networks, and ad hoc networks in particular are prone to two different types of attacks [1]:

- Active attacks—Actively alter the data with the intention to obstruct the operation of the targeted networks.
- Passive attacks—Steals valuable information from the targeted networks.

Nodes that perform such attacks with the goal of damaging rational nodes by causing network outage are considered as malicious. On the other hand, a node that does not forward others packets for routing, in order to save its own battery life for initiating its own communications are considered to be selfish. The security of this entire set of wireless networks greatly depends on utilizing secure routing protocols, communication mechanisms, and transmission technologies that are adopted by the participating nodes.

S. Biswas et al., *Adhoc and Sensor Networks: Security and Applications*, Studies in Systems, Decision and Control 653, https://doi.org/10.1007/978-981-95-5839-1_7

In this chapter, first the basic problem of resource limitation and its impact on providing confidentiality and hence, traditional cryptography has been discussed. Then, we detail the different attacks that could take place on routing of packets in MANET and WSN despite such cryptography techniques in place. Some feasible solutions are also discussed.

7.1 Resource Limitations

Confidentiality is one of the basic security services that is expected from any kind of networked systems. It refers to the availability of information only to the valid communicating parties. Encryption is a popular approach to establish this service. In secret key encryption, a secret key is shared among the valid users by a complex robust protocol. The sender encrypts the message to a cyphertext using the key. Upon receiving the cyphertext, the receiving user would apply decryption using the secret key to extract the message. Some widely used secret key encryption techniques utilized by existing systems include Advanced Encryption Standard (AES), Data Encryption Standard (DES), 3DES, Blowfish, and so on [2]. AES is one of the most studied secret key encryption technique [3]. However, the level of security depends on the complexity of the algorithm and sharing of the secret key is also an important issue for resource constrained environments like IoT or sensor networks. Secondly, new kinds of hardware attacks and side channel attacks are possible in such networks. So, lightweight techniques are needed to enforce confidentiality in such network scenarios. In [3], a power efficient AES Core was detailed by the authors for IoT constrained devices. They have fabricated it in UMC 130 nm technology. The authors applied Dynamic Voltage and Frequency Scaling (DVFS) technique to reduce the power consumption and hence make it lightweight.

Another approach to solve the problem of resource limitation could be found in [4] that applies fully Quasi Delay Insensitive asynchronous for AES algorithm. More research needs to be done to address the resource limitations and new kinds of security threats arising out of wireless network variants due to the absence of a guided medium.

Public key cryptography is another cryptographic technique where the encryption and decryption are performed through two different keys-public encryption key and a private decryption key. This is shown in Fig. 7.1. In such technique the two keys should not be derived from each other. Thus, no complex algorithm is needed for sharing the secret key among the parties.

Rivest-Shamir Adleman (RSA) is a robust and the most important encryption algorithm utilized by researchers. Though it is very stable it requires expensive resources to do the calculations. Elliptical Curve Cryptography (ECC) is the most popular resource constrained public key cryptography alternative that is widely used in systems with resource limitations. In [5], authors presented an implementation of an open source ECC for the Contici OS for IoT devices. Proper hardware implementation of ECC and its variants could even secure systems against side channel

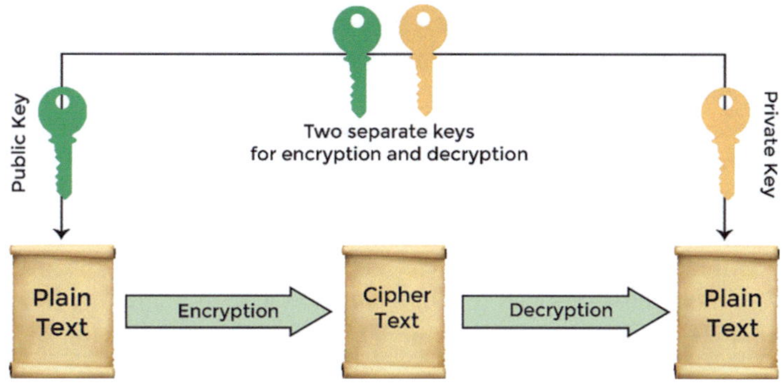

Fig. 7.1 Basic concept of public key cryptography

attacks. Since ECC has a low data requirement, faster crypto-processors could be utilized by the IoT devices.

7.2 Security Threats for Routing

Routing happens in the network layer. So, in this section, we study the network layer attacks that commonly occur for the wireless networks including MANET, WSN, and its variants. The discussion is mostly focused on MANET though; as it is the most crucial one as far as security threats are concerned. An attacker can absorb the entire network traffic, or alternatively, it may inject itself into the path between the source and destination to control the network traffic. The common security attacks are presented here as follows.

7.2.1 Flooding Attack

The aim of the flooding attack [6] is to exhaust network resources, such as, bandwidth. It may also consume a nodes resources, such as, computational and battery power or disrupt the routing operation to cause severe degradation in network performance. For example, in AODV protocol, a malicious node can send a large number of RREQs in a short period of time to some destination node that does not exist in the network. As the target node is not present that will reply to the RREQs, these RREQs will flood the network. As a result, the battery power, as well as network bandwidth of the connected nodes will be consumed and this could lead to denial-of-service. In [7], the authors have experimentally shown that a flooding attack can decrease the network throughput by 84%.

A mechanism to prevent flooding attack for the AODV protocol has been presented in [6]. As can be observed from the nature of the threat, it is important to monitor the RREQs and the rate at which a node is receiving them from its neighbors. If this rate exceeds a predefined threshold for any neighbor node then the node records the ID of this neighbor in a blacklist. The node would drop any future RREQs from nodes that are listed in the blacklist. The effectiveness of this approach depends on the threshold. If the threshold is set high then some flooding attacks would not be prevented. Moreover, if a malicious node A broadcasts a large number of RREQs in the name of a legitimate node B (could be done by impersonating its ID) then the node B might be blacklisted instead of node A that is actually malicious.

7.2.2 Blackhole Attack

In a blackhole attack [8], the aim is to route every packet in the network through the malicious node itself. As it tries to route every packet through itself, it falsely advertises that it has an optimum route. Consequently, the rational nodes would route data packets through the malicious one. For example, in AODV, the attacker would transmit a fake RREP to the source node. Such a message may contain fake destination sequence number that is fabricated to be equal or higher than the one contained in the RREQ. So, the recipient node would get the wrong impression that this node has a sufficiently fresh route to the destination node. As a result, the recipient node would start routing messages through the attacker. In this way, the attacker receives most of the routing traffic. The attacker could then discard the traffic or misuse it.

Many solutions have been designed by researchers to stop or prevent such attacks. In [9], the blackhole attack has been analyzed for any pattern. The authors observed that a malicious node must increase the destination sequence number sufficiently so that the legitimate nodes would trust that the route provided is sufficient. Based on this analysis, they designed an anomaly detection approach based on differences between the destination sequence numbers of the received RREPs.

Grayhole attack [10] is a slight modification of the blackhole attack where a malicious node may sometimes drop a few selective packets rather than all packets like the previous one.

7.2.3 Replay Attack

This attack utilizes the volatile nature of MANET links due to relative mobility of the nodes. This means that the network topology at a time instant might not exist in the future. In a replay attack [11], a malicious node records valid control messages received from other nodes and resends them later when the topology changes. Thus, other rational nodes would record stale routes in their routing tables. Replay attack can be misused to perturb the routing operations in a typical MANET configuration.

It can also be utilized by malicious nodes to impersonate some rational node in the network.

7.2.4 *Wormhole Attack*

A wormhole attack [12] is a sophisticated attack as compared to earlier ones that is comparatively difficult to detect in MANET. It may cause serious damage. This attack could be launched by a pair of colluding attackers are connected through a private high-speed network (the wormholes) who record packets at one location and replay them at another location. Thus, other nodes would get a false picture of the network topology and hence, gradually all packets would be routed toward the high-speed link. The severity of this attack is that it could be launched against all communications that provide authenticity and confidentiality. Thus, traditional cryptography and other techniques may not be effective here.

Interestingly, the researchers showed in [13] that the wormholes could be defined in terms of network graphs without knowledge of locations. Accordingly, a test on different properties of network connectivity can identify these wormholes with moderate accuracy.

7.2.5 *Colluding Misrelay Attack*

This attack [8] is similar to the Wormhole attack. Here also multiple attacker nodes are needed to launch the attack. The malicious nodes work in collusion to modify or drop routing packets in order to disrupt the routing operation in MANET. It is hard to detect such attacks by using the conventional methods such as watchdog and pathrater [14].

To detect such types of attacks, conventional acknowledgment-based approach could be adopted in MANET, especially for a proactive MANET.

7.3 Modelling Reputation Based Trust

Reputation is a fundamental concept that refers to the interaction among mutually distrusting parties. It is established among the nodes of a network through exchanging trust opinions.

In the literature, extensive works could be found on trust management and trust-based data routing in MANET [15].

The basic framework of a Trust Management System should consist of a Watchdog and a Reputation System (RS) [15]. The watchdogs normally monitor the event of data forwarding in such a way that they count the receipt of ACKs corresponding to data sent out/forwarded. Multiple feedbacks would be compressed together to tolerate link failure due to mobility. However, mobility is not bad for routing as it increases the probability of direct interaction with a node.

7.3.1 *Trust Based Reputation in MANET*

In MANET there is no central authority like a sink that is connected to all the nodes. Each node shares equal responsibility for communication and computation. Thus, a reputation system designed for MANET should be a distributed system. The main functions of such a distributed reputation scheme include:

- Updating and sharing data of respective nodes after a certain period of time,
- Integrating and calculating the trust rating of the nodes in the network and
- Detecting as well as preventing the rational nodes from possible security threats.

As we know, in MANET, each node maintains a routing table entry for each of its neighbors. Here, a mobile node computes the reputation values in the form of trust vectors and shares it with its one hop neighbors. These values reflect the experience of the past transactions.

We discuss here a simple trust-based reputation scheme that is designed in [16]. The trust vectors are defined as constant length binary vectors of L bits where L could get the values 8, 16 or 32 [17]. Each bit of L represents the experience of transaction with a neighbor where bit value 1 signifies an honest transaction and a 0 bit value indicates a dishonest one. The result of the new transaction is written on the most significant bit, shifting the present bits to the right. Figure 7.2 shows how a trust vector gets updated after a valid transaction. The number of trust vectors depends on the average no of neighbors the node has. However, such measures can be enhanced with longer trust vectors. The bit positions in the trust vector represent credits. Thus, the highest credit is held by the most significant bit and it indicates recent transactions. Thus, aging is incorporated to cope with the change in network topology due to node mobility. Hence, if a transient failure occurs at a node in MANET due to which it could not forward a packet, it then the node should not be treated as malicious. Instead, the node should get an opportunity in the future to demonstrate its credentials. Such a transient failure might happen due to battery run out or even buffer overflow. However, if its direct neighbors marked the node as malicious, then another chance would not be given. Thus, only when a node consistently drops packets in recent time for an appreciable interval that the scheme would mark the node as malicious. Here, the authors assumed that the data packets are encrypted by a suitable state-of-the art cryptographic algorithm [16].

Let the credit rating be R_k for the kth bit such that for 8-bit vectors, $k = 0,1,2\ldots0.7$ and $R_k > R_k - 1$. Here, *k* designates the significance of the bit in the m-bit trust vector.

The trust rating is assigned a weight by the credit rating of the corresponding bits. The credit rating is calculated using the credit vector that is stored in the nodes.

Thus, trust is calculated as follows

Fig. 7.2 Change in trust vector following a right shift after a genuine transaction

Table 7.1 Data structures utilized by the scheme

Data structure	Signicance
Trust vector	A vector containing 1's and 0's. The values are initialized to 1's
packet_sent	A variable denoting the no. of packets sent
packet_rcvd	A variable denoting the no. of packets received
Routing table	Tuple containing (node id, trust vector);

$$TE(V) = \frac{\sum_{k=1}^{m} R_k \times V_i}{\sum_{k=1}^{m} R_k} [\text{where } 1 \le \text{TE(V)} \le 0] \quad (7.1)$$

Here, V_k is the kth bit of V, trust vector and there are m bits in each trust vector. The total trust value, TE(V) is calculated by a node once a packet gets delivered. Accordingly, the distrust measure would be (1−TE(V)).

So, the authors have put a minimum threshold on the value of trust function required for a node in order to be trusted. This threshold is decided empirically through rigorous experimentation. If the trust of a node goes below this minimum threshold, then the node is treated to be malicious.

Based on the collected information regarding the trust function, a node is expected to eventually identify the malicious nodes in the neighborhood. The required data structures in the process of the calculation has been summarized as Table 7.1.

7.3.2 *Bayesian Network-Based Trust Model*

A Bayesian network [15] represents relationship probability among various elements. Every Bayesian network contains a root node T which can get either of the two values—"unsatisfying" (0) and "satisfying" (1). In the context of secure routing in MANET, $p(T = 1)$ could represent a node's overall trust for its neighbor that the neighbor would securely forward packets in time. It is calculated by the ratio of the no. of satisfying interactions with respect to the total number of interactions. On the contrary, the proportion of unsatisfying interactions is denoted by $p(T = 0)$.

$$p(T = 1) + p(T = 0) = 1 \quad (7.2)$$

We present here an approach of Bayesian network-based reputation mechanism suitable for MANET as discussed in [16]. A child node denotes a neighbor's ability of secure forwarding of the packets. Direct interaction experience of a node with its neighbor node is reflected in the trust calculation. Alternatively, a node when it first joins a new network or rejoins, it may accumulate recommendations about a neighboring node from its other neighbors. Aging should be considered in the process as it accounts for dynamics of the network.

Finally, residual energy of the neighbors is incorporated in calculating the aggregate trust value. A predefined threshold on aggregate trust value which is a positive value in $\{0, 1\}$ is taken as the default aggregate trust value. Before forwarding a packet to a node, the sender node must confirm that the aggregate trust value of the downstream node exceeds the corresponding threshold. A node may dynamically change its behavior for instance, a node may found to be a compromised one at some point of time while a selfish node can become a trusted node in future.

Direct trust is calculated based on direct experiences of the node. Once a node receives a packet, if the sender is trusted, it replies and then forwards the data packet to an upstream neighbor it trusts. According to the scheme, the source node could utilize RSA algorithm to encrypt the packets. The nodes along the route of a packet transmission keep a timer that is set to the *time-to-live* field mentioned in the packet. Upon receiving a reply in time, the node's trust table is updated accordingly. The node also relays the reply from the upstream neighbor. Consequently, the source could calculate the direct trust estimate for it's neighbors. If there is a time out, a node notifies it to the upstream neighbor concerned so that it is circulated to the source. If the aggregate trust for a neighbor node goes below a threshold, the node could choose another trusted neighbor node and look for a new route. In the trust calculation, both direct observations and recommendations by other nodes have been utilized. The direct positive outcomes as observed by node j resulted from direct interactions with node l is combined with the positive recommendations of node l as received by node j. A node then evaluates the aggregate trust by exploiting Bayesian network notions and the remaining energy ratio of that node. However, in malicious node detection direct observation has been given more importance. As aging has been incorporated through prioritizing recent experiences over past experiences it is viable to model dynamic behavior of nodes. Selfish node could be given better trust rating in the future once it's energy level is found to improve.

Active attacks as in gray hole attack, black hole attack instigate packet dropping or misrouting of packets causing timeout at senders. Such attacks could be mitigated. Denial of service attack can also be responded by discarding packets coming from malicious nodes. Due to monitoring of the *time-to-live* field, we can prevent jellyfish attack.

7.3.3 Dempster—Shafer Belief Theory

In the previous subsections we have seen secure routing solutions mainly targeted for MANET environment. However, WSN nodes could also face similar attacks. So, secure routing through reputation is required to be reinforced here as well.

Directed diffusion is a popular routing scheme for WSN discussed in Chap. 4. This scheme is susceptible to Sybil, sinkhole, selective forwarding, HELLO flood, and wormhole attacks [18].

In the threat model, selective forwarding attack and two new types of attacks-bad mouthing attack and good mouthing attack are considered. These attacks could pose threats to the reputation-based trust mechanisms as well.

- *Selective forwarding Attack*: Malicious nodes could be placed at arbitrary locations in the sensor network by an adversary. Such malicious nodes could drop packets arbitrarily that are relayed through them. Doing so would degrade the overall performance of the network.
- *Bad mouthing Attack*: In this attack, an adversary spreads negative information about a legitimate node. Thus, other nodes may treat this node to be malicious mistakenly.
- *Good mouthing Attack*: Such an attack is executed by a group of malicious nodes. It is the opposite of bad mouthing and thus the malicious nodes would spread good reputation for them so that others would trust them in forwarding packets for routing.

Due to the inherent distributed nature of WSNs, a sensor node can have an imperfect knowledge about other nodes. Hence, each node may have an opinion about other nodes although that may not be 100% correct. This opinion is based on three factors—belief (the extent a node is trusted), disbelief (the extent a node is distrusted), and uncertainty in case both belief and disbelief are not sufficient. This is expressed [19] following Dempster-Shafer belief theory as follows.

$$b + d + u - 1 \tag{7.3}$$

Here, b, d, and u represent belief, disbelief, and uncertainty, respectively. In [22], a reputation-based trust mechanism for MANET is presented to address such a scenario applying the concept of Dempster-Shafer belief theory. A node here considers observations from direct first-hand interactions as well as recommendation from other trusted nodes in shaping the overall reputation of a node. This is detailed as follows.

7.3.3.1 First-Hand Interaction

Any node A's direct interaction with a node B is recorded as direct experience. This direct experience information is broadcast periodically to A's neighborhood so that any other node C can use it as indirect information/recommendation from A. A node evaluates the trust depending on the direct observation along with recommendations applying Dempster Shafer Belief theory [22]. Here, a node could either be legitimate or suspicious. So, Beta(α,β), that is, beta distribution is applied where α and β both are updated for each direct interaction of node A with node B. Initially, the nodes pose Beta(1,1) for all their neighbors. If a node is found to successfully forward a packet that it received, then the α parameter would be updated; or else, β gets updated as the weighted (ω) mean of new and old observations following equations:

$$\alpha_{AB(new)} = \omega * \alpha_{AB(old)} + (1 - \omega) * \mu \quad (7.4)$$

$$\beta_{AB(new)} = \omega * \beta_{AB(old)} + (1 - \omega) * \mu \quad (7.5)$$

Let's say, a node *A* sends a packet to another node *B*. Now, node *B* successfully forwards the packet to another node *C*; then node *B* sends an acknowledgement (ACK) packet to node *A*. If the forwarding does not happen then ACK would not be sent. So, in that case, node *A* would not receive any ACK from node *B*. Accordingly, node *A*'s experience about node *B* is updated in the Beta(α,β) following Eqs. (7.4) and (7.5). Here, $\mu = 2$ if ACK has been received from node *B* and timeout, respectively. High value of $(\alpha + \beta)$ signifies that uncertainty (u) is low. Also, when $\alpha = \beta$; it means that success and failure both are equally likely. Thus, despite frequent communication, there is inconsistency in its behavior; hence, increasing the uncertainty (u). Uncertainty of $node_A$ in forecasting the legitimate behavior of $node_B$ could be represented as the expectation of the Beta(α,β) [17] is defined as follows.

$$u_{AB} = \frac{12 * \alpha_{AB}\beta_{AB}}{(\alpha_{AB} + \beta_{AB})^2 * (1 + \alpha_{AB} + \beta_{AB})} \quad (7.6)$$

Therefore, certainty is composed of both belief and disbelief as $(1 - u_{AB})$. Hence, belief of node *A* toward *B* could be calculated as the proportion of positive experience over total experience as follows.

$$b_{AB} = \frac{\propto_{AB}}{\propto_{AB} + \beta_{AB}}(1 - u_{AB}) \quad (7.7)$$

Similarly, disbelief would be quantified as the proportion of negative experience over total experience.

7.3.3.2 Second-Hand Recommendation

Nnode *A* gets first-hand information from other nodes about node *B*. We consider this second-hand recommendation information for faster convergence and detection of malicious nodes. Also, when a node newly joins anetwork, such recommendations are quite useful. Here, node *A* gathers an opinion in terms of (b,d,u) about node *B* from each of its neighbours. Then, it integrates the recommendation with the direct observation to calculate trust.

Thus, node *A* upon receiving $(b_B{}^C, d_B{}^C\ u_B{}^C)$ from node *C* about node *B*, calculates the indirect belief [21] as follows.

$$b_B^{A:C} = b_C^A * b_B^C \quad (7.8)$$

where $b_B^{A:C}$, $d_B^{A:C}$, $u_B^{A:C}$ denotes the belief, disbelief and uncertainty of node *A* for node *B* after getting recommendation from node *C*. Disbelief and uncertainty are calculated in a similar spirit and is further detailed in [23]. The indirect information would be updated periodically as a node receives a broadcast in its neighborhood containing direct interaction experience of the nodes.

7.3.3.3 Combined Trust Calculation

On receiving the broadcast messages containing indirect observations, node *A* combines the recommendation about node *B* from multiple nodes *j* as [19].

$$b_B^{A(indirect)} = \frac{\sum_{j=1}^{n} b_B^{A:j}}{n} \tag{7.9}$$

$$d_B^{A(indirect)} = \frac{\sum_{j=1}^{n} d_B^{A:j}}{n} \tag{7.10}$$

$$u_B^{A(indirect)} = \frac{\sum_{j=1}^{n} u_B^{A:j}}{n} \tag{7.11}$$

Such direct and aggregate indirect information would then be combined through weighted sum that is based on the uncertainty factor. Such combined belief, disbelief, and uncertainty of a node would be utilized to calculate the final trust value of node *A* for node *B* as [21].

$$T_{AB} = b_B^{A(final)} + 0.5\, u_B^{A(final)} \tag{7.12}$$

Here, it is expected that 50% of the uncertain states would be in the positive side of belief [21]. If T_{AB} falls below a predefined threshold of trust, a malicious node *B* is detected [22]. Node *A* then broadcasts this information in its neighborhood.

7.3.4 Role of Trust in Directed Diffusion

As discussed in Sect. 4.1.2 in Chap. 4, interest propagation and exploratory data transmission are the main steps of directed diffusion. Now, lets study how these two phases could be affected by selective forwarding attack how can trust model solve this problem.

Interest propagation-The sink periodically broadcasts an interest message to each of its neighbours. If the receiving nodes are not the source, they broadcast the message to their neighbours till the source of the data is reached.

- **Effect of malicious node-**The malicious nodes either forward the interest message or drop it. If the interest message is dropped by some malicious node, still it will reach the source by some other path as the message is broadcast.

Exploratory data transmission-The source on receiving interest message from its neighbors sends data message to each of its neighbors from which it had received interest message. This is followed till the data message reaches the sink.

- **Effect of malicious node-**The malicious nodes can randomly forward some data message and drop some.
- **Trust model-**For each data message received and successful forwarding, the upstream node sends an ACK to the downstream node. Based on receipt of ACK or in case of timeout, the downstream node updates its opinion about the upstream node and subsequently calculates its trust on the upstream node.

Thus, the trust model can further strengthen the packet transmission of directed diffusion. Similarly, other routing protocols could also be made more secure with such reputation-based trust models.

7.4 Summary

In summary, in this chapter, the security attacks on routing of data packets in MANET and WSN have been discussed. It has been discussed that cryptography, or so to say, lightweight cryptography cannot handle some security attacks due to the unguided open wireless medium. Threats such as, blackhole, grayhole, selective forwarding are in place. To solve such issues, the concept of reputation-based trust models could be utilized. Here, we have shown three such strategies based on bit manipulation, Bayesian networks, and Dempster-Shafer belief theory. The role of trust in in securing routing protocols is also shown.

References

1. Biswas, K., Md Ali, L.: Security threats in mobile ad hoc network. Master's thesis, Dept of interaction and system design, School of Engg, Blekinge Institute of Technology, Sweden (2007)
2. Dutta, I.K., Ghosh, B., Bayoumi, M.: Lightweight cryptography for internet of insecure things: a survey. In: 2019 IEEE 9th Annual Computing and Communication Workshop and Conference (CCWC), pp. 0475–0481 (2019). https://doi.org/10.1109/CCWC.2019.8666557
3. Agwa, S., Yahya, E., Ismail, Y.: Power efficient AES core for IoT constrained devices implemented in 130nm CMOS. In: Proceeding—IEEE International Symposium Circuits System, pp. 2–5 (2017)
4. Lu, M., Fan, A., Xu, J., Shan, W.: A compact, lightweight and low-cost 8-bit datapath AES circuit for IoT applications in 28nm CMOS. In: 2018 17th IEEE International Conference

Trusting Security Private Computer Communication 12th IEEE International Conference Big Data Science Engineering, pp. 1464–1469 (2018)
5. Pinol, O.P., Raza, S., Eriksson, J., Voigt, T.: BSD-based elliptic curve cryptography for the open Internet of Things. In: 2015 7th International Conference New Technology Mobile Security—Proceeding NTMS 2015 Conference Working (2015)
6. Yi, P., Dai, Z., Zhang, S., Zhong, Y.: A new routing attack in mobile ad hoc networks. Int. J. Inf. Technol. **11**(2), 83–94 (2005)
7. Desilva, S., Boppana, R.V.: Mitigating malicious control packet oods in ad hoc networks. In: The IEEE Wireless Communications and Networking Conference, pp. 2112–2117 (2005)
8. Kannhavong, B., Nakayama, H., Nemoto, Y., Kato, N.: A survey of routing attacks in mobile ad hoc networks. IEEE Wirel. Commun. 85–91 (2007)
9. Kurosawa, S., Nakayama, H., Kato, N., Jamalipour, A., Nemoto, Y.: Detecting blackhole attack on aodv-based mobile ad hoc networks by dynamic learning method. Int. J. Netw. Secur. **5**(3), 338–346 (2007)
10. Qian, L., Song, N., Li, X.: Detection of wormhole attacks in multi-path routed wireless ad hoc networks: a statistical analysis approach. Netw. Comput. Appl. **30**(1), 308–330 (2007)
11. Adjih, C., Rao, D., Muhlethaler, P.: Attacks against olsr: distributed key management for security. In: 2nd OLSR Interop/Wksp., Palaiseau, France (2005)
12. Hu, Y.C., Perrig, A., Johnson, D.: Wormhole attacks in wireless networks. IEEE J. Sel. Areas Commun. **24**(2), 370–380 (2006)
13. Ban, X., Sarkar, R., Gao, J.: Local connectivity tests to identify wormholes in wireless networks. In: The 12th ACM International Symposium on Mobile Ad Hoc Networking and Computing (MobiHoc'11) (2011)
14. Marti, S., Giuli, T.J., Lai, K., Baker, M.: Mitigating routing misbehavior in mobile ad hoc networks. In: The 6th Annual International Conference on Mobile Computing and Networking, pp. 255–265 (2000)
15. Li, N., Das, S.K.: A trust-based framework for data forwarding in opportunistic networks. Ad Hoc Netw. **11**(4), 1497–1509 (2013)
16. Banerjee, A., Neogy, S., Chowdhury, C.: Reputation based trust management system for MANET. In: the IEEE Proceedings of Third International Conference on Emerging Applications of Information Technology (EAIT 2012), pp. 376–381 (2012)
17. Roy, M., Chowdhury, C., Neogy, S.: Developing secured MANET using trust. In: 2014 Fourth International Conference on Advances in Computing and Communications, pp. 183–186 (2014). https://doi.org/10.1109/ICACC.2014.51
18. Karlof, C., Wagner, D.: Secure routing in wireless sensor networks: attacks and countermeasures. Ad Hoc Netw. **1**(2–3), 293–315 (2003)
19. Wang, Y., Vassileva, J.: Trust and reputation model in peer-to-peer networks. In: Proceeding of IEEE Conference on P2P Computing, pp. 150–160 (2003)
20. Kundu, K., Chowdhury, C., Neogy, S., Chattopadhyay, S.: Trust aware directed diffusion scheme for wireless sensor network, In: IEEE Proceedings of the Fourth International Conference on Emerging Applications of Information Technology (EAIT 2014), pp. 385–391 (2014)
21. Kota, C.M., Aissi, C.: Implementation of the RSA algorithm and its cryptanalysis. In: Proceedings of the 2002 ASEE Gulf-Southwest Annual Conference (2002)
22. Roy, M., Chowdhury, C., Anjum, M.N., Neogy, S.: Designing secure and reliable mobile agent based system for reliable MANET. J. Ad Hoc Ubiquitous Comput., Inderscience **32**(1), 43–58 (2019)
23. Chowdhury, C., Neogy, S.: Mobile agent security in MANET using reputation. In: Proceeding 1st International Conference on Parallel, Distributed Computing Technologies and Applications (PDCTA 2011), pp. 158–168 (2011)

Chapter 8
Case Studies: Disease Specific Healthcare Applications

Abstract This chapter entails several case studies on health monitoring systems. It is based on wearable sensors and other kinds of sensing devices. IoT-based applications for smart cities are also discussed here. Machine learning techniques have been applied to monitor the body vitals. Applications ranging from disease monitoring to walking assistant for the elderly people have been presented.

Keywords Health · Sensors · Machine learning · Deep learning · Smart walking assistant

Sensor, IoT, Smartphone, cloud, high speed connectivity and intelligent machine learning, deep learning based models have been exploited to develop smart health monitoring and care system prototypes. These kind of smart systems are in demand since outbreak COVID 19. In [1], some of these prototypes have been summarized. Few alarmingly increasing disease prototypes are being described in this chapter.

8.1 Brain Cancer

Cancer growth is alarming all over the world. Brain tumors vary by type of tumor, location, and size and these variations make diagnosis difficult as symptoms also vary. Thus, detecting which part is affected by the tumor is an extremely challenging task in segmenting the cancerous part from the non-cancerous part. Many researchers have addressed such challenges by using various datasets like BRATS, BTI, and BMI. Few case studies on related research addressing the challenges are discussed in [1] (Table 8.1).

A brain cancer classification model developed by adopting deep transfer learning models for feature extraction, GoogleNet was implemented for feature extraction. Three types of brain cancer were classified: (i) meningioma, (ii) glioma, and (iii) pituitary tumors. The efficiency of models depend on training the system with fewer

S. Biswas et al., *Adhoc and Sensor Networks: Security and Applications*, Studies in Systems, Decision and Control 653, https://doi.org/10.1007/978-981-95-5839-1_8

Table 8.1 Literature summary on algorithms and datasets used

Authors	Algorithms used	Datasets	Types of tumors
Guo et al.	2D-CNN, 3D-CNN	2D and 3D image data	Not specified
Zhao et al.	Fully CNN (FCNN) and Conditional Random Fields (CRF)	BRATS2013, BRATS 2015, and BRATS 2016	
Heba et al.	DNN and DWT and PCA for feature extraction	66 MRI real images were collected from Harvard Medical School website (https://www.med.harvard.edu/AANLIB/home.html)	Three types of Malignant brain tumors: glioblastoma, sarcoma and metastatic bronchogenic carcinoma

samples and accuracy achieved would be higher. The proposed model has addressed this challenge. Details of modeling are as follows (Table 8.2).

8.2 Breast Cancer

A profusion of research has taken place in the last research in the field of breast cancer detection and diagnosis; some of this research is specified in the present section (Table 8.3).

8.3 Sleep Disorder Monitoring

Exploiting the power of smartphone and Artificial Intelligence, the authors in [2] have designed and developed a system to identify sleep apnea or disorder through snoring detection. The flowchart below tries to depict the step by step procedure in Fig. 8.1.

8.4 Diabetics Detection—Non-Invasive Method

Invasive Diabetic Detection [3] is applied in healthcare system for accurate measurement. Often for the people with prolonged diabetes history grow with dislike with this invasive process because of many reasons. Non-invasive method to measure diabetes accurately is still a research challenge.

Figure 8.1 illustrates the prototype for necessary breath sample collection, sample processing and recording, etc.

Table 8.2 Models used for multiclass brain cancer classification

Models used	Purpose	Feature values	Dataset
Dense-Net201 and deep transfer learning algorithms	Multiclass brain tumor classification	Entropy–Kurtosis-based High Feature Values (EKbHFV)	BRATS2018 and BRATS2019

Table 8.3 Works done on breast cancer classification

Authors	Algorithms	Datasets	Types of tumor
Spanhol et al.	*CNN variant ALexNet*	Histopathological images	*Breast cancer, malignat, benign classification*
Ertosun and Rubin	*CNN, output fed to SVM*		detect the subsistence of mass in mammography (input) images and later it localizes the mass from those images
Xu et al.	Stacked Sparse Autoencoder (SSAE), greedy algorithm was used for optimizing SSAE	Histopathology breast images, mammography image dataset	*Classifying nuclei from histopathology breast images*

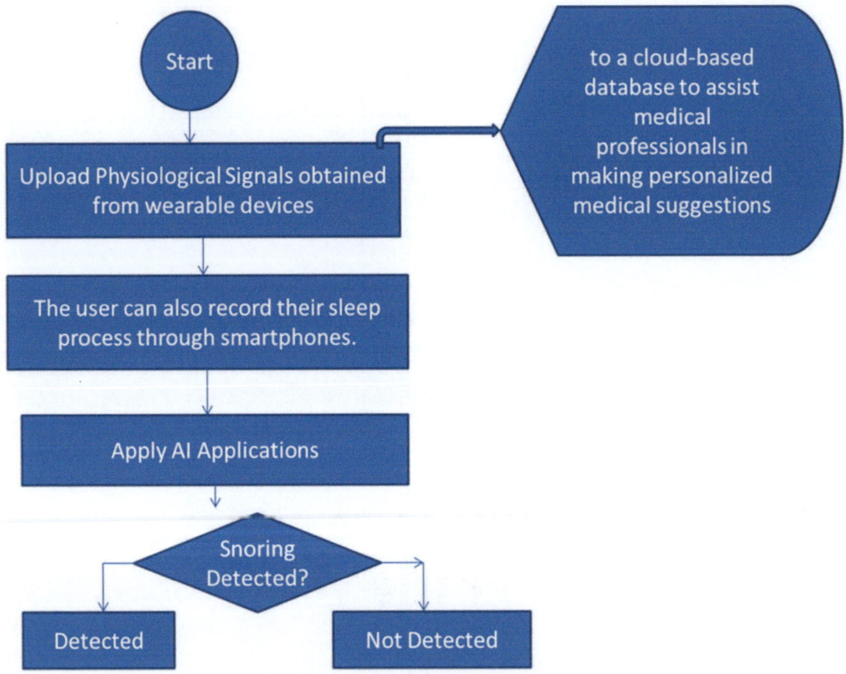

Fig. 8.1 Workflow of the sleep disorder monitoring mechanism

Collection of the Breath Sample to Be Infused into the Device

Into the sensor-based setup using a drip pipe mounted on top of the soda cup cap, a breath sample in fasting sugar condition was collected in a balloon and was infused.

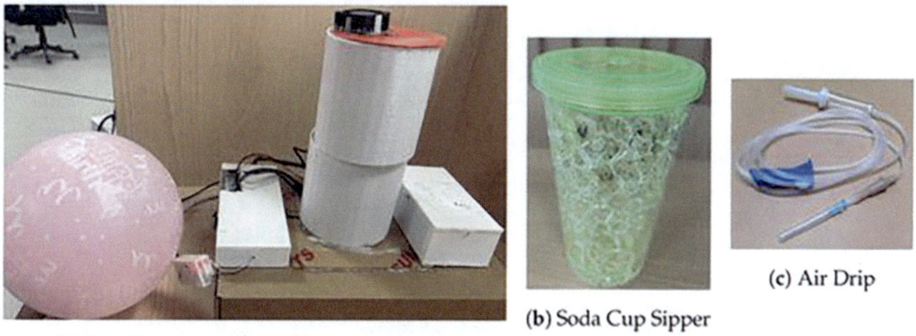

(a) Non-Invasive Diabetes Detection Device

(b) Soda Cup Sipper

(c) Air Drip

Fig. 8.2 Breath sample collection and analysis device arrangement

Processing of the Breath Sample and Recording of the Data

The sensors showed deflection from their baseline upon interaction with the VOCs present in the breath sample. Into an InfluxDB time series database, the recorded deflection data are directed.

The sensor voltage readings are related with the concentration of VOCs in the breath sample.

In Fig. 8.2a, the small prototype named "DiabeticSense" is represented. It consists of an array of sensors of various MOS-type electrochemical sensors. These sensors are arranged in a cylindrical manner. This is integrated into a soda sipper cup and have a very tightly closing cap, please refer to Fig. 8.2b. Breath sample collection was done through birthday balloons. The breath sample was infused into the device slowly using a drip pipe as shown in Fig. 8.2c.

(i) ML Model Development for Non-invasive Diabetes Monitoring [3]:

Breath samples have been collected for diabetes prediction task applying state of the art Machine Learning models. Feature matrix obtained by processing the breath samples are divided into training and testing as 80:20 split. fivefold cross validation has been used.

The ML models applied are Gradient Boosting (G-Boost)

1. Decision Tree (DT)
2. Ridge
3. Lasso
4. Elastic Net (ENet)
5. Logistic Regression
6. Support Vector Machines (SVMs)
7. eXtreme Gradient Boosting (XG-Boost)
8. Random Forest (RF).

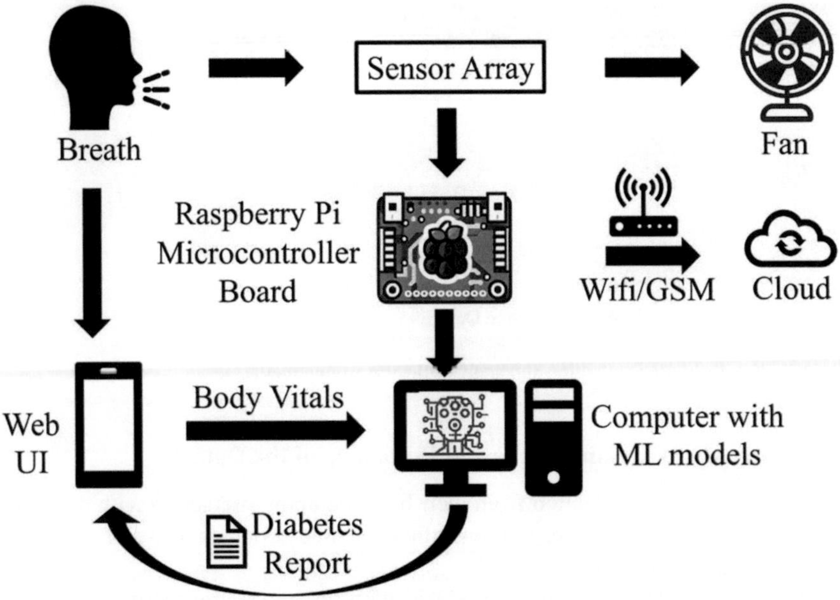

Fig. 8.3 Block diagram of proposed diabetes detection system

8.5 Assessing Pain in Pediatric Hospital Wards [4]

The children generally experience and express pain very differently than adults. With this variation, it can throw challenge in hospital settings. To determining accurate treatment, where accurate pain assessment is crucial to determine appropriate treatment. Children cannot express the feeling of pain like adults. Also they may not clearly tell but may try to express by crying or showing some discomfort. Moreover, due to fear of being criticized or may be ignored, often children may refrain themselves from expressing. These may affect pediatric health specifically due to poor pain management in children. State of the art literatures also lack benchmark effective solution approaches toward pediatric pain management methodologies, etc.

Current Method: There are influencing factors such as hospital admission, tiredness, and heightened emotions, etc., while using a 1 to 10 scale or happy to sad faces to assess pain. The research project TAME is aimed to co-design a technology tool to help healthcare professionals in assessing pediatric pain with more accuracy [5, 6].

At the initial pain assessment moment in the Emergency Room, if the clinicians can do the initial pain assessment, it would really be much better to diagnose the problem early. The enhancement of the decision-making ability of the clinicians was emphasized. And this may ensure a positive experience for both the child and the clinician in diagnosing the problem and to start recovery process in time. The children recovery rates and overall healthcare experiences will also improve pain.

8.6 Smart Walking Assistant for Elderly Monitoring-Fall and Posture Monitoring [7]

This work implements a fall and posture detection system that utilizes cost-effective sensors and leverages machine learning to assist individuals, both indoors and outdoors [7]. This intelligent system can identify falls, whether with or without recovery, within a specified time frame. In cases where a fall is detected without recovery, the system promptly sends an alert message to a designated relative or caregiver, including the date, time, and location of the fall. This real-time feature ensures timely assistance, preventing potential critical situations due to delays. Additionally, the system notifies about the immediate posture before the fall, providing insights into a person's vulnerability to falling from a particular posture. This information can be valuable for healthcare professionals to take preventive measures against future falls. The system can also handle unresponsive devices after a fall, if applicable. We have developed and implemented this intelligent real-time fall and posture detection system by utilizing sensors in the MPU6050, in conjunction with the low-cost ESP8266 microcontroller MCU using WiFi connectivity. A schematic diagram of it is presented in Fig. 8.4. Kinematic sensor data is collected at a rate of 40 Hz, utilizing Accelerometers and Gyroscopes. The results demonstrate that the system can consistently identify the location and posture of the subject, along with the date and time of a fall without self-recovery (if any). An emergency help system is integrated with an audio-visual warning at the Raspberry Pi-based monitoring station, as well as the capability to send distress SMS messages. The system can be operated in either manual or auto mode. The dataset used for testing comprises individuals of various age groups (ranging from 10 to 70 years) and both genders. The system was randomly tested on 10 volunteers, achieving an overall detection accuracy of up to 98%.

Figure 8.4 illustrates the smart walking assistant (SWA) with detailed components embedded for its working as described above.

8.7 IoT-Based Air Pollution Monitoring System

Air pollution is a global concern today. In developing countries, due to rapid urbanization, city areas have high density of population where air quality is becoming poorer for health. People are unknowingly exposed to harmful gases. Its effect is even more severe in elder adults. So, monitoring a city's overall pollution level at macro level by deploying large weather monitoring stations is not sufficient. Devices should be developed to monitor an individual's pollution footprint and its associated health hazards should be assessed. So, with this objective, *AirSense,* an IoT-based system for air quality monitoring has been designed in [8] that when deployed can monitor air quality both indoors and outdoors. This system could encourage the citizens to participate in a participatory-sensing initiative. In this work, an air quality

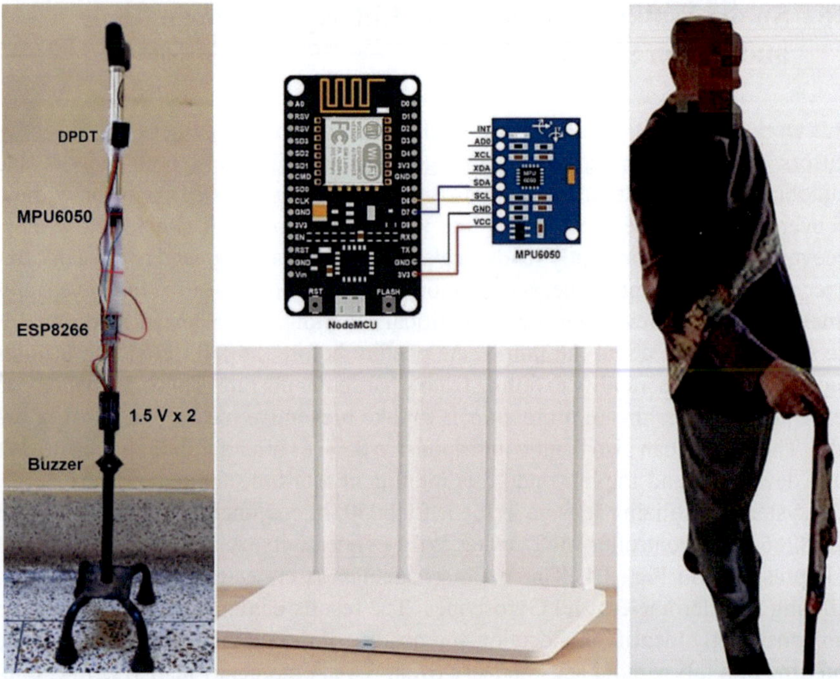

Fig. 8.4 [clockwise] Smart walking stick, the connection diagram, WiFi router with internet connectivity, one of our volunteers with the prototype

monitoring device was developed that contains sensors such as MQ 135, MQ 2, MQ 7, and MQ9. Such a device connects with smartphone to get the GPS coordinates of the location it senses and sends the entire data that is also location tagged to a remote server over the internet. Based on REST API, an OPENSHIFT channel had been created to store the data in the cloud. MySQL database was used by the authors for storing data in OPENSHIFT. Data were collected by the team from the adjoining areas of Jadavpur University and a bus stop near the university [9]. The authors also collected data from indoor environments such as, faculty rooms. The air quality indexes were evaluated. Real-time updates in air quality could be monitored using the device. If different users utilize such a device and can share their sensing data then a detailed pollution map of the city area could be obtained from such a device.

8.8 Summary

In summary, this chapter covers different applications of IoT and sensor networks. Real-life case studies and implementation aspects have been discussed. Here, data analysis has been found to play a role in assessing the sensor readings and mining patterns from it. Mostly, IoT-based approaches have seen a wide range of real-life applications in disease detection, remote healthcare, eldercare to air quality monitoring.

References

1. Chiu, P.C., Su, K.W., Wang, C.H., Ruan, C.W., Shiao, Z.P., Tsao, C.H., Huang, H.H.: Development and testing of the smart healthcare prototype system through COVID-19 patient innovation. Healthcare **11**(6), 847 MDPI (2023)
2. Shiao, Z.-P.: A study of audio feature learning of snoring using convolutional and recurrent neural networks. Unpublished Master's Thesis, National Kaohsiung University of Science and Technology, Kaohsiung, Taiwan (2022)
3. Kapur, R., Kumar, Y., Sharma, S., Rastogi, V., Sharma, S., Kanwar, V., Dutt, V.: DiabeticSense: a non-invasive, multi-sensor, IoT-based pre-diagnostic system for diabetes detection using breath. J. Clin. Med. **12**(20), 6439 (2023)
4. Hurley-Wallace, A., Wood, C., Franck, L.S., Howard, R.F., Liossi, C.: Paediatric pain education for health care professionals. Pain Rep. **4**(1), e701 (2019)
5. Montana-Hoyos, C., Chamorro-Koc, M., Scharoun, L.: The role of design in healthcare innovation and future digital health. In: Digital Health: From Assumptions to Implementations. Springer, pp. 155–175 (2023)
6. Chamorro-Koc, M., Gomez, R., Dwyer, J., Wannenburg, E., (eds.): TAME: Paediatric pain empathy device. Health Excellence Accelerator Lab (HEAL) Symposium: HEAL Showcase (2021)
7. Bhattacharjee, P., Biswas, S.: Smart walking assistant (SWA) for elderly care using an intelligent realtime hybrid model. Evol. Syst. **13**(2), 265–279 (2022)
8. Dutta, J., Roy, S., Chowdhury, C.: Unified framework for IoT and smartphone based different smart city related applications. J. Microsyst. Technol. **25**, 83–96 Springer (2019)
9. Dutta, J., Chowdhury, C., Roy, S., Iqbal, A., Gazi, F.: Towards smart city: sensing air quality in city based on opportunistic crowd-sensing. COMNET-IOT, ICDCN **2017**, 1–6 (2017)

Chapter 9
Demonstration of Smart Healthcare System Prototype Using IoT Application

Abstract With the advancement in Wireless Sensors Network, communication technologies, Internet of things, Cloud, Machine Learning, etc., smart applications such as smart healthcare system development has become achievable with ensured efficiency, reliability, security, affordability, usability, etc. Biomedical sensors spanned over human body forming Wireless Body Area Network (WBAN) to sense and transmit human body vitals to the processing server through communication links are variedly available with acceptance range of accuracy, reliability ensuring continuous, remote health monitoring. Enabling technologies such as high speed Wi-Fi, internet connectivity, cloud storage and processing have aided such automated healthcare prototypes to be in place for use in parallel to the traditional healthcare system. This chapter illustrated different aspects of healthcare prototype development, development and working of different health monitoring prototypes for body vitals monitoring, Human Activity Monitoring, Fall monitoring, etc., to aid the people specially elderly ones to lead a quality living.

Keywords Prototype · Demonstration · Healthcare

9.1 Introduction

In rural areas there is a need of biological sensor-based health data sensing for patients or elderly people. This sensed health data is sent to Doctor's device through internet, the doctor can see the data and can provide necessary advice to the patient. In urban areas also, there is a demand and need of smart, auto-health monitoring system to the people specifically elderly citizens who are suffering from prolonged diseases such as Alzheimer's, Parkinson's, Diabetes, Heart related ailments, Breathing discomfort like Asthma, COPD, Lung disorder, etc. In such diseases the health parameters need to be examined on regular basis and appropriate medication, diagnostics, examinations by the doctor are to be continued. Biomedical sensor based health vitals monitoring system can read health data on regular interval and send the aggregated data through sink or coordinator device to the remote server for analysis by applying

S. Biswas et al., *Adhoc and Sensor Networks: Security and Applications*, Studies in Systems, Decision and Control 653, https://doi.org/10.1007/978-981-95-5839-1_9

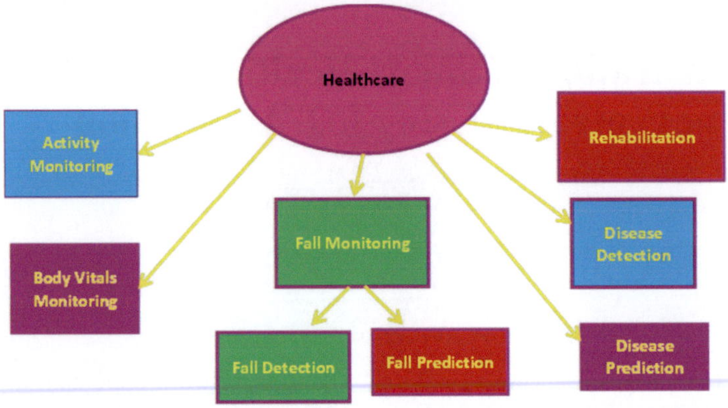

Fig. 9.1 Smart healthcare utilities

intelligent models using Machine Learning, deep learning, Artificial Intelligence, etc. With the raw health parameters and the analyzed results, the doctor can give advice immediately even from remote end. This would avoid the manual error of Telemedicine where the patient or the manual support needs to verbally report the health parameters. Also, the health vitals could be stored as Electronic Health Record (EHR) for future health condition variation pattern analysis specifically at the time of rehabilitation of the patient. IoT based smart healthcare could deliver various services as illustrated in following figure (Fig. 9.1).

The EHR are sent through insecure channel, hence data may suffer from security attacks and threats. Attackers can try to steal data, access and update data through different attacks such as Eavesdropping, man-in-the middle attack, Denial of Service attack. If adversary alters the vital health information doctor will provide advice based on altered data which can be life threatening. So this vital information should be kept confidential. Since confidentiality is not enough to secure the data, integrity of the data should be maintained. Proposed project work will ensure confidentiality, integrity of the sensitive health data during transmission from patient to doctor and storage in cloud. Lightweight and faster encryption will be applied to protect the data from being disclosed, Message Digest algorithms will be applied to verify the intactness of the data. This proposal aims to provide end-to-end remote secure healthcare solutions.

IoT based healthcare services or utilities that may facilitate quality living of people specifically diseased elderly are

1. human activity Monitoring,
2. body Vitals Monitoring,
3. fall Monitoring—(i) Fall Detection, (ii) Fall Prediction,
4. disease Detection,
5. disease Prediction, and
6. rehabilitation.

Here we illustrate prototype demonstration of (i) Human Activity Monitoring, (ii) Body Vitals Monitoring, and (iii) Fall Monitoring.

9.2 Prototype Demonstration of Body Vitals Monitoring

Body vitals monitoring prototype is used for different vital parameters measurement and analysis as per medical guidelines to monitor the physical condition of a person in real time using biomedical sensors either wearable or implanted spread over the human body. Biomedical sensors form a network over the human body called Wireless Body Area Network (WBAN) [1]. The biomedical sensor kit used in this prototype is Mysginals HW development sensor kit [2, 3]. Mysignals HW is a hardware development platform for medical device which is used to build e-health system. It is a package of several biomedical sensors such as body temperature, blood pressure, pulse rate, heart rate, oxygen saturation (SPo2) in the blood, breathing rate, muscle electromyography signals, ECG sensor, blood glucose levels, airflow, body position, galvanic skin response, lung capacity, etc. Arduino UNO act as a microcontroller integrated with MySignals HW. Arduino UNO works as both sink device and gateway device. The sensors can work both in wired or wireless connection. The sensory data can be analyzed at local server or at cloud server using WiFi module.

9.2.1 Fundamental Biomedical Sensors

Body Temperature Sensor

The parameter that gets affected primarily due to any abnormality in the human body such as fever, indigestion, stroke, hypertension. During COVID-19 this was the basic and primary parameter to monitor the disease.

Pulse Sensor

Pulse rate is a very significant parameter to detect any abnormality in health condition, pulse sensor measures pulse rate.

Respiratory Rate Sensor

This sensor measures number of breathes per second. This parameter can signify the status of a person having lung issues, hyper tension, heart problems, etc.

Blood Pressure Sensor

This parameter changes as impact of other diseases or bad health condition. This is not a primary health parameter. If blood pressure is abruptly high, the condition may hypertension, or high blood pressure can cause cardio-vascular disease, low blood pressure may cause weakness in human body, etc.

Pulse Oximeter (SPo2)

This sensor is significant in measuring oxygen saturation level in blood and can help to find if there is any health issue of respiratory function, hypoxia, etc.

Red nodes are biomedical wearable sensors spread over the human body, blue one is smartphone attached at waist position working as a sink or coordinator node to receive and aggregate sensor data. The biomedical sensor nodes communicate using short range communication protocols such as Bluetooth and Wi-Fi.

We may wonder how the body vitals are being analyzed by the experts at remote end and necessary advice given to the subject in concern in real time? The answer is clearly depicted in Fig. 9.2 (Fig. 9.3).

This architecture is self-descriptive of the fact that the person wearing Wireless Body Area Network (WBAN) [4–6] formed by different biomedical sensors is being monitored continuously. The parameters are being sensed and sent to the sink/coordinator/edge device through short range communication protocols such as Bluetooth, WiFi, Zigbee. From edge device the body vitals are being sent to the WiFi Access point which acts as a gateway to transfer the sensory data to the outside world through the internet, 3G/4G to the Cloud medical server. From cloud medical server, the experts/doctors, etc., can access the data, analyze, and share extracted knowledge about the health condition of the subject in concern on the basis of medical guideline. Accordingly proper advice could be sent to the person in concern or relatives or caregiver of the person through mobile-app or SMS in real life.

Figure 9.4 depicts a general framework of Sensor Network based data collection from physical world and transmission to the Processing unit for information generation enabled with Internet of Things technology (IoT). Middle layer is the communication layer consisting of heterogeneous links for seamless data transmission. At the Processing layer, once the data is processed and knowledge is gathered, the information to be shared with intended/authorized entities to maintain privacy and security of data.

In Fig. 9.5, a more illustrated 3 tier architecture of MBSN is shown. In tier I, sensors form the WSN known as MBSN which is spanning over human body. Heterogeneous Biomedical sensors sensing body vitals such as body temperature, heart rate, pulse rate and sending the data to the sink node shown as personal number in the following figure in 1-hop wireless transmission. The short range wireless links here can be WiFi, Bluetooth, Zigbee, etc. The sensor nodes are connected in star topology in MBSN. In tier II, Sensed biological data are sent to the cloud medical server over the internet through access networks. In tier III, the data are analyzed or processed through intelligent models or algorithms such as Machine Learning, Deep Learning, Artificial Intelligence. The doctor or caregiver or any stakeholder concerned can access the time series health data or the result after data processing in the cloud for further intervention.

From the above study so far, it is clear to all that WSN is applied in health monitoring and care with the specialized form of WBAN/WBSN/MBSN, etc.

Basic differences between WSN and WBAN are (Table 9.1).

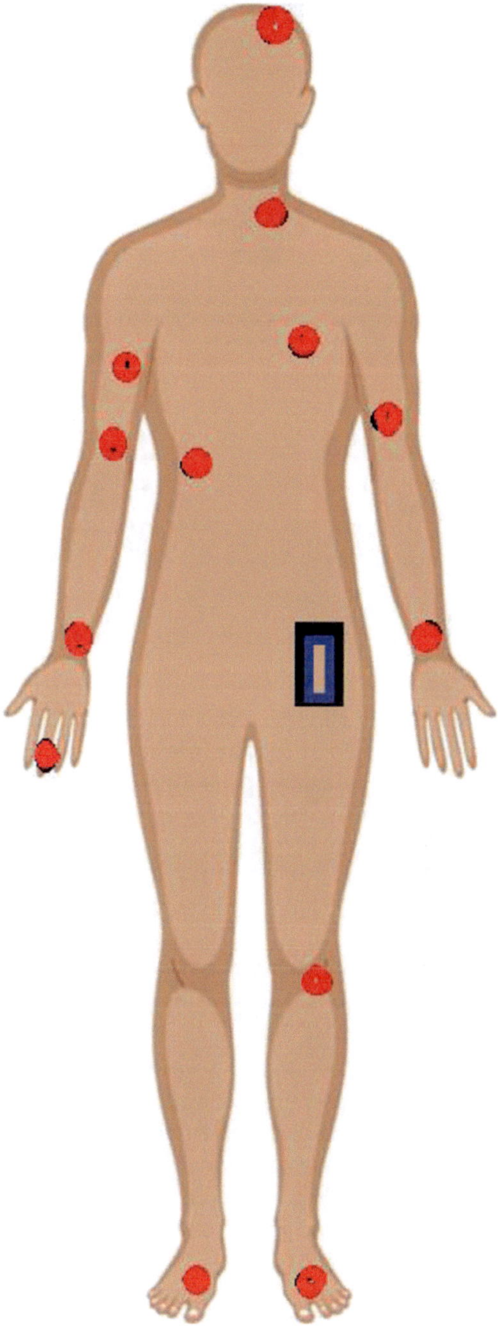

Fig. 9.2 WBAN formed with a number of body vitals monitoring sensors

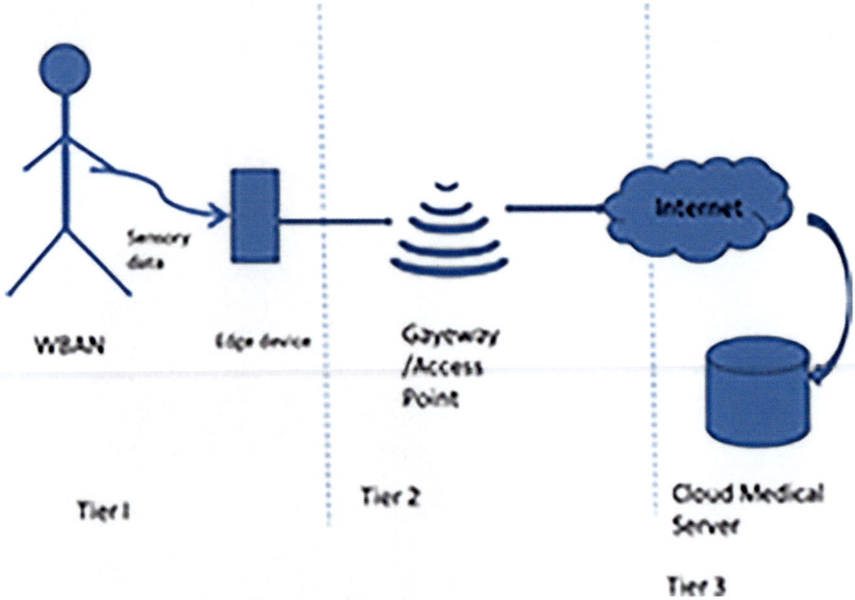

Fig. 9.3 A 3-Tier architecture of smart health monitoring system

So, utilizing all these technologies discussed so far, the smart and remote health monitoring and care system has received risen popularity among the healthcare professionals, researchers and users. Due to sudden deadly pandemic outbreak like Covid 19, these remote health monitoring systems are getting more popularity and acceptance among all the stakeholders. The lifespan of the world population above the age of 60 is analyzed. In 2017, the death rate from chronic diseases such as cancer and heart disease were said to be 70%. In 2017, the elderly death rate was reported to be 9.62%. It will gradually increase in the year 2050 to 21.1%, and in the year 2100, it is expected that the increase in the death rate will be 31.1%. Due to the rapid increase in the growing population, it is expected that the need for healthcare will also increase rapidly, and there will be a heavy monetary scarcity in the future, as per the records. So, developing a suitable and futuristic healthcare system is necessary for developing generations of evolution. Information and communication technology (ICT) over the past years has led to tremendous development in diagnosing diseases that occur in patients and monitoring their health condition with the help of data collected by wireless sensor devices. Correspondingly, the life time of the patient has increased and he gets relief from several chronic diseases.

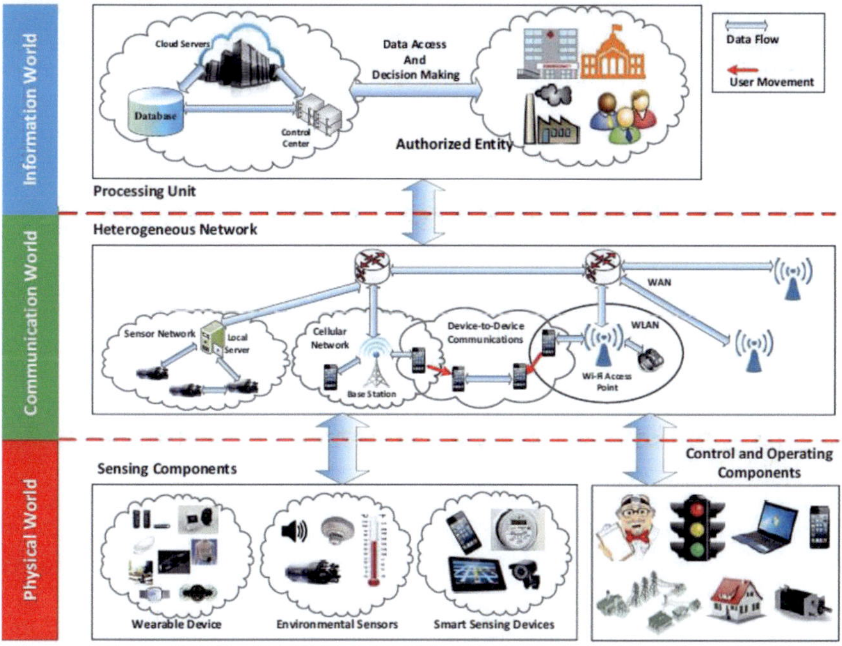

Fig. 9.4 Sensor network at physical world to cloud server at information world through communication world. This figure illustrates IoT based smart framework demonstrating the components involved in data collection from physical world by heterogeneous sensors, data transmission through communication world comprising different heterogeneous links and and data processing at information world where the raw data is processed into information for further appropriate actions by the appropriate authorities

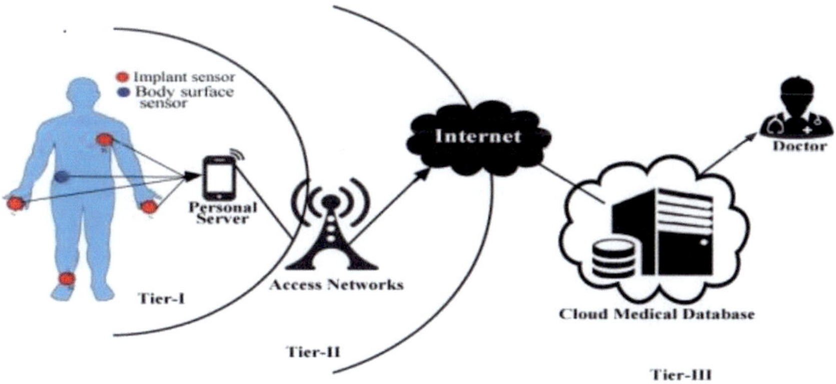

Fig. 9.5 The 3 tier framework of medical body sensor network (MBSN)

Table 9.1 WSN versus WBAN

Parameters	WSN	WBAN
Node density	256	<= 64
Communication range	10–100 m	2–5m
Data rate	250 kbps	1–10 kbps
Reliability, stability	Less	more
Communication bands used	315 MHz, 433 MHz, 868 MHz (Europe), 915 MHz (North America), and 2.45 GHz industrial-scientific-medical (ISM) band	Wireless Medical Telemetry Services (WMTS) and Medical Implant Communications services (MICS)

9.2.2 Objectives of Prototype Development

1. To simulate Medical Body Sensor Network based e-healthcare environment.
2. To make hardware prototype for health data collection.
3. Design and implementation of light weight encryption algorithm for resource constraint device.
4. To encrypt and decrypt health data with different cryptographic algorithms using shared key.
5. Performance evaluation of the proposed algorithm in terms of QoS parameter such as end-to-end delay.
6. Design and implementation of machine learning based intrusion detection systems.

Standard for WBAN has been defined in IEEE 802.15.6 with data transmission rate in the range of 75.9 Kbps to 15.6 Mbps. WBAN interacts with Internet and Bluetooth, ZigBee, WPAN, as well. WBAN can support up to 256 nodes. Sensor nodes should be able to transmit at 0.1 mW with the maximum being not more than 1 mW [7–9]. WBAN monitors human physical conditions and transfers data to a central node via wireless channel as shown in Fig. 9.6.

In this section, the most significant and recent research works based on e-health monitoring [10–13] and COVID patient monitoring which includes systems and solutions to monitor human health.

9.3 Security and Privacy Issues

Since these health information are sent through shared insecure wireless channel, data suffers from lack of security and privacy. Adversary can apply different security attacks like Man-in-the-middle, replay attack, impersonation attack, modification attack, etc., to gather private information of the patient or can alter the information. The hardware prototype developed for the remotely monitoring of health condition

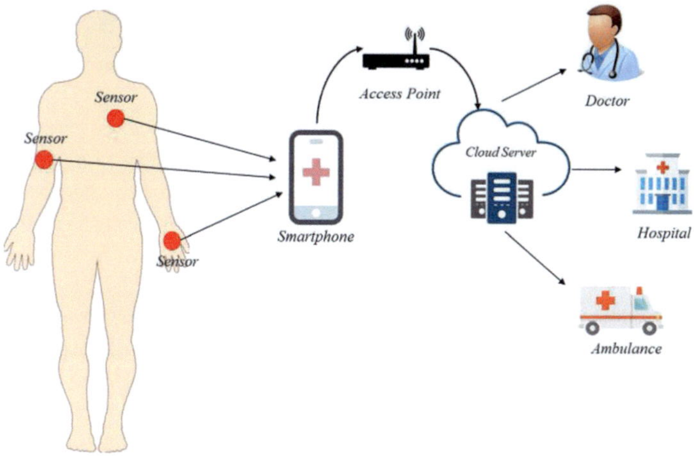

Fig. 9.6 Architecture of WBAN, IoT and Cloud based smart healthcare

can health vitals form human being and then to handle the data securely, necessary security measures are being applied.

Secure frameworks applying traditional and lightweight cryptographic algorithms to ensure the security of the health data has been proposed. Traditional encryption algorithm such as AES and DES and novel lightweight cryptographic algorithm called LSEA has been considered for the secure frameworks. Also, machine learning based intrusion detection framework is proposed. All proposed schemes have been verified against the several security attacks. Performance evaluation has been done in terms of end-to-end delay.

Data Confidentiality

Sensitive health data to be transmitted in encrypted form so that the data could be shared securely between the intended parties only ensuring confidentiality.

Data Integrity

Health data integrity is utmost important for accurate diagnosis and medical advice. Integrity ensures that health data reached to the receiver in its original form or the data is not tampered or altered by any intermediate entity illegally.

Data Availability

The doctors or health professional in concern should get or access patients' biological data as and when required. Data availability must be ensured by any trusted entity.

Data Authentication

In accessing and handling with sensitive health data, all stakeholders must be authenticated with secret credentials such as user ID, password, secret code by trusted third party.

Non-Repudiation

The sender should not be in a position to deny that he or she has sent the message and the non-repudiation can only ensure that.

Data Authorization

While accessing the EHR on server, the entities must be authenticated by the trusted third party every time to ensure if they are authorized to get access to the health data or not.

Data Freshness

Data freshness ensures that the data in concern is received by the receiver close to the time of generation of the data. For health data this property is utmost important for accurate medical advice based on current data.

Access Control

The authorized and authenticated users must be given specific permissions to handle with health data based on their roles. Based on specific roles of the user, the particular permissions should be well defined.

9.4 Why Security and Privacy is Important in IoT Based Smart Healthcare Systems?

The WBAN IoT based smart healthcare system architecture is enabled with various technologies in different tiers or layers. In tier I or layer I it is sensors but they are heterogeneous in nature. Now the sensor data are being transmitted to the Tier III, i.e., cloud layer through either edge layer or Fog layer (Fig. 9.7).

Here, life cycle of medical data generated in WBAN sensors is represented. The sensory data generated by body-worn sensors are sent to the remote clients. In between there are edge devices, fog devices, etc., to provide connectivity to the local client or remote client. From edge layer data reaches to local clients such as doctors, nurses, physicians or local computing server through fog devices at fog layer. Whereas if data needs to be sent to the remote clients like doctors, healthcare professionals, nurses, insurers, etc., through cloud layer. Performance metrics such as latency, end-to-end delay, turn-around time, mean-response time, packet drop rate get varied based on the path selection data forwarding.

Also the security and privacy issues of the privacy sensitive health data also get varied if it is forwarded through fog layer to the local end or to the remote clients through the cloud layer.

Here as we can see health data gets transmitted or processed in difference heterogeneous nodes and links with various security attacks and vulnerabilities, security and privacy of sensitive health data is a big concern. The security attributes that have been listed above are common to all types of data in different smart applications.

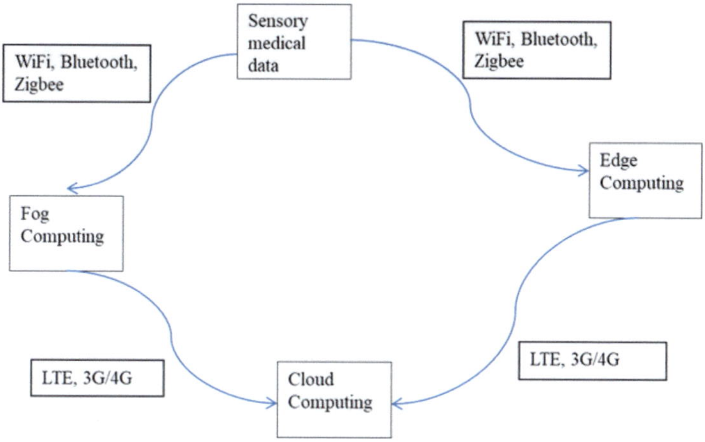

Fig. 9.7 Sensory data transmit to processing layer through heterogeneous devices and links

What attributes are significantly and differently important in healthcare domain? Among others, the data freshness, data availability are very much significant in all healthcare data specifically for life critical scenarios such as heart attack, stroke. Now, data freshness may not be ensured if data is not delivered to the receiver or the processor unit as close as the time of data generation. So to ensure that, emergency health data should be given a priority to be processed as close to the data generation point. Hence, based on the situation, emergency health data would be processed at edge end, fog end instead of cloud end to avoid latency or delay. And that decision needs to be taken dynamically based on the scenario.

9.5 Prototype Development and Demonstration on Smart Walking Assistant Device for Independent Remote Monitoring and Care

The smart walking stick, as highlighted in *The Times of India* article [14], integrates cutting-edge sensors to monitor the user's posture and detect changes indicative of an imminent fall. This system preempts accidents by sending alerts to caregivers, allowing for timely intervention, shown in Fig. 9.8. Designed with affordability as a priority, the device is affordable, making it accessible to a wide audience, especially in rural and low-resource settings. The technology is not only a pioneering solution in assistive devices but also an affordable and scalable healthcare tool for widespread adoption. This initiative utilizes engineering and technology to meet humanitarian needs, particularly for underprivileged communities with limited access to traditional healthcare.

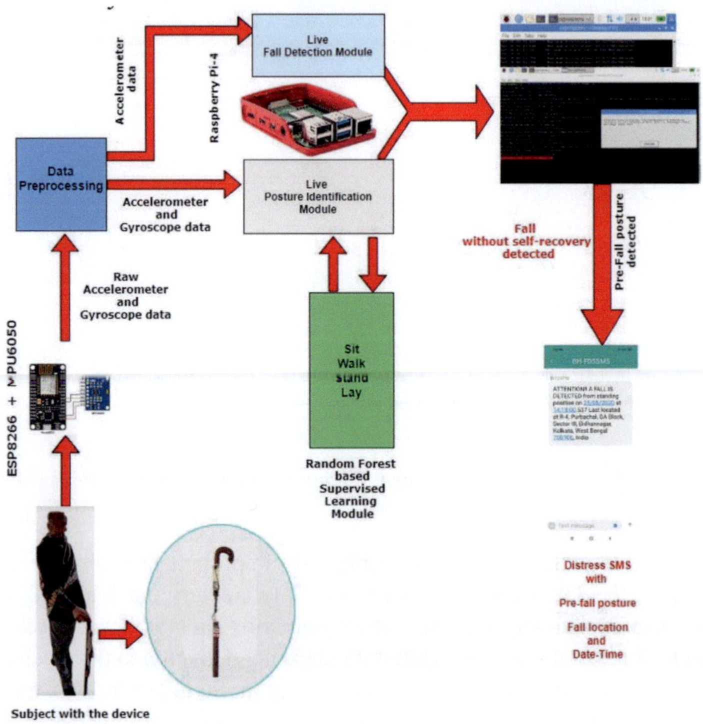

Fig. 9.8 Working diagram of smart walking assistant (SWA) [16]

9.5.1 Background and Motivation

The aging population in India and worldwide faces increasing risks related to mobility and health, with falls ranking as one of the leading causes of severe injury and mortality among older adults. Often, elderly individuals live alone or with limited supervision, especially in rural areas where access to emergency care is scarce. Traditional healthcare monitoring fails to address these immediate needs, leading to a demand for innovative solutions that offer continuous, preventive support.

In response, this sensor-enabled smart walking stick was developed, prioritizing affordability and usability for elderly individuals. The project, anchored in their 2021 publication in Evolving Systems (Springer), combines theoretical insights and practical applications to create a device that addresses fall prevention in real time. This device is unique in its predictive capabilities, continuously monitoring posture and providing alerts when the user is at risk of falling. This pre-fall detection mechanism and immediate alert system aim to mitigate injuries while offering peace of mind for both users and caregivers.

9.5.2 Technological Innovation and Features

The smart walking stick is a comprehensive system integrating multiple innovative features, specifically designed to serve the elderly [15, 16]. It is not just a mobility aid but an intelligent health monitoring tool that enhances personal safety. The unique features include:

1. ***Pre-fall Detection Sensors***: Equipped with motion sensors, the walking stick detects abnormal changes in posture, such as swaying or sudden imbalance, that indicate a high risk of falling. By predicting such events, the device gives caregivers crucial time to intervene. This predictive system has been granted patent protection by IP Australia (certificate number AU 2,021,102,699), which further emphasizes the novelty and international recognition of this technology.
2. ***Real-time Alerts***: The stick is designed to send instant alerts via a connected mobile app or SMS to the caregivers, family members, or healthcare providers. The system ensures that help is on hand even if the user is alone, thereby reducing response times in critical situations.
3. ***User-friendly Design***: Recognizing the ergonomic needs of elderly users, the stick is designed for comfort and ease of use, requiring minimal setup. Lightweight and durable, it ensures long-term usability.
4. ***Affordable and Scalable***: Unlike most healthcare devices that are cost-prohibitive, this walking stick was designed with affordability in mind. At around INR 700, it is accessible to economically disadvantaged communities, making large-scale deployment feasible.
5. ***Long Battery Life and Durable Build***: The device supports prolonged use on a single charge and is built to withstand regular wear and tear. This feature is particularly critical for elderly users, who may not be able to charge devices frequently.

9.5.2.1 Social Impact and Benefits

The walking stick is not only a tool for mobility but also a proactive safety device, revolutionizing the way elderly care is approached in resource-limited settings [17]. This project has yielded the following social benefits:

Reduced Injuries and Healthcare Costs

By preventing falls, the smart stick reduces medical costs associated with injury treatment. This is particularly impactful in rural regions where healthcare facilities are distant, and travel expenses can be prohibitive.

Improved Quality of Life for the Elderly

The device gives elderly users a greater sense of security and independence, allowing them to navigate daily activities with confidence. It also reduces the psychological burden on caregivers, who can monitor loved ones from afar.

Accessible Health Technology for Rural and Underprivileged Communities

By ensuring affordability, the project aims to reach marginalized groups, addressing a critical gap in accessible health monitoring technologies. The smart stick is an ideal solution for the elderly in rural India, where healthcare infrastructure is limited.

Promotes Independent Living

One of the greatest challenges for elderly individuals is the fear of losing independence. This device supports independent living, as it offers a safety net, reducing the need for constant caregiver presence.

9.5.2.2 Recognition and Media Coverage

The innovative nature and societal impact of this project have gained significant media attention. Notably, The Times of India highlighted the smart walking stick, emphasizing its potential to transform elderly care by providing a practical solution to fall prevention. The article underscored the stick's relevance to public health and its contribution to the safety and well-being of elderly users. This recognition is a testament to the device's relevance and its anticipated positive impact on society.

9.5.2.3 Scalability and Future Prospects

The smart walking stick is designed to be scalable, making it adaptable to various settings. The team envisions expanding its functionality by adding health-monitoring sensors, such as heart rate and oxygen level monitors, to provide a more comprehensive health overview. Additionally, plans are underway to develop a GPS-enabled version to aid in location tracking, further enhancing the device's utility.

9.6 Prototype Demonstration and Performance Evaluation in Terms of Delay—A Case Study

In this demonstration [17], our aim is to show the difference in computation delay in heterogeneous processor with varying resources. A test prototype has been developed using a pulse sensor to collect pulse rate from human body. The pulse rate from the sensor has been sent on encrypted form considering the security vulnerability and attacks while in-transit through wireless short range communication such as Bluetooth, Wi-Fi or Zigbee. The encrypted sensor data would be decrypted at the processing unit, the local Desktop considered here.

Table 9.2 Experimental setup

Parameters	Arduino Uno	Desktop
CPU	ATmega328	Intel core i3 2310
Clock speed	16 MHz	2.10 GHz
Storage	32 KB	500 GB
RAM	2KB	4 GB
Software	Arduino IDE	MATLAB

Fig. 9.9 Pulse rate in encrypted format getting collected

The proposed algorithm is implemented using MATLAB simulation software. The processing is done at local end, i.e., in laptop. The software and hardware specifications of the experimental setup are given in Table 9.2. The experimental hardware prototype to collect physiological parameter, i.e., pulse rate is shown in Fig. 9.9.

Here the security sensitive health parameter sensed by the pulse rate sensor is encrypted using symmetric key algorithm, AES. AES with 128 bit key is applied here. For data processing, data is processed at local computing unit, i.e., a laptop here. Execution time is measured and plotted in Figs. 9.10 and 9.11 with varied size of plain text data. Figure 9.10 represents execution time in Arduino and Fig. 9.11 represents execution time in laptop. This is done to see the difference between the execution time when it is Arduino or it is laptop to have a comparative idea. Execution time is the total encryption-decryption time of input plain text data.

It can be observed from Fig. 9.10 that it requires 1.25 ms time to complete the encryption and decryption process for 16 byte data. In Fig. 9.11 it shows that proposed algorithm requires 7.4 ms for 512 byte of data and it is less than the time required in AES. Similarly, it requires 0.14 ms for 16 byte and 0.88 ms for 512 byte when executed in a laptop equipped with more hardware resources. Hence the experimental results prove that proposed Lightweight Symmetric Encryption Algorithm (LSEA) in [17, 18] can execute in resource constrained device ensuring the equivalent level of security of the data.

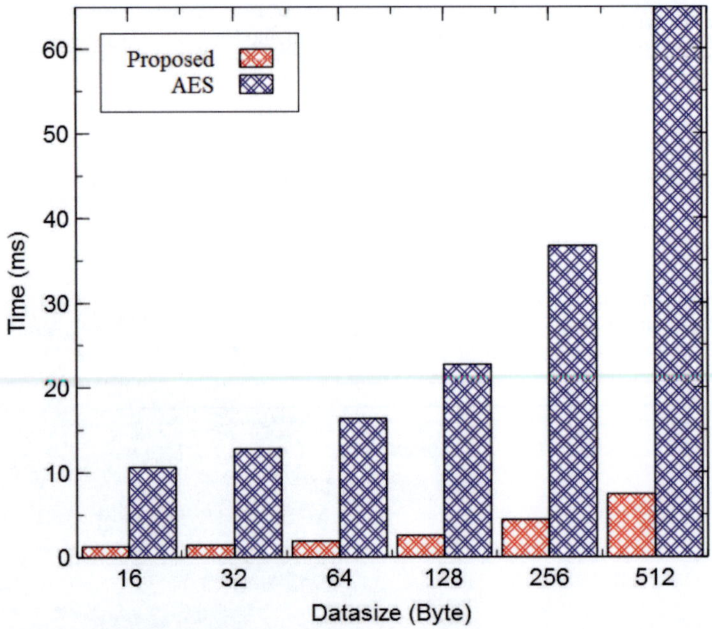

Fig. 9.10 Execution time required in Arduino UNO

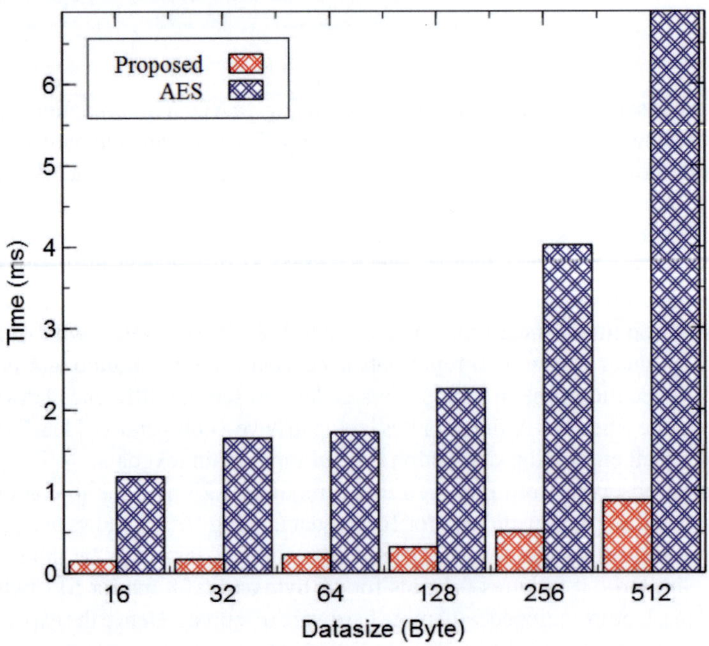

Fig. 9.11 Execution time required in Laptop

9.7 Problems

Question 1. Which layer of IoT based healthcare framework senses health data?

Answer: The biomedical sensors spanning over human body collected health data in sensing layer of IoT.

Question 2. Differentiate between WSN and WBAN.

Answer: Refer to Table 9.1, page no. 7.

Question 3. What are the important security concerns are there in IoT based smart healthcare system?

Answer:

Data Confidentiality

Sensitive health data to be transmitted in encrypted form so that the data could be shared securely between the intended parties only ensuring confidentiality.

Data Integrity

Health data integrity is utmost important for accurate diagnosis and medical advice. Integrity ensures that health data reached to the receiver in its original form or the data is not tampered or altered by any intermediate entity illegally.

Data Availability

The doctors or health professional in concern should get or access patients' biological data as and when required. Data availability must be ensured by any trusted entity.

Data Authentication

In accessing and handling with sensitive health data, all stakeholders must be authenticated with secret credentials such as user ID, password, secret code by trusted third party.

Non-Repudiation

The sender should not be in a position to deny that he or she has sent the message and the non-repudiation can only ensure that.

Data Authorization

While accessing the EHR on server, the entities must be authenticated by the trusted third party every time to ensure if they are authorized to get access to the health data or not.

Question 4. What is data freshness? Why it is significant in smart healthcare? How security attack can affect this security attribute?

Answer:

Data Freshness

Data freshness ensures that the data in concern is received by the receiver close to the time of generation of the data.

For health data this property is utmost important for accurate medical advice based on current data.

Routing attack, replay attack, Delay attack, Denial of service attack can cause delay to the delivery of data to the receiver, thus this parameter may get affected.

Question 5. What type of attacks the health data can suffer from while being transmitted through network layer?

Answer: Health data may suffer from Sinkhole attack, Wormhole attack, Greyhole attack, Blackhole attack, Routing attack, DoS attack, Man-in-the-middle attack, Eavesdropping, etc., while being transmitted through network layer.

Question 6. In WBAN or MBSN, which network topology is used and why?

Answer: Star topology. To support direct communication between nodes and sink, to enable scalability.

Questions 7. In WBAN, which device acts as coordinator or sink node in layer.1?

Answer: A smart computing device with mobility support and wireless connectivity, preferably smartphone, laptop, tablet computer, etc.

9.8 Conclusion

The development of the smart walking stick for fall prevention in elderly users represents an immense contribution to humanitarian engineering. This project demonstrates how engineering innovation can directly address the challenges faced by vulnerable populations, providing them with safety, independence, and a better quality of life. By making the device affordable and scalable the innovation has ensured that this solution is accessible to a broader population, particularly benefiting rural and underserved communities in India.

References

1. Rajasekaran, A.S., Sowmiya, L., Maria, A., Kannadasan, R.: A survey on exploring the challenges and applications of wireless body area networks (WBANs). Cyber Secur. Appl. 2, 100047 (2024)
2. Saif, S., Saha, R., Biswas, S.: On Development of MySignals based prototype for application in health vitals monitoring. Wireless Pers. Commun. **122**(2), 1599–1616 (2022)
3. https://development.libelium.com/mysignals/documentation/mysignals-sw-technical-guide
4. Movassaghi, S., Lipman, J., Smith, D., Jamalipur, A.J.: Wireless Body Area Networks: A Survey. Commun. Surv. Tutor., IEEE **16**(3) (2014)

5. Chen, M., Gonzalez, S., Vasilakhos, A., Cao, H., Leung, V.C.M.: Body area networks: a survey. Mob. Netw. Appl. **16**(2), 171–193 Springer (2011)
6. Ullah, S., Hignis, H., Braem, B., Latre, B., Blondia, C., et. al.: A comprehensive survey of wireless body area networks. J. Med. Syst. **36**(3), 1065–1094 Springer (2012)
7. Smith, Varshney, U.: Pervasive healthcare and wireless health monitoring. In: 2007 Springer: Mobile Network and Applications **2**(2–3):113–127 (2007)
8. Kwak, K., Ullaha, S., Ullaha, N.: An overview of IEEE 802.15.6 standard. In: 2010, 3rd International Symposium On Applied Sciences in Biomedical and Communication Technologies (ISABEL), pp. 1–6 (2010)
9. Ullah, S., Higgin, H., Siddiqui, M.A., Kwak, K.S.: A study of implanted and wearable body sensor networks. In: 2008, Proceedings 2nd KES International Conference on Agent and Multi-agent Systems: Technologies and Applications, pp. 464–473, Springer-Verlag, Berlin, Heidelberg (2008)
10. Naranjo-Hernández, D., Reina-Tosina, J., Roa, L.M.: Special Issue Body Sensors Networks for E-Health Applications. Sensors **20**, 3944 (2020)
11. Hassen, H.B., Ayari, N., Hamdi, B.: A home hospitalization system based on the internet of things, Fog computing and cloud computing. Inform. Med. Unlocked **20** (2020)
12. Hosseinzadeh, M., Koohpayehzadeh, J., Ghafour, M. Y., Ahmed, A. M., Asghari, P., Souri, A., Rezapour, A.: An elderly health monitoring system based on biological and behavioral indicators in internet of things. J. Ambient. Intell. Hum. Comput 1–11 (2020)
13. El Attaoui, A., Hazmi, M., Jilbab, A., Bourouhou, A.: Wearable wireless sensors network for ECG telemonitoring using neural network for features extraction. Wireless Pers. Commun. **111**(3), 1955–1976 (2020)
14. A walking stick that sends alert on elderly user's fall, pre-fall posture. The Times of India (2023). https://timesofindia.indiatimes.com/city/kolkata/a-walking-stick-that-sends-alert-on-elderly-users-fall-pre-fall-posture/articleshow/97832931.cms
15. . Bhattacharjee, P., Biswas, S.: Smart walking assistant (SWA) for elderly care using an intelligent real-time hybrid model. Evol. Syst. pp. 1–15. SCIE, Springer (2021). https://doi.org/10.1007/s12530-021-09382-5
16. Bhattacharjee, P., Biswas, S.: A system and method for Smart walking assistant for elderly care. Patent AU 2021102699, granted by IP Australia (2021)
17. Bhattacharjee, P., Sarkar, I., Biswas, S.: Enhanced fall prevention: A real-time hybrid analysis with smart walking stick and Edge-based IoMT. Comput. Electr. Eng. **124**(Part A), 110312 (2025). ISSN 0045–7906. https://doi.org/10.1016/j.compeleceng.2025.110312
18. Saha, R., Biswas, S., Sarmah, S., Karmakar, S., Das, P.: A working prototype using DS18B20 temperature sensor and arduino for health monitoring. SN Comput. Sci. **2**(1), 33 (2021)

Chapter 10
Conclusion

Abstract This is the conclusion Chapter. This chapter summarizes the contents of the book.

Keywords Computer networks · Wireless networks · Fault tolerant network · Adhoc network · Security

Computer networks truly are the unseen yet vital framework underpinning our modern world. They are as if the intricate nervous system of our digital society. They not only connect devices; but also enable seamless flow of information, resources, and even experiences or history data across any distance imaginable. This connectivity is the fuel for everything from global commerce and scientific collaboration to social interactions and entertainment. The ability to share printers in an office, access files on a remote server, stream a movie from across the globe, or engage in a video call with someone on another continent—all of this is made possible by the power of computer networks.

When we talk about how data travels, we encounter the fundamental distinction between wired and wireless networks, which hinges on the transmission medium.

Wired networks, exemplified by Ethernet, generally translates to high bandwidth, meaning a large capacity for data transfer, and reliable connections with minimal signal degradation. This makes them ideal for applications demanding speed and stability, such as transferring large files, online gaming, or industrial control systems. However, the inherent limitation is mobility; devices are tethered to the physical cable, restricting movement.

Wireless networks, on the other hand, embrace the freedom of electromagnetic waves to carry data through the air. Technologies like Wi-Fi (using radio waves) and Bluetooth (for shorter-range communication) offer greater flexibility and mobility, allowing devices to connect without the constraints of physical cables. However, this freedom comes with potential trade-offs: lower bandwidth compared to wired connections in many scenarios, and susceptibility to interference from other electromagnetic sources or physical obstacles, which can impact connection stability and speed.

S. Biswas et al., *Adhoc and Sensor Networks: Security and Applications*, Studies in Systems, Decision and Control 653, https://doi.org/10.1007/978-981-95-5839-1_10

Beyond the physical layer, we can also categorize networks based on their need for a central access point or infrastructure.

Infrastructure-based networks are commonly encountered especially in homes, offices, and public Wi-Fi hotspots. They rely on dedicated network devices like routers and access points to act as central hubs. These devices intelligently manage and direct network traffic. This centralized approach offers advantages in terms of security, management, and scalability, making it easier to add or remove devices and control network access.

In contrast, ad-hoc or infrastructure-less networks are more spontaneous and decentralized. They allow devices to communicate directly with each other without the need for a central coordinating device. Think of a temporary file transfer between laptops or a direct connection between wireless headphones and a phone. This offers simplicity for temporary connections and can be useful in situations where setting up infrastructure is impractical or unnecessary. Consequently, they are less suitable for larger or more permanent deployments. Security and management can also be comparatively challenging as the number of devices in an ad-hoc network grows.

Another critical design consideration is mobility support. Networks are designed with different levels of user movement in mind.

Mobile networks, such as cellular networks (like 4G LTE and 5G), are specifically engineered to maintain continuous connectivity as users move across a wide geographical area. They employ sophisticated technologies like handoffs, where a user's connection is seamlessly transferred from one network cell tower to another without interruption. This enables ubiquitous communication on the go.

Fixed networks, on the other hand, assume that the connected devices remain in a relatively stable or permanent location. Traditional wired networks and many Wi-Fi setups in homes or offices fall into this category. These different network types each possess distinct characteristics that make them suitable for various applications.

Wired networks are prized for their high speed, providing the fastest data transfer rates. They also generally offer higher security due to the physical connection and are less susceptible to eavesdropping. Low latency is another key advantage, crucial for real-time applications.

Wireless networks are convenient due to ease of deployment. Infrastructure-based networks provide robust management and scalability. Network administrators can centrally configure security settings, manage user access, and expand the network capacity as needed. Ad-hoc networks offer simplicity for localized communication, requiring minimal setup for direct device-to-device interaction.

Mobile networks prioritize continuous connectivity during movement, ensuring users stay connected as they travel. Each network type also has its own limitations. Wired networks are inherently constrained by physical cabling. Wireless networks are susceptible to interference from other electronic devices, physical obstructions, and environmental factors, which can degrade performance. They often have a limited range depending on the technology and environment, and in many scenarios, they offer lower bandwidth compared to wired alternatives. Infrastructure-based networks require network devices like routers and access points, as well as ongoing management and maintenance. Ad-hoc networks can be less secure due to the lack of centralized control and may become harder to manage as the number of participating devices increases. Mobile networks grapple with issues like signal strength variations depending on location and distance from cell towers, as well as the complexities of handovers between network cells, which can sometimes lead to brief interruptions. These inherent characteristics and limitations lead to various challenges in designing and managing computer networks. Ensuring security against cyber threats is a constant concern across all network types. Maintaining quality of service (QoS), ensuring that critical applications receive the necessary bandwidth and have low latency, is vital. Managing network congestion, especially during peak usage times, is an ongoing challenge. And the need to support increasing user demands for more bandwidth and connectivity continues to drive network evolution. For wireless and mobile networks, allocation and regulation of radio frequencies, is a critical aspect. Interference mitigation, developing techniques to minimize the impact of unwanted signals, is also paramount for reliable performance. Addressing these multifaceted challenges requires continuous innovation in networking technologies and protocols. Researchers and engineers are constantly developing new ways to improve network speed, security, reliability, efficiency, and mobility, ensuring that computer networks can continue to serve as the robust backbone of our increasingly interconnected world.

Wireless networks are no longer a novelty but a fundamental infrastructure that underpins much of modern life. This global connectivity empowers social interaction, facilitates business on a worldwide stage, and providing access to education and entertainment at the same time.

Delving into the shorter distances, short range wireless technologies like Bluetooth play a crucial role in the seamless interaction between our personal devices and peripherals.

Building upon the foundation of wireless and sensor networks is the transformative concept of the Internet of Things (IoT), which integrates these technologies to connect everyday objects, ranging from household appliances to industrial machinery. This interconnectedness generates a wealth of data that can be analyzed to enable intelligent automation and create smarter environments.

In smart homes, IoT devices allow for the remote controlling of lighting, temperature, security systems, and even kitchen appliances, offering convenience, energy efficiency, and enhanced security.

Smart cities leverage IoT technologies on a larger scale for efficient traffic management through smart traffic lights and congestion monitoring, smart parking systems that guide drivers to available spaces, optimized waste collection based on fill levels, and enhanced public safety through interconnected surveillance and emergency response systems.

Healthcare IoT is further advancing patient care through remote patient monitoring devices that provide continuous health data, telehealth platforms that enable virtual consultations, and the development of personalized medicine approaches based on individual data.

The Industrial IoT (IIoT) is a key driver of efficiency in manufacturing by enabling real-time data analytics from interconnected machinery, optimizing production processes, and facilitating predictive maintenance on a larger scale.

Across these various sectors, IoT applications are creating smarter, more efficient, and interconnected environments, promising to revolutionize how we live, work, and interact with the world around us. The synergy between wireless connectivity and sensor technology is the engine driving this profound transformation.

Networks with infrastructure support provide managed connectivity, particularly in environments with a significant number of users and devices, such as businesses, educational institutions, and other similar institutions. These generally consist of servers, routers, switches, and access points.

Routers act as intelligent traffic directors, determining the best path for data packets to travel between different networks. Switches, on the other hand, operate within a local network, efficiently forwarding data packets between connected devices based on their unique addresses. They create dedicated communication pathways, and try to prevent collisions. Access points are the gateways to wireless connectivity in infrastructure-based networks, allowing wireless devices to connect to the wired network.

Wired Ethernet networks, with their physical cable connections to switches and routers, and managed Wi-Fi networks, where access points are centrally managed and integrated into the wired infrastructure, are prime examples of infrastructure-based designs. These networks offer high bandwidth and reliable connections. The centralized control allows network administrators to have granular control over network access, security, and performance. This makes them particularly suitable for deployments where reliability, security, and manageability are paramount.

In contrast, networks without infrastructure support, also known as ad-hoc networks, offer a fundamentally different approach to connectivity. They enable direct communication between devices without the need for a central coordinating entity. In these networks, devices are more autonomous, acting as both hosts (end-user devices) and routers, meaning they can forward traffic to other nodes in the network to reach a destination that is not directly connected.

Familiar examples of ad-hoc networks include Bluetooth networks that connect personal devices like smartphones, headphones, and keyboards, and Wi-Fi Direct, which allows for peer-to-peer file sharing and direct connections between devices like laptops and printers without needing a traditional Wi-Fi access point.

The design of ad-hoc networks is often simpler and more flexible for temporary connections and localized communication. Setting up a Bluetooth connection or using Wi-Fi Direct is typically straightforward and does not require any pre-existing network infrastructure. However, the lack of central infrastructure introduces complexities in other areas. Routing in ad-hoc networks can be more complex. Since there is no central router to determine the best path, devices must rely on distributed algorithms to discover routes to other nodes and forward traffic accordingly. These routing protocols need to be dynamic and adaptive to changes in the network topology as devices join or leave.

While ad-hoc networks offer ease of deployment and lower initial costs (as no dedicated infrastructure hardware is required), they can face significant challenges in scalability, security, and network management as the number of devices increases. As more devices join an ad-hoc network, routing becomes inefficient, potentially leading to increased latency and reduced throughput. Security can also be a concern as there is no central authority to enforce security policies, and each device is responsible for its own security. Managing a large ad-hoc network can be difficult due to the lack of centralized control and visibility.

In essence, the choice between infrastructure-based and infrastructure-less networks depends heavily on the specific requirements of the environment. Infrastructure-based networks provide a robust, managed, and scalable solution for larger and more permanent deployments, while ad-hoc networks offer simplicity and flexibility for temporary, localized connections. Each architecture has its own set of trade-offs in terms of cost, complexity, performance, security, and manageability.

Then comes the time to delve deeper into the fascinating world of protocols that orchestrate communication, manage movement, and guide data in these dynamic network landscapes.

Ad-hoc networks, by their very definition, operate without a fixed infrastructure. This property itself presents unique challenges so that devices find and communicate with each other, especially when devices are on the move. Thus, requirement of hitherto unknown protocols come into play.

Wireless Sensor Networks (WSNs) operate under a different set of constraints, primarily limited energy resources and processing power. These limitations heavily influence the design of their lightweight communication protocols, such as Zigbee, which is designed for low-power, low-data-rate applications. Their routing protocols, like Low-Energy Adaptive Clustering Hierarchy (LEACH), often prioritize energy efficiency over pure speed.

The Internet of Things (IoT) presents an even more complex landscape, encompassing a diverse range of devices and network types, from tiny, battery-powered sensors to more powerful embedded systems, connected via various wireless and wired technologies. This heterogeneity necessitates a variety of protocols tailored to the specific needs and constraints of different IoT devices and applications.

Routing in IoT networks often aims to bridge the gap between low-power wireless devices and the internet. Standards like IPv6 over Low-Power Wireless Personal Area Networks (6LoWPAN) enable devices using protocols like IEEE 802.15.4 (the underlying technology for Zigbee) to integrate with the internet using IPv6, the next generation of the Internet Protocol. This allows IoT devices to have globally unique addresses and communicate seamlessly with other internet-connected devices and services.

Mobility management in ad-hoc networks is a core concern. Since nodes can move freely and unpredictably, the network topology can change frequently. Mobility management mechanisms focus on adapting to these frequent topology changes to ensure that routes remain valid and data can still be delivered. This might involve detecting broken links, discovering new routes, or proactively maintaining existing routes to minimize disruptions caused by movement. Mobility in WSNs is typically limited or predictable, depending on the application. In some cases, sensors might be static, while in others, they might be attached to moving objects but with relatively predictable movement patterns. This characteristic of limited or predictable mobility significantly influences the design of communication and routing protocols, allowing for optimizations that might not be feasible in highly mobile ad-hoc networks. Several mobility models have been included in this book. Mobility in IoT varies greatly depending on the specific application. Some IoT deployments involve static sensors in smart buildings or agricultural fields, while others involve mobile assets like tracking devices on vehicles or wearable health monitors. The mobility requirements influence the choice of communication and routing protocols, as well as the power management strategies employed.

Evaluating the performance of these dynamic network environments is crucial for understanding their capabilities and limitations. This involves measuring key metrics such as throughput (the rate of successful data transfer), delay (the time it takes for data to travel from source to destination), packet loss (the percentage of data packets that fail to reach their destination),1 and, particularly important for battery-operated devices, energy consumption. These metrics are often assessed through simulations using specialized network simulation software and testbeds, which are real-world deployments of the network under controlled conditions. A few frameworks that support evaluation of different protocols are discussed as well.

A fault-tolerant network is engineered with a paramount goal: to sustain its intended functionality even when faced with the failure of one or more of its constituent parts. Think of it as designing a system with built-in resilience, capable of weathering disruptions and continuing to operate reliably. The core principle behind achieving fault tolerance is redundancy. This involves strategically duplicating critical components or communication pathways within the network. If a primary component malfunctions or a primary link goes down, the system can seamlessly switch to backup resources upon detecting the failure. This automatic failover mechanism ensures continuous and reliable operation, minimizing any interruption to the services the network provides. Imagine having a spare tire for your car—if one goes flat, you can quickly replace it and continue your journey. Fault-tolerant networks employ similar strategies at a network level.

However, there are specific challenges faced by ad-hoc and sensor networks when it comes to reliability. The probability of failure in these networks can be relatively high compared to more traditional, infrastructure-based networks. This heightened risk stems from several key factors. Firstly, the resource-constrained nature of nodes—often battery-powered with limited processing capabilities and memory—makes them more susceptible to failure due to energy depletion or processing overloads. Secondly, they are frequently deployed in potentially harsh operating environments, where they might be exposed to extreme temperatures, humidity, physical damage, or other adverse conditions that can lead to malfunctions. Lastly, the dynamic network topology inherent in ad-hoc networks, caused by the mobility of nodes, and the potential for node depletion in sensor networks as batteries die or sensors become damaged, further contribute to the likelihood of failures.

In ad-hoc networks, the very characteristic of node mobility can lead to frequent link failures as devices move out of range of each other. This constant flux can also result in network partitions, where the network splits into isolated segments that can no longer communicate, significantly increasing the likelihood of communication disruptions. Imagine a group of robots collaborating wirelessly; if too many move too far apart, they might lose their ability to coordinate.

Sensor networks, often deployed in large numbers over potentially vast and unattended locations, face their own set of vulnerabilities. Battery exhaustion is a primary concern, as many sensor nodes rely on limited battery power for their operation, and replacing these batteries can be impractical or impossible in many scenarios. Environmental damage from weather, wildlife, or accidental human interference can also lead to physical failure of sensor nodes. Furthermore, communication interference from other wireless devices or environmental factors can disrupt the transmission of data, effectively causing a node to appear as if it has failed. All these factors collectively contribute to node failures in sensor networks.

To counteract these inherent vulnerabilities and build more resilient networks, fault-tolerant algorithms are employed. One powerful and widely used technique is checkpointing. Checkpointing is a process where the state of a node (its current data, configuration, and operational status) or even the entire network is periodically saved to a stable storage medium. Think of it as taking a snapshot of the system at a particular point in time.

Upon detection of a failure in a node or the network, the system can perform a rollback to the last saved checkpoint. This allows the system to effectively "rewind" to a known good state before the failure occurred, minimizing data loss that might have occurred since the last checkpoint and reducing the overall downtime of the network. Instead of starting from scratch, the system can resume operation from the saved state, significantly speeding up the recovery process.

However, implementing checkpointing strategies in ad-hoc and sensor networks requires careful consideration of their unique constraints. These strategies need to be highly energy-efficient to avoid rapidly draining the limited power resources of the nodes. They also need to be coordinated across the network to ensure consistency and avoid excessive communication overhead associated with saving and restoring checkpoints.

The frequency and granularity of checkpoints are critical design parameters. Taking checkpoints too frequently can consume excessive energy and bandwidth, impacting the network's overall performance and lifetime. On the other hand, taking checkpoints too infrequently can lead to significant data loss and longer recovery times in the event of a failure. Designers must carefully balance the need for effective fault recovery with the inherent resource constraints of the network.

By strategically implementing checkpointing in conjunction with other fault-tolerant mechanisms like redundancy in routing paths or the use of backup nodes, the overall reliability and resilience of ad-hoc and sensor networks can be significantly enhanced. This ensures that these networks, despite the challenges posed by their dynamic nature and resource limitations, can provide continuous and dependable operation for their intended applications, whether it's monitoring critical environmental conditions or enabling seamless communication in mobile scenarios.

Next in the discussion is the critical security landscape of Wireless Sensor Networks (WSNs), the Internet of Things (IoT), and ad-hoc networks. The chapter highlights the inherent weaknesses, the ways attackers might exploit them, and the security measures being developed to fortify them.

The security landscape of WSNs, IoT, and ad-hoc networks is complex and constantly evolving, largely due to their unique characteristics and the environments in which they operate. Unlike traditional wired networks with well-defined boundaries and more powerful devices, these wireless and often distributed networks present a significantly expanded attack surface and are often more vulnerable to a range of threats.

Wireless Sensor Networks (WSNs), with their resource constraints (limited battery power, processing capabilities, and memory) and often unattended deployment in potentially hostile environments, are particularly susceptible to various security attacks.

The Internet of Things (IoT) dramatically expands the attack surface due to its diverse range of interconnected devices, from smart thermostats and refrigerators to industrial control systems and medical devices. This heterogeneity introduces vulnerabilities at multiple levels:

- Device Level: Many IoT devices have limited security features, weak default passwords, and unpatched software vulnerabilities, making them easy targets for exploitation.
- Network Level: Communication between IoT devices and cloud platforms can be intercepted or manipulated if not properly secured. Wireless communication protocols used by IoT devices might have inherent weaknesses.
- Cloud Level: Cloud platforms that manage and store data from IoT devices are also potential targets for data breaches and unauthorized access.

This expanded attack surface makes IoT environments prone to a wide array of threats, including:

- Data Breaches: Attackers can gain unauthorized access to sensitive personal information, health data, or industrial secrets collected by IoT devices.
- Botnet Recruitment: Compromised IoT devices can be recruited into botnets and used to launch large-scale distributed denial-of-service (DDoS) attacks against other targets on the internet.
- Physical Tampering: Some IoT devices, especially those in public or industrial settings, might be vulnerable to physical manipulation that could compromise their functionality or security.

Ad-hoc networks, characterized by their lack of a centralized authority or infrastructure, face unique security challenges. The absence of a central point of control and the reliance on distributed cooperation make them vulnerable to.

- Routing Disruptions: Malicious nodes can inject false routing information, disrupt the establishment of communication paths, or create routing loops, preventing data from reaching its destination.
- Impersonation Attacks: Attackers can impersonate legitimate nodes to gain unauthorized access to network resources or to intercept communication intended for other nodes.
- Absence of Clear Trust Boundaries: In the absence of a central authority, establishing trust between nodes can be difficult, making the network susceptible to attacks launched by compromised or malicious participants. This makes secure communication a significant challenge in ad-hoc networks.

Across all these network types, some common security issues persist:

- Lack of Strong Authentication and Authorization Mechanisms: Many devices and protocols lack robust ways to verify the identity of communicating entities and control access to network resources. Weak or default credentials are often exploited.
- Insufficient Data Encryption: Sensitive data transmitted wirelessly might not be adequately encrypted, making it vulnerable to eavesdropping.
- Vulnerabilities in Routing Protocols: As seen in ad-hoc networks, routing protocols themselves can be exploited by malicious nodes to disrupt network operation or redirect traffic.

Attack models for these networks often consider two main categories of adversaries:

- External Attacks: These originate from outside the network and aim to disrupt operations, gain unauthorized access, or steal sensitive information.
- Insider Threats: In these scenarios, a compromised node that is already part of the network (either maliciously introduced or a legitimate node that has been taken over) launches attacks from within, making detection and mitigation more challenging.

To address these multifaceted threats, a variety of secure solutions are being developed and implemented.

Simulation and implementation of secure solutions in realistic testbeds are essential for evaluating their effectiveness in real-world conditions. This includes assessing their security strength against various attack models, analyzing their performance overhead in terms of resource consumption and network latency, and determining their feasibility for deployment in different application scenarios with varying constraints. The ultimate goal is to build resilient and trustworthy wireless and IoT ecosystems where users can confidently rely on the security and privacy of their data and the integrity of the network operations.

Establishing trust among nodes is paramount for secured and reliable operation of decentralized networks. In networks without a central authority, like ad-hoc, WSNs, and IoT deployments, nodes must cooperate to perform tasks such as routing data, sensing the environment, or actuating physical systems. However, without a central entity to vouch for the trustworthiness of each participant, the network becomes vulnerable to malicious or faulty nodes that might disrupt operations, disseminate false information, or compromise the security of the entire system. Therefore, trust management aims to create mechanisms by which nodes can assess the trustworthiness of their neighbors and make informed decisions about which nodes to interact with, which data to believe, and which requests to fulfill.

To provide essential security services like confidentiality, integrity, and authentication in these resource-limited environments, lightweight cryptography techniques are indispensable. Traditional cryptographic algorithms, while offering strong security, often demand significant computational power, memory, and energy, making them impractical for tiny sensors or battery-powered IoT devices. One key approach to establishing trust is through modeling reputation-based trust. This involves assessing the past behavior and interactions of nodes within the network to quantify their trustworthiness. Nodes that have consistently behaved reliably and cooperatively are assigned a higher trust score, while those that have exhibited malicious or faulty behavior receive lower scores. This assessment often uses metrics like packet forwarding rates (how often a node successfully forwards data intended for others) or data accuracy (how reliable the data reported by a sensor node has been in the past). By observing these behaviors over time, nodes can build a reputation profile for their neighbors and use this information to make trust-based decisions.

Beyond simple reputation scores, more sophisticated Bayesian Network-based models offer a probabilistic approach to trust evaluation. These models represent trust relationships and influencing factors as a probabilistic graph. They allow nodes to update their trust beliefs based on observed evidence (e.g., a neighbor successfully forwarded a packet) and prior probabilities (initial beliefs about a node's trustworthiness). As more interactions occur and more evidence is gathered, the Bayesian network automatically updates the trust probabilities, providing a dynamic and adaptive way to assess trustworthiness in the face of changing node behavior.

However, it's crucial to acknowledge that the effectiveness and complexity of these trust management and cryptographic techniques are significantly impacted by the inherent resource limitations of the network nodes. Constraints on computation (how fast they can perform cryptographic operations or run complex trust evaluation algorithms), memory (how much data they can store, including cryptographic keys and trust-related information), and battery life (how long they can operate before needing recharging or replacement) all pose significant challenges. Trust management models that require extensive computation or large amounts of memory might be too resource-intensive for small sensor nodes. Similarly, complex cryptographic algorithms might drain their batteries too quickly.

Therefore, designing secure and trustworthy systems necessitates a careful balance between the strength of security mechanisms and the resource overhead they introduce. Lightweight solutions are crucial for practical deployment in these constrained environments. Trust models, while needing to provide meaningful assessments of node reliability in the face of potential malicious behavior or dynamic network conditions, must be computationally efficient to be viable for implementation on resource-limited devices. Addressing these resource limitations is a central challenge in developing secure and dependable wireless and IoT systems. Researchers and developers are constantly exploring novel lightweight cryptographic primitives and efficient trust management algorithms that can provide robust security and reliability without exceeding the capabilities of these increasingly pervasive networks.

A couple of compelling real-world examples that vividly illustrate the transformative power of sensor networks and the Internet of Things (IoT) lie in the critical domains of healthcare and defense.

In the realm of healthcare, sensor networks and IoT are ushering in a new era of proactive, personalized, and accessible care. Imagine a future where health issues are detected in their earliest stages, interventions are tailored to individual needs, and healthcare reaches individuals wherever they may be. This is the promise being realized through these technologies.

Continuous remote patient monitoring is becoming a reality, enabled by networks of wearable and ambient sensors that track vital signs such as heart rate, blood pressure, oxygen saturation, and body temperature, as well as activity levels, sleep patterns, and even physiological indicators of stress. This constant stream of real-time data allows healthcare providers to gain a comprehensive understanding of a patient's health status outside of traditional clinical settings. This is particularly beneficial for managing chronic conditions, monitoring recovery after surgery, and facilitating early detection of health issues before they escalate into more serious problems. Early detection can lead to timely interventions and significantly improved patient outcomes. Furthermore, the rich data collected through sensor networks enables the development of personalized care plans that are tailored to an individual's specific needs and health profile, leading to more effective and patient-centric treatment.

Wearable IoT devices are empowering individuals to take a more active role in managing their own well-being. Smartwatches, fitness trackers, and specialized medical wearables continuously collect and share health data—ranging from activity levels and sleep quality to electrocardiogram (ECG) readings and glucose levels—with healthcare providers. This direct involvement of patients in data collection fosters greater awareness of their own health and facilitates more informed discussions with their doctors, leading to more proactive health management and lifestyle adjustments.

The concept of smart hospitals is also gaining traction, leveraging IoT technologies to enhance operational efficiency and patient safety. Sensor networks and IoT devices are being used for asset tracking, allowing hospital staff to quickly locate critical equipment like wheelchairs, infusion pumps, and medical devices, saving valuable time and improving resource utilization. Automated medication dispensing systems, integrated with IoT, can ensure that patients receive the correct medication at the right time and dosage, reducing the risk of medication errors. Furthermore, IoT devices are being deployed for environmental control, monitoring and adjusting temperature, humidity, and lighting in patient rooms to optimize comfort and create a healing environment. These applications collectively demonstrate the potential of sensor networks and IoT to streamline hospital operations, reduce costs, and, most importantly, improve the quality and safety of patient care.

These diverse applications in healthcare underscore the profound potential of sensor networks and IoT to revolutionize healthcare delivery, making it more proactive by anticipating health issues, more personalized by tailoring treatments to individual needs, and more accessible by extending care beyond the walls of traditional medical facilities.

Turning our attention to the realm of defense, sensor networks and IoT are proving to be invaluable assets, transforming capabilities across various domains. The need for enhanced situational awareness, real-time intelligence, and operational efficiency in challenging and often hostile environments drives the adoption of these technologies.

Defense applications heavily rely on sensor networks for battlefield surveillance, deploying a multitude of interconnected sensors to monitor vast areas, detect enemy movements, and gather crucial information about the terrain and environmental conditions. These networks enable target tracking, providing real-time data on the location and movement of personnel and vehicles. They are also essential for environmental monitoring in hostile terrains, collecting data on weather patterns, chemical or biological agents, and other factors that can impact military operations. The information gathered by these sensor networks provides critical real-time intelligence that is vital for informed decision-making and mission success.

IoT devices are being increasingly integrated into various defense applications, further enhancing operational effectiveness. Smart logistics leverages IoT sensors to track the location and condition of equipment, supplies, and personnel, optimizing supply chains and ensuring that resources are available where and when they are needed. Personnel tracking using wearable IoT devices can improve troop safety and accountability in the field. The integration of IoT with unmanned aerial vehicles (UAVs) allows for enhanced control, autonomous operation, and real-time data collection, significantly expanding their capabilities for reconnaissance, surveillance, and other missions. These applications collectively contribute to enhanced situational awareness, providing commanders with a more comprehensive and up-to-date understanding of the operational environment, and improved operational effectiveness by automating tasks, optimizing resource utilization, and enhancing the capabilities of personnel and equipment.

Border security is another critical area benefiting from the deployment of sensor networks. Networks of unattended ground sensors can be strategically placed along borders to detect intrusions, monitor remote and difficult-to-patrol areas, and provide early warnings of potential threats. These sensors can detect movement, seismic activity, or even the presence of specific materials, providing valuable intelligence to border security forces.

These compelling case studies in defense highlight how sensor networks and IoT are fundamentally transforming defense capabilities. They provide enhanced sensing capabilities, allowing for the collection of vast amounts of data from diverse sources and environments. They enable enhanced communication, facilitating the real-time sharing of critical information across distributed forces. And they support automation of various tasks, freeing up personnel for more strategic roles and improving the speed and efficiency of operations. Ultimately, these technologies contribute to improved security by providing better threat detection and situational awareness, and enhanced decision-making by providing commanders with timely and accurate intelligence in challenging and critical environments.

These examples in both healthcare and defense underscore the profound and far-reaching impact of sensor networks and IoT, demonstrating their potential to address critical challenges and create significant advancements in diverse and vital sectors.

This book aims to portray an overall idea about wireless and adhoc network and computing. The idea is not restricted to architectures or protocols only. The book with its different chapters also provides detailed concept and existing solutions for providing fault tolerance and reliability, and security to wireless and adhoc networks.